Preface

A high ranking corporate executive from Scotland arrived in St. Louis to meet with his new local manager for the first time. Having mentioned that he had never seen a baseball game, the manager, anxious to please his boss, purchased tickets to see the hometown Cardinals play both Saturday and Sunday games.

The Saturday game turned out to be quite a thrilling pitcher's duel which the Cardinals won to the wild cheers of the hometown crowd. Sunday's game turned out to be quite different. By the third inning the Cardinals' pitcher was being shelled when the Scotsman turned to his host and said, "I don't understand. Why did you guys change pitchers? The fellow that pitched yesterday was much better than this guy."

For some reason the innocence of that story (which is true) has stuck with me for many years. It's like an Aesop's fable which ends with a thoughtful moral to the story: "If you don't know the rules, you can't play the game." Or, in the case of the Scotsman, he didn't understand the rules having never played or seen the game before.

For some strange reason I was reminded of the Scotsman's remark while listening to the awful story of a hard working single mom who had been cajoled into purchasing a house well beyond her means by a smooth talking loan originator. Overwhelmed by the thought of living in a dream setting, she trustingly signed all the documents and settled into her new surroundings.

The results were wonderful for two years. That's when she received notice that the interest rate on her mortgage had been increased from 6½% to 13½%. Needless to say there was no way she could afford such an increase, and I don't need to describe for you the traumatic outcome. When asked, she really did not have a clue as to what she had signed. The originator had told her he would take care of all the details and for her not to worry. The house was hers. If only she had understood the rules of the game. When it comes to money, there is very little room for innocence.

PEARSON ALWAYS LEARNING

Fred Selinger

The Missing Link: from College to Career and Beyond

Personal Financial Management

Sixth Edition

Back Cover Image: Courtesy of Fred Selinger

Pearson Education, Inc., 330 Hudson Street, New York, New York 10013
A Pearson Education Company
www.pearsoned.com

Printed in the United States of America

000200010272152808

KR

ISBN 10: 1-323-85057-0
ISBN 13: 978-1-323-85057-2

TABLE OF CONTENTS

CHAPTER 1

INTRODUCTION

Living in the Midst of a Complex World

> **We are living in the midst of a complex world moving at a pace that man has never experienced.**

We live in a world of contradictions and complexities, mixed priorities, complicated interrelationships, unintended consequences, greed and frugality, and poverty and enormous wealth. It is a 24/7 whirl of personal computers (PCs), laptops, tablets, smart phones, videos, YouTube, Facebook, Twitter, Snap Chat, LinkedIn, Google, Yahoo, Instagram, electronic mail (email), messaging, 24 hour news coverage, bloggers, and political pundits. Thousands of satellites, drones, and even smart phones watch us every day taking pictures, tracking our movements, watching where we shop, what we buy, and how we look. The data is collected and sold to advertisers who bombard us with ads hoping to get our attention and our money. There appear to be no more secrets. We are constantly being inundated with information. Some is relevant. Some is not. For many people, it's too much to handle.

In our grandparents' generation, earning the money first and then getting what you wanted was how it worked. Over the years, that concept became almost obsolete, almost non-American. Instead of paying cash, we began to use credit cards. The new mantra became, "Buy it now and pay for it later" (plus interest, fees, and penalties). Instead of worrying about saving money, we began to worry about our credit score. Instead of a house being a place where you live, it became our personal mint that printed money for cars, boats, vacations, education, and retirement.

So now we face a world of credit cards, debit cards, prepaid cards, student loan debt, credit reports, credit scores, identity theft, IRAs, 401(k) plans, endless investment options in stocks, bonds, mutual funds, real estate, soaring medical and retirement costs, dwindling pension plans, complex subprime and adjustable rate mortgages, car leases, and exploding college tuitions. It is within this environment that you will confront the many financial decisions needed to make a living, make a life, and take care of your "financial" future.

Money is something you will deal with virtually every day of your life. Yet, the financial awareness which is so vital to making good decisions is notoriously lacking. Worse is the fact that there are people (and institutions) consumed by greed and power who spend their days and nights trying to figure out how to get more of your wallet into their wallet, legally or illegally, morally or immorally.

Many of the financial decisions you will make should be based upon factors about which you may have little or no knowledge or experience. Unfortunately, mistakes and missteps can be very costly and difficult to undo. When it comes to money, there is little room for innocence or ignorance.

Along the way you will likely have dealings with accountants, lawyers, bankers, stockbrokers, insurance agents, real estate brokers, and estate planners. Some of these "professionals" may be more concerned about their own financial future than yours. In some instances you will be faced with having to make important financial decisions. How prepared are you to manage and protect your financial self?

If you are going to play the game, you need to know the rules.

Knowing the rules is the starting line for the hike to financial independence. This is where we begin to level the playing field for you. Opportunities to save and invest money are everywhere. So are pitfalls. You will need to make some serious choices along the way.

The world is about choices. Your life is about choices. And the choices you make matter to you, your family, your community, and your country.

What surprises most people is that you can actually choose to become a "millionaire," the term we define as, "People who are financially able to take care of themselves throughout their adult lives and live the life they want to live without help from government programs such as welfare, Medicare, and Social Security."

We live in the richest country the world has ever known. Do you think Social Security will be there to take care of you when you retire 20, 30, or 40 years from now? Do you think the government will be there to take care of your medical bills when you retire? If not, who will take care of you?

Even though we live in the richest country the world has ever known, we need to be aware of some pertinent facts:

- Some 47 million people are receiving food stamps. That is about 15% of the population needing help just putting food on the table.

- 1 of every 6 Americans receives a Social Security check each month.

- According to the Census Bureau, 40% of the children born today are born out of wedlock.

- In California, arguably the richest state, half of the children are born to mothers who do not have a high school diploma.

- 1 of every 140 people living in America now resides in jail or prison. And we are all paying for this at an annual rate of about $30k to $50k per inmate.

- The cost of college education is soaring, with parents and children struggling over how to pay the expenses.

- Student loan debt, at $1.5 trillion and rising, now exceeds credit card debt.

- Obesity afflicts 25% of the population. The cost of treating diabetes and

- Alzheimer disease is skyrocketing.

- 7,000 students drop out of high school every day.

- 11,000 seniors reach age 65 each day, and that number is growing.

You can make a "living" if that is all you want. The question is how high above that do you want to go? The Nightingale/Conant Institute reported a study that showed that of 100 people who start working at age 25, by the time they reach age 65,

- 1 will be rich.

- 4 will be financially independent, able to take care of themselves.

- 45 will have some funds but will still need some form of continuing financial aid.

- 50 will essentially be broke.

Let us think about these facts. In the richest country the world has ever known, after 40 years of working, only 5% of the people become financially independent – able to take care of themselves – the ones we define as "millionaires."

Do not outlive your money!

As it turns out, retirement is not the biggest problem. On the contrary, it is **longevity.** Consider the facts:

- A male age 65 has a 50% chance of living beyond 85, and a 25% chance of living beyond age 92.

- Women live 2 to 3 years longer.

- If **both** your birth parents reach 65, there is a 50% chance that one will live beyond 92, and a 25% chance that one will live beyond 97.

Most people will live long past the age they planned for, save too little along the way, and deplete their assets far too soon. How do you plan to live another 20 to 30 years after you retire from a full-time job without a steady paycheck?

At the beginning of this century, many people looked upon the soaring value of their homes as banks to fund consumption throughout their retirement. Sadly, as a result of the Great Recession, millions of those homes were repossessed, their owners were left with nothing, and dreams were crushed. You need a different strategy!

The question is, "Who is going to take care of you?" The "who" is YOU!

According to the IRS, only 4.9% of households have a net worth of at least $1 million, which is very close to the 5% figure the Nightingale/Conant survey found to be rich or financially independent. Where do rich people come from? Rich people come from poor people. Find a rich person and you will probably find a parent or grandparent who was poor. Obviously, it is not just where you start that counts. It is what happens to you along the way, and where you finish that matters.

In my mind, there is a BIG difference between being "rich" and being "wealthy." Rich has to do with money. **Wealth is lifestyle**; living the life you want and pursuing your passions. The goal is for you to be wealthy and financially independent.

4

Whatever path you take, whatever your passion, I want you in the top 5% of your craft and in the top 5% financially, able to take care of yourself without your lifestyle being overwhelmed by what you owe to financial institutions, or relying on aid from shrinking government support programs. In short, manage your money and do not let your money manage you.

Invest in yourself now.

I believe the best investments you will ever make are those you make in yourself, such as:

- Education, in the classroom and on the job.

- Continuing education, a life-long endeavor.

- Doing what it takes to achieve your personal goals.

I applaud you if you are investing in yourself now by preparing for your financial future.

Let us begin to think about the issues by taking a look at the demographics and financial realities you will encounter. This may be a bit depressing but the problem will become crystal clear.

As you read this, ponder these questions: Will the younger generation have the opportunity to acquire as much wealth as their parents, which in itself can be shockingly insufficient? Will young workers and those yet to be born be willing and able to repay the massive societal debts incurred by previous generations? Are we looking at a potential breakdown of major proportions between the young and the old?

Baby boomers are reaching age 65 at an accelerating rate and a growing percentage of government spending is devoted to their needs. These same people are living longer, while the birthrate is declining. As a result, younger people will end up working longer to support them and there is likely to be a serious shortage of skilled workers. The trend will benefit those who are educated and have marketable skills.

President Obama said, "It's a screwed up mess out there due to the irresponsibility of both the public and private sectors … from the executive suites of finance and industry, to the seats of power in Washington, DC." There is plenty of blame to go around!

There is no question the gap between rich and poor households is widening. That is not opinion, it is the data. Take a look at the breakdown of the federal tax brackets which are approximately as follows:

- The top 1% of households earn $400,000 plus, and pay 40% of income taxes.

- The top 5% of households earn $160,000 plus, and pay 60% of income taxes.

- The top 10% of households earn $113,000 plus, and pay 70% of income taxes.

- The bottom 50% of households pays less than 3% of income taxes.

- 47% of households pay no federal income taxes.

- The bottom 10% of households receives checks from the government.

- Only 10% of households have income of more than $113,000 even though an estimated 78% have **two people working.**

- Most people pay more in Social Security and Medicare taxes than federal income taxes.

In most years, if you, or you and your spouse together earn more than $113,000, you are already in the top 10% of income earners.

The educational system is broken. In many inner-city schools, less than half of the students graduate. Who will support all these young people, very few of whom have marketable skills, yet many of whom will live very long lives and save little or nothing?

The medical system is broken and a whole new comprehensive healthcare program is in its infancy. As we go to print, we still do not know how the Health Care Reform Act will actually be implemented over the next several years.

As we go to print, we have no national energy policy, we have no national immigration policy, and there is no plan for reducing our skyrocketing national debt. By 2024, the annual interest on the national debt could reach $1 trillion, which would be about half of all income tax revenue. And that is just the interest, with nothing going toward paying down the debt.

The cost of political campaigns is out of sight. There are thousands of registered federal lobbyists. Congressmen spend 80% of their time raising campaign funds. The Supreme Court decision allowing unlimited campaign contributions by corporations, unions, and special interest groups has dramatically changed the political landscape at the national, state, and local levels of government.

The population is aging. The "boomers" are coming. Social Security now pays out more than it takes in and Medicare costs are soaring.

The total cost of college education has been increasing about 15% per year. Borrowing for college expenses is up 85% over the last five years. Parents and children are beginning to struggle over how to pay for college. Entry-level pay for most college graduates has not kept up with the cost of education. How will these student loans be repaid?

College costs are competing with the retirement needs of many families. Boomers have not saved enough. Heads of household age 55 to 64 typically have retirement savings of only about $65,000. That will not last long.

The burden of saving and investing for retirement and health care is shifting ever more from the employer to the employee.

Gone is the American dream that all one needed to do for a lifetime of security was join a union and go to work for General Motors.

Pensions and lifetime medical care paid by employers is becoming a thing of the past; businesses can no longer afford it and remain competitive in a global marketplace. The Great Recession and record low interest rates have stunned both pension funds and individual investors, wiping out billions of dollars of retirement funds. Private industry has made the adjustment; however, many government agencies have not.

Our government has spent us into a huge deficit to be paid by your generation and that of your children and grandchildren. In this environment will you be able to take care of yourself?

Here are a few projected demographics as of 2030. Keep them in mind as you ponder your future:

- 360 million people will be living in America, 20% of whom will be over age 65.

- The world's population will reach 8 billion people.

- China competes with the United States for the largest economy.

As global population ages and birth rates decline, governments will need to cut benefits to seniors and raise taxes on younger workers. Moreover, 40 years from now it is estimated that 1.5 billion people on the planet will be over 65. As the population of a country ages,

7

the economic growth rate tends to slow, which means that growth alone will not solve financial and social problems.

Debts are increasing. Growth is slowing. The number of "boomers" is growing. Birthrates are declining. In emerging economies there are billions of people who want cars, dishwashers, computers, and refrigerators. They will compete for energy, natural resources, and food, and continue to pollute the planet.

Notwithstanding all of these issues, America will still be a great nation, and you can carve out your future while learning to manage your personal finances and becoming financially independent. By the end of this book, you will have learned how to save hundreds of thousands of dollars and create future wealth in the millions.

Suppose you borrow $500,000 to buy a house with a 30-year-fixed-rate loan.

- At 6% interest, the monthly payment is $2,998. Total interest is $579,191.

- At 8% interest, the monthly payment is $3,669. Total interest is $820,776.

That is a difference of $241,585 which can be saved and invested for your future. Why the higher rate of interest? Maybe it's your credit score.

In this book, among other things, you will learn how important your credit score is, and how to increase it. You will learn how and when to start saving; how and when to invest; and what to invest in. You will learn how to deal with debt if you have it, and how to avoid it if you do not. You will learn how to mix love and money in a relationship; the best way to buy a car, a house, medical care; and save for retirement and your long life.

Most importantly, you will learn the importance of living within your means, setting priorities for spending, and the need to devote more time to managing your personal finances.

Let's get started!

Notes and Updates

CHAPTER 2

WHO ARE THE MILLIONAIRES?

Why Not You?

> By our definition, "millionaires" are those who are financially independent, living the life they want to lead, and able to take care of themselves without financial help from government sources.

Becoming a millionaire is a choice…a choice you can make. The vast majority of millionaires did not choose their occupation on the basis of how much money they would make, although most everyone wants good pay and benefits. The first responders who ran into the World Trade Center Towers on 9/11 were not doing it for the money. The high school teacher who loves kids and also coaches the basketball team after school is not doing it just for the money. It is true that some occupations typically pay more than others. But because someone chooses to be a firefighter or teacher does not disqualify them from financial success.

Surprise! Many millionaires do not earn over $100,000 per year. They usually live in lovely homes and drive nice cars. Well over 50% are self-employed or own a business. They tend to be compulsive savers and investors. Many have never bought a car "new," preferring to let someone else absorb the major depreciation expense. They strive for and become financially independent.

Millionaires tend to enjoy life because they are doing something they want to be doing and doing it well. What they enjoy most may be their profession or career, or it may be something outside of their employment that is also very gratifying. They are among the top of their craft. Only about 10% are men and women who are highly paid senior executives in large businesses. Some 80% became millionaires in one generation. Almost all came from ground zero. No inheritance. No trust funds. However, 20% of the millionaires are retired.

Outside of a mortgage or a business loan, they have little or no debt. They are not credit card "junkies." **Being frugal, not cheap but value oriented, is the cornerstone of their wealth.** They became millionaires by working toward their goals, budgeting, and controlling expenses.

They spend time planning their major expenses and investments and often consult with professional advisers. It is less about investing in real estate or the stock market than investing in themselves, their careers, their businesses, and their passions. They balance financial success with enjoying life. They realize you cannot enjoy life if you are addicted to consumption and the use of credit. They understand if you are credit dependent you are in fact controlled by someone else, some institution, or you are consumed by living beyond your means.

> **Most millionaires budget and spend carefully, live within their means, work (or worked) very hard, and want to be financially independent.**

Although over 80% of the millionaires are college graduates and some have advanced degrees, most were not Phi Beta Kappa, magna cum laude, or summa cum laude. Some are professional people such as accountants, lawyers, and doctors. Some are in sales, such as real estate brokers and insurance agents. Some own small businesses like dry cleaners, pest control firms, and restaurants. Others have created unique branded products sold in stores, over the internet, or through distributors across the nation. Many are franchisees in fast food and other industries. An increasing number may not only work for a large organization, but also have a "second" business operating from their home which may account for 50% or more of their household income. The IRS calls them, "Homepreneurs."

To be a millionaire does not require one to compromise their integrity. When millionaires work hard, they work really hard. However, 40-hour weeks may be rare. They are motivated by goals, not just pleasant activities. They allocate their time properly. They often do things that others do not like to do. They are disciplined.

One common trait of millionaires is that they have the ability to communicate and sell their ideas. A study was done in which English comprehension tests were given to all the employees in several companies. The scores generally reflected the positions of the employees. The conclusion was that command of the language (not necessarily your accent) is very important in communication, and that communication skills are important to success.

Millionaires tend to make accurate judgments about people, especially those they hire and with whom they do business. They tend to be honest with everyone and try to get along with people. Further, 80% are married, and most high-income couples are two-earner families. They recognize the importance of having a supportive spouse or life partner. They take great satisfaction in helping people.

Millionaires are willing to play for higher stakes to realize their goals. They do not follow the crowd. Many were told at some time or another that they were not intellectually gifted or would never amount to anything. They just didn't believe it. Millionaires learn from their mistakes and never give up. Millionaires are attracted to innovation.

Just like most of us, millionaires worry about their kids, college expenses, good health, and retirement.

People who succeed have goals.

Successful people know where they are going, even if they do not know exactly how they will get there. Millionaires focus on maintaining a positive attitude about what they are doing, regardless of setbacks. They have learned that one success can outweigh a hundred failures. They look for new ideas and are willing to try new things. Many volunteer their time and money to help others in need.

You know yourself better than anyone else. You are the captain of your own ship, and you can point your ship in any direction. As you read this chapter, did you see how "ordinary" millionaires really are? Is there anything here YOU can't do?

You can be a millionaire; financially independent and able to follow your passions to the fullest. It is your choice. It was Earl Nightingale who said it best, "We become what we think about." Are you thinking that you too can choose to be a millionaire?

Is there anything here YOU can't do?

Notes and Updates

CHAPTER 3

CREDIT, DEBT, AND MONEY

Make the World Go Around

For too long a period of time we were living in a consumption oriented, easy money, "I've got to have it now" or "Buy now….pay later" society. Mailboxes were full of solicitations for credit cards and home loans with very tempting "teaser rates" with low interest and small minimum monthly payments. Financial institutions lowered their credit standards to keep money flowing. Their goal was to collect more interest, fees, and penalties, and report record profits as the value of their stocks soared to new highs. Very few customers read the fine print. Even fewer understood what it said. Eventually, the bubble burst and the Great Recession began as asset values plummeted.

Overspending and overconsuming have no social boundaries. Rich people do it. Poor people do it. Males, females, young, and the elderly do it.

Good Debt vs. Bad Debt

That being said, there is a valuable role for debt in our society. It is often a necessary part of achieving your goals. There is what I call "good debt" and "bad debt." Here is what I mean.

Good Debt
By good debt, I mean the following:
>   Education
>   Car
>   Mortgage
>   Starting a well thought out business

Bad Debt
By bad debt, I mean the following:
>   Borrowing money to support a life style beyond one's means
>   Shopping to feel good on a bad day
>   Borrowing more than you can
>   repay.
>   Shopping to kill time
>   Keeping up with, or ahead of, your peers

Do you see that "good debt" is investing in yourself? When you invest in these items they help you on your path to financial independence. Think about a better job or your own business; a car to get to work; a secure family; and real estate ownership. Can you also see that "bad debt" is sheer consumption, and in some cases you may still have the debt to repay long after your purchase is eaten, worn out, out of style, or just a fading memory?

If you do borrow money, you should know in advance how you're going to pay it back. You cannot enjoy life if you are addicted to consumption and the use of credit. We call it "credit dependent," controlled by someone else, some institution somewhere.

When you borrow money from financial institutions, whether a bank or "nonbank," you are dealing with a service industry that makes money through the interest, fees, and penalties they charge you. So it is in their interest to keep you coming back for more. Just like anything else you buy, it is "buyer beware." You should be thoughtful about your real needs before undertaking any loan and, by all means, make sure you understand the contract you're signing, including the fine print.

Monetary Instruments

Ironically, to establish "good" credit you need to borrow money and pay it back on time according to its terms. So that you do not get tripped up by jargon, let us start leveling the playing field by identifying many of the common monetary instruments that are in use today.

Credit card

A credit card is an **unsecured line of credit**, which represents the fact that a bank or other lender is willing to lend you money. The loan is based upon your good faith and your credit history. The lender can access your credit reports which track your financial history.

- If you do not pay back the loan according to its terms and conditions, the lender can then alert other potential lenders, landlords, employers, etc. via your credit reports that you are a poor credit risk.

- The lender cannot take the money out of your bank account or, for example, force you to sell your house or other assets to pay them back. An exception may be if your credit card is with the same bank as your checking or savings account, in which case the bank may be able to take the funds out of that account to offset your credit card debt if you are delinquent and just refuse to pay.

- Because the lender is unsecured, its bad debt may be difficult or impossible to collect even if it is turned over to a collections agency.

Why even use a credit card if you can pay cash or write a check? Cash is becoming less fashionable. There are a growing number of places that don't even accept cash anymore. And isn't it frustrating to wait in the checkout line while someone actually writes a check? Furthermore, paying cash does not establish good credit. **<u>The best time to establish credit is when you don't need it.</u>**

Another reason, aside from establishing your good credit, is that these days you cannot really check into a hotel, rent a car, or purchase anything over the internet without a credit card. When you check into a hotel, the first thing they ask to see is your credit card. If the room is $200 they may put a "hold" on your credit card account for $350 to cover any damages or other purchases you make. It is only after you check out that they release the hold money if it is not needed. And that may take a few days.

And here is why lenders like credit cards:

- Over 50% of credit card holders do not pay off their balances each month.

- The average American household carrying a monthly balance has over $9,000 in credit card debt and may have several credit cards.

- Credit cards have become an important factor in financing college education. One recent survey reported over 75% of college undergraduates had at least one credit card, and the average balance owed exceeded $3,000. Other surveys have shown similar results.

In addition to the interest you will pay on outstanding credit card debt, additional credit card related fees and penalties may be charged. Make sure you know what fees and penalties your financial institution may charge, such as:

- Annual membership fees including extra fees for "status" cards.
- Fees when using another bank's automated teller machine (ATM), up to
- 5% per transaction with a minimum charge.
- Foreign exchange transaction fees, sometimes even if they are in dollars,
- 3% to 5%.
- Overdraft fees for charging more than your credit limit.
- Late payment fees.

- Returned check fees from payments not honored by your bank.
- Miscellaneous services, like receiving paper statements.
- Duplicate card fees for lost cards.
- Cash advance fees even from your own bank.
- Balance transfer fees of 2% to 5% if you move your account.
- Account closing fees.

Be aware that interest can be charged on penalties and fees. This means if you are carrying balances forward, you may be paying interest not only on your purchases, but on the added penalties and fees, usually at a higher interest rate.

Getting a credit card had been relatively easy until a few years ago. Because of the Great Recession issuers began raising rates, cutting limits, increasing fees, canceling inactive cards, reducing or eliminating teaser rates and award programs, and making it more difficult to qualify for a credit card.

Consumers responded to these economic times by reducing their use of credit, slowly paying down their debts, and purchasing more items with debit cards or cash. Credit card issuers were required to write off as uncollectible billions of dollars of credit card balances, absorbing large financial losses.

However, as the economy recovered, and money began flowing again, credit standards eased, and solicitations increased. Warning! Do not be lured by easy money and the mistakes that led to the Great Recession. Think twice before paying high annual fees for the so-called "status" cards that are flashy gold or mysterious black. If you are searching for a new credit card, see www.cardtrak.com or www. creditcards.com for additional information, news, and updates.

Debit card
A **secured** bank card that takes money out of your bank account immediately to pay for purchases you have made. Debit cards gained popularity as an alternative for those having difficulty managing credit cards. However, using a debit card does not necessarily help you establish credit since the money is already in your account and the **bank is taking no risk**.

Though debit cards may not be as advantageous to you as credit cards, merchants prefer them because the fees they pay to the banks or issuers for each transaction, called interchange fees, are usually about one-third of the fees for processing credit cards. This amounts to savings for the merchant, though the consumer will probably not see any of it through lower prices at the cash register.

Banks like debit cards because the money is in your account and they incur no risk. However, some banks add fees of about $30 if you exceed your limit (overdraft), though they can do so only with your prior approval.

When using a debit card, take your receipts, especially if no personal identification number (PIN) is required. In fraud cases involving hackers or data breaches, with a debit card it may take 2 to 3 months for the money to be reimbursed into your account, as opposed to credit cards where it is usually handled within a few days. I recommend not using a debit card for hotels or car rentals, since they will probably put a large hold on your account for several days.

Charge card

A credit card is issued by a "retailer" allowing you to charge purchases made only with their store. Stores frequently offer discounts at the register on all purchases made that day in the store to entice you to open an account. It may be hard to resist when you're offered 10% to 20% savings that day, but there is a downside.

Store credit cards usually carry high rates of interest, as high as 20% to 30% on unpaid balances. Some store cards have no grace period, so interest begins on the date of purchase. And if you're thinking about taking advantage of the discounts and quickly canceling the card, be aware that your credit score may be lowered. You might be better off asking if they have a "friends or family" discount. I just tell them I am a "friend," and I am surprised how often that works.

If you do decide on a store credit card, you should be prepared to pay it off every month and not carry a balance or pay interest. The additional card means one more card in your wallet, one more statement to look at each month, and possibly one more chance to get hacked. And if you get miles or cash back on your regular credit card, you will not get them when using a store card.

Prepaid card

Prepaid cards may be the fastest growing segment of the plastic money industry. They are offered by banks and nonbanks. They are not linked to a bank account. Prepaid cards were initially designed to provide the less affluent, those without bank accounts, a secure way to carry money. But banks have found they can be quite lucrative with fees such as:

- Activation fees of up to $39.95, according to Consumers Union

- Inactivity fees

- Fees to load money onto the card

- Fees if you **do not** load any money, or at least a minimum amount, onto the card each month

- Fees to check balance information

- Fees to use an ATM for cash

- Fees for using a check to close an account

How bad can it get? I read about one lady with a $500 prepaid card, which she did not use for a year and was charged $186 in fees.

Prepaid cards are not subject to most credit card restrictions. They are used like debit cards but are not subject to interchange fee requirements. Banks can charge merchants negotiated fees. Banks can also charge "shortage fees" without permission or restriction if purchases exceed the amount of the card.

The biggest downside to prepaid cards is that if they are lost or stolen, the money is probably gone forever.

Payday loan

A high interest short term cash loan is intended to be repaid by future paychecks.

These loans have been around for many years, often solicited from mobile units stationed outside military bases, factories, or in strip mall offices. Payday lenders may also cash paychecks and write checks for rent and utilities, taking in fees for service. By attempting to reach the "underserved," they compete with pawn shops and similar providers.

Some banks, looking to increase profitability, are marketing loans for cash advances of up to $500, to be repaid by future paychecks. One bank charges $2 per $20 borrowed or about 10% every 35 days for amounts up to $500. Another bank charges $7.50 per month for each $100 borrowed but limits the length of the loan to six months. The annual percentage rates (APR) commonly reach 300% or more.

Installment debt

Money that is borrowed to purchase large items such as a car or furniture, paying for them over time. The borrower purchases the item and pays for it at regular intervals until the loan is paid back in full. Usually the payments are monthly in equal amounts, with interest comprising most of the payment in early installments, and principal being most of the payment in later installments.

Deferred interest plan

A plan that enables a consumer to purchase big-ticket items paying no interest or a low "teaser" rate of interest over a promotional period. The promotional period may be a specific number of months or years. They are usually applied to things such as cars, mattresses, furniture, appliances, and electronic devices. However, there are pitfalls to watch out for, making deferred interest plans very expensive. For example:

- If the entire balance is not paid off by the end of the period, not only will interest begin, but you may also be retroactively charged for the interest on the entire balance during the promotion.

- If you are late in your payments, usually 60 or more days, you may be charged interest on the entire balance retroactively.

Gift cards

Gift cards are stored value cards, usually for use at a specific retailer or merchant. They are quite flexible in that gift card expiration dates have now been eliminated or restricted to no fewer than five years, and fees and other deductions from the card's value are severely limited. However, be aware that loss of a gift card probably means you have lost all its value.

Cashier's check

A check purchased by you from a bank, payable to a third party designated by you. It is issued by the bank for the value of the check plus a service fee. Because it is issued by the bank after they have received your funds, it has the reputation of being a "good" check.

Certified check

A personal check the bank guarantees as being supported by funds in your account. It is made payable to any third party you designate. The amount of the check is immediately deducted from your account along with a service fee.

Common Credit Terminology

Now that you are familiar with the most common monetary instruments you have available, let us gain some familiarity with the terms frequently used when describing them. Whether you are planning your budget, talking to a bank, or reading an agreement, do not let yourself be in for a big surprise just because you don't understand what the words mean.

Credit: The amount of money a lender is willing to lend subject to repayment terms and conditions such as interest, fees, and penalties.

Debt: The state of owing something such as money.

Debtor (or borrower): A person or entity with debt which owes or has the obligation to repay the debt.

Principal: The amount of money borrowed or loaned.

Interest: The cost of money paid by the borrower to obtain use of the principal, or received by the lender for providing the principal. It is often expressed as an Annual Percentage Rate ("APR") of the principal. The more often interest is calculated or compounded, the higher the interest rate becomes.

For example, when you carry a balance in your credit card account from month to month, and do not pay it off in full, the bank will usually calculate your interest on a daily basis which will earn it more than the stated rate. This means a 12% annual rate could actually be 12.74%. The banks know this. Now, you do too!

Fixed rate of interest: A loan with an interest rate that will remain at a predetermined or "fixed" rate for the life or term of the loan. The rate does not fluctuate during the period of the loan.

Adjustable rate of interest: A loan where the rate of interest is not fixed, but may change at various specified times. This is most commonly found in home loans where the interest rate is established for a few years and is then changed to a new rate for the balance of the loan.

Variable rate of interest: An interest rate that moves up and down based upon a benchmark interest rate which is not controlled by the lender. It is now commonly used by credit card issuers. One example would be to base the variable rate on the "prime rate" of interest which is supposedly the lowest interest rate banks charge their best customers.

"Go-To" rate: The interest rate you are charged on unpaid credit card balances, in addition to the variable rate, to determine the total rate of interest on your account.

Your go-to rate is based on your credit history. As your credit history improves or declines, so is the likelihood that your go-to rate will rise or fall on future borrowings.

For example, if your go-to rate is 8% and the variable rate is 3%, your total rate of interest on unpaid balances is 11%. If interest rates rise and the variable rate increases to 5%, your total rate of interest will rise to 13%.

Revolving credit: Credit or funds made available to you for your use, at any time, subject to the terms of repayment. Credit cards provide a revolving line of credit which, when you use the funds, will require you to make at least a minimum payment each month. As you repay all or a portion of the funds you have used, you can make new charges up to your maximum credit limit. Thus, you can reuse your credit line over and over again up to its limit......it revolves.

Default rate: An accelerated rate of interest, typically 28% to 35%, charged on your credit balance as a penalty when either of the following occurs:

- The issuer did not receive at least the minimum payment by the due date and time.
- Your payment is not honored by your bank, such as a bounced check.

Balance transfer fee: The fee which might be charged by a new lender if you transfer the balance from your credit card provider to another. Typically, this fee is 2% to 5% of the balance being transferred, unless special promotions are being offered to incentivize you to move your business. If you are transferring a balance to reduce the interest rate charged, the transfer fee may negate your savings.

Grace period: A period in the billing cycle during which no penalty is due as long as payment is received on time by the lender.

Stop payment: Requesting the bank to reject payment of a check when presented. If the need to stop payment on a check arises, contact your bank with the information and be ready to pay a fee (my last one being $30). Be sure to clarify how long the stop payment period is. Some expire every 30 days and your account may automatically be charged another fee if you do not cancel the stop payment. Some do not expire for 90 days and may or may not charge a fee. It is up to each bank so be aware of their policy. Odds are if the check is not presented within 2 to 6 months it probably won't be.

Always read the fine print!

Agreements with financial institutions may be long and loaded with jargon. That is no excuse for not reading them. Always read and understand each document before you sign. You may be surprised at what you find.

Though you might be attracted to a particular card for its travel rewards or cash benefits, there are other more important questions to ask when applying for credit:

- What is the interest rate on unpaid balances?

- What is the credit limit?

- What is the minimum payment required each month to avoid a penalty? This is usually 2.5% to 3% of the outstanding balance, but some banks under certain circumstances are raising it as high as 5%.

- Is there a grace period, the period for which no penalty is due?
    o If you carry a balance, there may be no grace period on new purchases.
    o The grace period may not apply to cash advances or balance transfers.

- If you are being offered a low interest teaser rate, what are the conditions?

- Is there insurance or warranty? Some cards include insurance coverage for stolen items and a warranty benefit which extends the terms of the original US manufacturer's warranty on "eligible purchases" charged to the card. Eligibility comes with restrictions so know what they are.

Other pitfalls you should be aware of include the following:

- To avoid a late payment fee always make sure your credit card payment is made two days before the due date if paying online, or five days before the due date if paying by mail. When mailing, payment must be **received,** not postmarked, by the due date.

- If you make payment using a live person, you may be charged a fee for the privilege. I'm not kidding! Ask first.

- When making an overpayment above the minimum, but less than the total balance in the account, make sure it is first applied to the principal, not interest or future payments. Use your overpayment to reduce the amount of the loan, which will reduce future interest charges as well.

- Never use "convenience checks" that connect to your credit card account due to their minimum charge, shown in small print, and high rate of interest. Shred them. They may have your account number on them. You are better off using the credit card.

- Never use a credit card in an ATM to get cash except in an emergency. Issuers typically charge a fee of 3% to 4% for the privilege, and that is not counting any other ATM charges or future interest charges on the advance.

- If you carry a balance, there may be different rates of interest charged for purchases, cash advances, balance transfers, and convenience checks.

- You can negotiate some terms and conditions with credit card companies. Try to reduce the annual fee. Providers now promote high-end cache or reward cards for extra fees for services you may not need.

Interest rates should come down as you pay on time over time. Do not be afraid to ask for a lower rate of interest if you make payments on time. Be nice---try twice. Many requests are granted. 35% is the highest default rate I have seen. Any single digit interest rate is as low as you can get.

Make every effort to reduce and eliminate your credit card debt as soon as possible.

- Stop using your credit card.

- Save first and then make your purchase.

- Take an extra job or allocate extra money to pay down the balance.

- Use gifts and bonuses to pay off the highest interest rate charges.

- If you are carrying balances on several credit cards, make the minimum payment on all cards. If you can afford it, pay more on the account with the highest rate of interest, not the card with the smallest balance.

- Call your credit card issuer and ask for a lower rate.

Seek help from your lenders if you are not able to pay on time. It does not hurt to ask for help. Describe your circumstances. Be polite. Do not argue, yell or use profanity. Calls are recorded. If you are not successful, wait a day and call back. Be nice.....try twice.

Credit card issuers may waive over limit fees and late penalties the first time. Also consider consolidating your debts into a single low-interest monthly payment loan to reduce high interest rates, speed up the payment of debts, and improve your credit score. Such loans may be available from your bank or credit union at substantially lower rates. You may even be better off selling some assets and using the proceeds to reduce or eliminate high interest debt.

If your account continues in default you can expect calls and letters that will get more aggressive over time. Keep your composure and document everything. In time, your account may be turned over to a collection agency and the contacts may seem downright threatening. Work hard to have default interest rates and late payment fees removed so you are dealing only with the principal amount. That could eliminate up to 40% of the total due. If you can reach a settlement, get it in writing with a letter stating the matter has been fully resolved. With the settlement letter you can try to get the credit reporting agencies to remove all negative mention of default from your account. It's worth a try.

Credit card theft is when your credit card is missing or stolen. Contact the credit card issuer or bank immediately. Current law states your loss is limited to $50 if you contact the issuer within two days of discovery. Beyond two days of discovery, you may be liable for up to $500 in losses. Beyond 60 days after discovery, you may be liable for the full amount of charges. Close the account immediately. Ask for a new card on a new account. If, after all this, you find a "lost" card in an old coat pocket or seat cushion, just destroy it so that it cannot be used.

Finally, always check your credit card statements every month. Look for erroneous charges and report them immediately.

And, never give your credit card number to anyone who calls you, unless you know them personally. If you need to make a payment, you call them!

Credit card fraud is commonly caused by a dishonest clerk, waiter, cashier, or thief who copies your account number and expiration date directly from your card or from a discarded receipt. Notify the issuer immediately if you suspect your card information has been compromised.

And, never create a fake new credit identity yourself. That is criminal fraud.

Avoid bankruptcy. This is not an easy way out. It is a last resort. Bankruptcy can negatively impact your credit score for up to 10 years. Additional credit, if available, will be at increased rates of interest. It may even make it difficult for you to rent an apartment or buy a car. It is that serious. Bankruptcy does not relieve you of obligations for taxes, alimony, child support, or most student loans.

Always get legal advice if bankruptcy is a consideration. Many lawyers will want to be paid their fee in advance of a filing. Be sure to have some cash in reserve, for living expenses and the legal fees. Brace yourself. Legal fees and expenses can add up to many thousands of dollars depending on the situation.

Contact a credit counseling agency before missing a monthly payment or deadline. Get names at www.nfcc.org or www.aicca.org. Beware of "credit repair" companies that advertise their services to consumers who need help with their credit. They may charge fees of hundreds or thousands of dollars mostly up front. They may promise to clean up your credit report, but most of the time they cannot deliver. Some are known to advise clients to stop paying their bills and then try to negotiate a better deal on a larger amount.

Latest Developments

There is more technology coming. Historically, credit cards and debit cards were made out of plastic and had a magnetic strip on them containing your specific account information. This technology, which has been around for years and carries static data, is relatively easy for thieves to steal, sell, or use to purchase items without your permission.

To counteract criminals, credit card issuers are shifting from magnetic strip cards to chip cards using Europay, MasterCard, Visa (EMV) technology, which encrypts the data from each transaction. In some cases, they are pairing EMV technology with a PIN or even a fingerprint sensor.

In fact, some especially sensitive accounts may require a user name and password, plus another layer like a one-time code, a second password, a fingerprint, or the correct answer to a deeply personal question such as the middle name of the bridesmaid at your first wedding.

One of the biggest issues in converting to EMV is the need for a compatible payment terminal at the vendor's location. Some countries have already made the switch, in which case your old magnetic strip card may not work. Check with your credit card issuer if you plan to use your credit card internationally. In the United States most vendors have made the switch, but it may be only a matter of time before some new currency or technology arrives on the scene.

Next in the credit and debit card technology explosion is using your mobile phone to pay for goods and services by "waving" it in front of a scanner to pay for purchases. Waving is looking to replace "swiping" a plastic credit or debit card at checkout time. It's already being done at quite a few merchants such as Starbucks, and in Japan, UK, and parts of Africa.

The incentive for all of the card usage is "money," but not for you or me. Every time a credit or debit card is used, a small transaction fee results. The fee is paid by the merchant to the card issuing bank, the merchant's bank, and the payment network. The sum total of these fees is many billions of dollars.

With the entry of Apple Pay and Google Wallet, the competitive battle among corporate giants becomes even greater. Major direct providers of products and services, such as Amazon, AT&T, Verizon, Wal-Mart, and Target, may want to keep these fees for themselves. New technologies and corporate alliances are sure to follow. Stay tuned!

Credit Card Accountability Responsibility and Disclosure Act, or "Card Act."

The Card Act and the Federal Reserve's new rules apply **only** to **consumer** credit cards, **not business** credit cards. That's why credit card providers are now flooding the mailboxes of businesses with tempting offers of credit based upon the old, more flexible and profitable, rules.

But make no mistake, they are also still flooding the mailboxes, emails, and mobile phones of consumers too, to lure customers with all kinds of ads and "teasers" that are within the law, such as zero transfer fees and zero introductory interest rates.

In response to massive consumer complaints, the US Government passed a major piece of financial protection legislation. Following is a summary of the Card Act which is currently the law of the land:

- When a new account is opened, there can be no interest rates increase for the first 12 months unless an **introductory rate** has come to an end, or you are more than 60 days late with a payment, or unless you are on a variable interest rate tied to an index. When your introductory rate expires, the interest rate will revert back to your "go-to" rate plus the variable rate.

- After one year or the introductory rate expires, the card holder must be notified **45 days** in advance of any rate change.

- If you are more than 60 days **late in making the minimum payment**, the issuer may charge you the interest default rate, which is typically 28% to 35%. However, if you make your payments on time for six consecutive months, the original rate must be restored. Some banks may refund part of the default rate for each month you pay on time as an incentive to get the account "cleaned up."

- For an account in good standing, **interest rate increases** can only be applied to **new charges.**

- **Promotional rate periods** must be for a minimum of six months.

- **Overdraft fee**s may not be charged unless the cardholder agrees to allow them. When you "accept" most modern-day contracts you are probably agreeing to overdraft fees. Otherwise, the issuer would reject the charge. How embarrassing!

- Overdraft and late payment fees, as high as $39, are added to your balance and will increase your interest charges if not paid. That means you might end up **paying interest on the interest and fees** which were added to your balance.

- An **unused credit hold**, such as those placed by hotel or car rental companies, may not create an overdraft charge unless the hold is executed.

- Cardholder **statements** must show how many months it will take to pay your balance if only the minimum payment is made. Plus, it must show the total you will pay in principal and interest over that time.

- Cardholder statements must also show how much will have to be paid each month to pay the **entire balance in 36 months.** Plus it must show the total you will have to pay in principal and interest over that time.

- **Activation fees, annual fees, and other specified fees** may not exceed 25% of the credit limit during the first year of use. **After one year, there is no limit or "cap" on fees.** If your initial credit limit is $500, first year fees cannot exceed $125, excluding penalty fees such as a late payment fee.

- There is **no legal limit or cap on interest rates on outstanding balances.** Let the buyer beware!

- Statements must be mailed at least 21 days before the payment due date, and various **finance charges, penalties, and fees cannot be charged prior to the 21st day.** This 21-day period is commonly referred to as the grace period. Some banks are allowing up to a 25-day grace period.

- The **payment due date** should be the same day each month, and some issuers will adjust it for you to coincide with paydays or some other preferred day of the month.

- Consumers with existing accounts must be informed of any **rate increase or new charges at least 45 days** in advance of the effective date. Thereafter, the issuer **must review the account once every six months** to determine if the rate increase or charges should be dropped.

- Credit card issuers may not raise interest rates on **prior charges** solely on the basis of current changes in a credit report or a credit score.

- If you are notified 45 days in advance of a **significant change in terms**, such as a rate or fee increase, the issuer must give you a chance to close

- the account and **pay off the balance at the old interest rate(s).** However, the credit card company may increase your monthly payment so it will be paid off in five years, or double the percentage of the minimum payment. No new charges will be allowed.

- No fees can be charged for making credit card **payments online or over the phone** unless you make the payment on your due date or later. The due date fee may actually be less than the late payment fee. Think about it.

- Payments are "on-time" if **received by 5 pm** at the location of the payment office on the due date or the next business day after a holiday or weekend.

- Credit cards cannot be issued to anyone **under age 21** unless the applicant has a responsible cosigner, usually a parent or guardian, or can demonstrate independent means to repay the debt.

- Issuers are not allowed to **solicit students** on or "near" campuses and offer T-shirts, pizza, etc. as gifts or incentives for completing an application for credit. The law does not prohibit such solicitations at off-campus sites.

- Credit-limit increases for those under 21 must be subject to the **co- signer's permission**. For as long as the cosigner is on the account, the cosigner will be jointly responsible for repayment even after age 21. Issuers will have the option of keeping the cosigner on the account.

- Statements must include a toll-free phone number you can call for **credit-counseling services.**

- Payments in excess of the minimum must first be applied to the balance with **highest interest rate**. This is a major change, and a benefit to the consumer.

- Statements must include a "**Late Payment Warning**" and a "**Minimum Payment Warning.**"

- Customers must be notified **30 days in advance before their account is closed.**

- And finally, believe it or not, H.R. 5244, the Credit Cardholders' Bill of Rights Act of 2008, signed by President Obama and which amends the Truth in Lending Act, includes an amendment that allows people to carry guns in National Parks and wildlife refuges as a concession to Sen. Tom Coburn (R-Oklahoma).

Federal Reserve Rules

The Federal Reserve also issues consumer credit card protection rules. Updates are available at www.federalreserve.gov/creditcard.

- Your credit card company cannot charge you a fee of more than **$25** unless one of your last six payments was late, in which case your fee may be up to $35.

- In addition, your credit card company cannot charge a **late payment fee that is greater than your minimum payment.** So, if your minimum payment is $20, your late payment fee cannot be more than $20. Similarly, if you exceed your credit limit by $5, you cannot be charged an over-the- limit fee of more than $5.

- Your credit card company cannot charge an **inactivity fee** for not using your card.

- Your credit card company cannot charge you more than one fee for a **single transaction or event** that violates your cardholder agreement. For example, you cannot be charged more than one fee for a single late payment.

- If your credit card company increases your card's APR, **it must tell you why**.

- If your credit card company increases your **APR**, it must reevaluate that rate increase every six months. If appropriate, it must reduce your rate within 45 days after completing the evaluation.

- Issuers that have increased rates are required to **evaluate whether the reasons for the increase have changed** and, if appropriate, to reduce the rate.

- Current providers of consumer credit cards must post their credit card agreements at www.federalreserve.gov/creditcardagreements.

Consumer Financial Protection Agency (CFPA)

This federal agency is to protect the consumer by eliminating "unfair, abusive, and deceptive" practices. Operating within the Federal Reserve, "CFPA" will enforce regulations dealing with credit cards, as well as checking accounts, deposit accounts, student loans, check cashers, pay-day lenders, home mortgages, and other consumer related financial products. The mere existence of this agency is a point of political controversy. It publishes new rules and regulations, and accepts consumer complaints at: www.consumerfinance.gov.

Ultimately, you need to protect yourself.

If you monitor your statements and pay your bills on time, most of these issues will go away!

Notes and Updates

CHAPTER 4

CREDIT REPORTS AND CREDIT SCORES
"I Spend, Therefore I Am."

Your **credit report** is your individual financial report card which tells whether you have been making your credit card and loan payments on time. It also includes a lot of other personal information about you. The total information about you on your credit report determines your **credit score.**

Nearly every financial decision you make is being watched, tracked, and reported to one or more of the major credit bureaus. The scope and depth of the information in your credit report might surprise you. Some of the information may be incorrect; perhaps an account you never had, or an account showing an overdue balance which was, in fact, fully paid. Like it or not, this is what lenders, landlords, employers, and others will want to see when judging you.

There are three major reporting agencies as listed hereunder:
- Transunion (Empirica score)
- Equifax (Beacon score)
- Experian (Experian model)

Credit reports cover the previous 7 to 10 years and may include employment history, lawsuits, judgments, arrests, DUI's, bankruptcies, and records of all loans, including student loans, rents and mortgages, credit cards, charge cards, credit limits, credit usage, monthly payment records, delinquencies, items turned over for collection, checking and savings accounts.

Recently, lenders seeking new customers have begun to reach out to underserved groups such as seniors, minorities, and those who have had mortgage debt problems, but who otherwise might be good credit risks. In response, credit reporting agencies and their customers are now looking more closely at individuals' debit and prepaid card use, length of employment, utility bill payments, and the frequency of address changes.

For each account listed, the report shows the account number, balance, credit limit, monthly payment, past due amounts, and late payments. It also includes the number of accounts you have applied for recently, and the number of requests which have been made recently to see your report.

Voluntary requests to see your report are those authorized by you so that a lender, landlord, employer, etc. can legally get a copy of your credit report.

Involuntary requests usually come from lenders interested in soliciting you by mail for a preapproved credit offer. They have no bearing on your score.

It is estimated that about 50% of employers are using credit checks as part of the hiring process. This is legal. However, the **employer must have your written permission to do** so. If you know there is an issue you may be able to correct it in advance or address it upfront along with an explanation.

You are legally entitled to one free copy of your credit report per year from each of the three major bureaus, or 1 per 4 months, for example January, May, and September. The only **federally mandated** website for free credit reports is **www. annualcreditreport.com** or call 877-322-8228. Other sites typically will solicit you for credit watching services with fees or, in some cases, may be imposters looking to use your information to open accounts in your name.

While making these reports available is helpful, there are now firms in the private sector which will enable you to get free credit reports and scores as frequently as you wish. This includes customers of certain financial institutions along with independent websites such as creditkarma.com, credit.com, and mint.com. They are free provided you are willing to view some ads of course, and they can provide you with some valuable information.

So, if you are concerned about your creditworthiness, or planning to buy a car or a house, you can see it is possible to get this information, plan ahead, and put a shine on your credit report.

Those three important numbers

Your three-digit **FICO score** is the mathematical number used by lenders to determine if you are a good or bad credit risk. Your FICO score is based upon the delinquency and default rate of a large number of people with credit history similar to yours. This indicates how likely you are to repay a loan or credit card balance as agreed. The higher the delinquency rate, the lower the score, and therefore the less chance you have to get a favorable deal, or any deal at all. For example, look at these projected delinquency rates and you will clearly see why few lenders will want to risk lending to someone with a low score:

Credit Score	Delinquency Rate (in %)
800–850	1
750–799	2
700–749	5
650–699	15
600–649	31
550–599	51
500–549	71
300–499	87

People you do business with are constantly reporting your financial activity to one or more of the three major credit bureaus. The same information may not be transmitted to all bureaus by every merchant or creditor. Therefore, each credit bureau may have slightly different information about you which will result in **three different FICO scores**. Credit scores can change almost daily as new information is submitted.

The minimum criteria required for a score is based upon at least six months of history, including:

- at least one reported "account" which has been open for at least six months,
- at least one account that has been reported by a lender in the last six months, and
- nothing that indicates you're deceased.

It is not uncommon for crooks to assume the identity of a dead person and open accounts in that person's name.

The Standard **FICO formula** includes five basic categories.

Record of paying bills on time over time	35%
Debt-to-credit ratio, which is the total balance on your credit cards and other loans compared to your total credit limit	30%
Length of credit history	15%
New accounts and recent applications for credit	10%
Mix of credit cards and loans	10%

Paying your balance each month will not hurt your credit score.

Ranges and exact cutoffs can vary from lender to lender, but this is believed to be a typical representation:

780–850	Best
720–779	Good
661–719	OK
620–660	Subprime
560–619	Bad
500–559	Worst
300–499	Toxic

FICO scores are designed to show how you handle credit. As far as we know, they do not consider factors such as age, race, sex, marital status, where you live, occupation, or salary.

Importantly, FICO's latest version will no longer consider medical debts just because adults are having trouble paying them. Some medical bills relate to an emergency, and many others are ultimately covered by insurance. Additionally, when calculating credit scores according to a recent model, FICO will not consider collections which have been paid.

From time to time you may encounter other scores, but FICO is still the most commonly used. Your score tells how you have handled credit in the past, a proxy for how you are likely to handle credit in the future.

Why is your credit score so important? Remember when I said a higher score will get you a better deal?

Assume a four-year car loan for $20,000. A FICO score of 775 vs. 575 is equal to about $5,000 of interest saved. If you invested the $5,000 at 8% compounded over 40 years, you would have $107,000.

Your credit score is **not** part of your credit report. In fact, it is your credit report that is used to generate your credit score, so it is most important to pay attention to the details in the report. You can dispute items in a credit report such as a closed or nonexistent account. But the score it generates is not negotiable. It is your score. **Want to change your score**? Change the information on your credit report. Be a better credit risk.

Check reports for accuracy
In this regard, 25% have serious errors or list old accounts.

- Make sure it is **your** credit report. Sometimes people apply for credit under different spellings of their name, like Fred, Fredric, or Frederick.

- Check for an error with the Social Security number or some other clerical error.

- Payments or charges might be mistakenly reported to the wrong account.

- Years later, a closed account may still show up on your credit report and may be included in determining your score for some period of time.

To correct an error, call the customer service department of the business which reported the problem or call the credit bureau to correct the problem, depending on the source. Sometimes you can get unflattering items removed from your credit report by asking the company or agency that reported the information to have it removed. This can only be done after the item has been resolved, but it is worth a try. Be nice. No arguing or profanity. If necessary, wait a few months and try again.

You can also file, or threaten to file, a lawsuit under the Fair Debt Practices Act. But this can be time consuming and expensive. Getting the party that supposedly reported the error to make a change and put it in writing is a far better way to go.

If there is no error, another option to handle problems is to try to negotiate a settlement. All offers, and counter offers, along with the settlement agreement need to be in writing. With that in hand you can try to have the item removed from your credit report.

Check for identity theft.
Identity theft usually begins when someone gets hold of your personal information. It could be your Social Security number, password, credit card number, phone number, address, bank account number, or any other piece of personal information which can be used to open accounts in your name and make purchases.

There are a number of ways for strangers to get this information, for example, **loss or theft of** a purse or wallet, dumpster diving or going through your trash, stealing from your mailbox, and postal forwarding of your mail such as bank or credit card statements to another address or post office (PO) box. Other methods include **phishing** via email or over the phone with fake messages, sometimes enticing you to validate or update your personal information; and **hacking** or stealing your information from other computers or data centers which you believed were secure.

Never give your Social Security number or other personal information to a stranger.

What to do if your identity has been stolen?

- Immediately contact the three major credit bureaus and put a **"fraud alert"** on your account which requires all creditors contact you directly before granting any new credit:

Transunion	+1-800-916-8800
Experian	+1-888-397-3742
Equifax	+1-800-525-6285

- Close all of your accounts as soon as possible (ASAP) and reopen new accounts, not just bank and credit card accounts but remember places like Amazon, iTunes, Macy's, and AT&T.

- Contact all of your creditors.

- File a police report and keep the number of the report.

- Keep a detailed record of who you contact and when.

Usually identity theft and stolen credit cards are afforded some protection by your bank, the card issuer, or some insurance policies.

Protect yourself from fraud and identity theft

The following steps will help you in protecting yourself from fraud and identity theft.

- Do not respond to phone calls or emails supposedly from the IRS. **The IRS does not call people or email them.** If there is an issue, then you will be contacted only by snail mail. That's it! And remember, they already have your Social Security number.

- Create unique passwords and personal identification numbers.

- Change passwords periodically.

- Keep your personal information secure at home and away.

- "Sign out" of sensitive personal websites when using public computers.

- Shred or otherwise destroy documents that contain account numbers and other personal information such as your Social Security or other ID numbers.

- Be extremely careful about giving out personal information over the phone or internet, especially when the contact is initiated by another party. In that case, it may be best to call them back to make sure you know who you are talking to.

- Carry with you as few credit, debit, charge, and bank cards as possible. Do not carry your Social Security card or number with you. Memorize it!

- Keep a separate copy of all your account numbers in a secure place.

- Review all monthly statements for unfamiliar transactions including checking, savings, brokerage, and credit card accounts. Report them immediately.

- Check your credit reports regularly.

Additional protection

A new technique that has become popular due to large-scale hacking of business and governmental data centers is **"security freeze."** If your Social Security number or other information is stolen, then hackers may try to open new credit accounts in your name. A security freeze can be used to deny access to your credit information so that a potential new creditor is not able to access your information in order to approve the request. To **initiate a credit freeze** you need to individually contact each of the three major credit bureaus.

With a freeze in place, only certain entities can access your file, including existing creditors and firms you specifically authorize to monitor your credit file to prevent fraud. Almost all states have security freeze laws which govern fees which are quite small and are usually free for victims of identity theft.

Know the score!

In some instances you might need to pay or reimburse a third party to get a FICO score and a credit report for a specific loan. That is another reason to periodically check your credit report for accuracy, clear up errors, or take necessary steps to improve your score. You want it to be as high as possible when the need arises.

Improve your FICO score

You can improve your FICO score by following these steps:

- **Pay at least the minimum balance due** on time and over time. Minimums are usually 2 .5% to 3% of the outstanding balance, but may be as high as 5%.

- Always mail your payment at least five days before the due date or pay online at least two days before the due date. You will avoid **a late payment fee** this way.

- **Manage your total debt/credit ratio.** Stay below a 50% debt-to-credit ratio on each credit card. A 30% ratio is best for top scores. Pay down what you owe or increase your credit limits to lower your credit ratio. Do not charge any more purchases on these cards!

- **Preserve history.** Cancel newer cards first, but be careful. Canceling a card may increase your overall debt-to-credit ratio which might lower your FICO score. Do not destroy or cancel older cards if you can help it.

- **Create the right credit mix.** Your credit mix can impact your credit score. For example, a person with eight credit cards and no other debt, paying minimum balances on time would probably not have as high a score as someone with two credit cards paying the minimums, a mortgage and a car loan with no late payments.

- **Do not apply for a lot of additional credit at once.** Each time you apply for credit you are creating an "inquiry." Lenders may view several inquiries for a car loan or a mortgage as a single event, assuming you are just shopping for the best deal. However, multiple inquiries for revolving credit cards might indicate financial stress and could impact your score. According to www.myfico.com, people with several such inquiries have a greater risk of declaring bankruptcy.

FICO score simulators, available on the internet, will help you understand how your future behavior will change your score, up or down. They can be helpful at times by telling you which bills or loans you should pay first to lift your credit score the most.

Credit reporting agencies are constantly looking for new ways to judge you and build their own businesses. TransUnion, Equifax, and Experian periodically introduce credit scoring systems of their own to try to compete with FICO and save paying fees. These new scores may be numerically different than FICO's because they are weighted differently.

Sometimes the scores consumers get are not the same scores that are sold to lenders, landlords, insurers, or employers. They may be more interested in how you handle specific areas such as rent, utilities, insurance, phone, day care, and other payments in calculating your score. Some lenders also look more carefully at where you spend your money. Charges at bars, pawn shops, massage parlors, and tire retread shops are frowned upon.

Credit score confusion is common. For example, FICO rolled out a new scoring program with Transunion which ignores collection accounts under $100, along with isolated delinquencies such as a single phone or utility bill.

Finally, agencies continue to look for new ways to attract some 50 million people living in the United States including many immigrants, young adults, and seniors with little or no credit history, many of whom pay their bills on time.

> **Pay your bills on time over time,**
> **keep your debt-to-credit ratio near 30%,**
> **and avoid DUIs, bill collectors, and other "character flaws."**

Notes and Updates

CHAPTER 5

CONTRACTS CAN BE DANGEROUS TO YOUR HEALTH

Read Them!

We are all getting way too casual about signing contracts.

It seems every time we sign up for an "app" or computer software program we are asked to click "accept." I don' t know about you, but I cannot remember ever reading one of these contracts. I could be signing away my house and never know it until it's too late.

That's what happened to millions of Americans who signed home mortgages and credit card applications without reading or understanding them. In some cases, it led to financial ruin.

Generally speaking, a contract is a **binding agreement** entered into voluntarily by two or more competent parties. Two party contracts are often referred to as **bilateral** contracts, while contracts with three or more parties are generally called **multilateral**. Contracts create legal obligations between the parties.

- Commitments in a contract may last a long time and may have serious consequences if they are broken or violated.

- Many of the terms and conditions may be "hidden" in fine print or terminology that only a lawyer or judge fully understands. Sometimes, things are unintentionally ambiguous.

- Some definitions, terms, and conditions may be found in footnotes or the last few pages of a lengthy document.

Assume nothing. Get it in writing.

Some of the most common personal contracts involve marriage, employment, real estate, credit cards, debit cards, buying a house, renting an apartment, insurance, buying or leasing a car, joining a health club, or signing up for cable or cell phone service.

In common law, before a contract can be binding, all parties to the contract must offer what is called **consideration**, which means there is a mutual obligation to perform, and that something of value is to be exchanged. It presumes there is an offer of some type by a competent party, and acceptance by another competent party. Consideration could be money, services, physical objects, future actions, promised actions, etc. Without adequate consideration from all parties, there is no valid contract. To be enforceable, the consideration must be deemed **adequate** or **sufficient** when tested in a court of law.

Contracts may be written or oral, but in most cases written is better because it is more definitive than "he said, she said" and print does not fade the way memory does. If it's an oral contract, have good witnesses and document with dated notes.

When a party does not adhere to the terms and conditions of the contract, the contract is considered **breached**. If guilty, that party could then become liable for any damages or consequences. Certain contracts, such as home loans or insurance policies **must be in writing** to be binding and enforceable.

Always read the contract before signing it, and make sure you understand all of its terms and conditions.

There are certain items to look for in **every contract**. I suggest keeping this **checklist** handy as a guide, but always consider professional legal advice if you are at all concerned.

- Always be sure you know how much you are required to pay or be paid and when.

- Know how long the term of the contract will be. Know what constitutes the "end" of the contract.
  Is it a particular date or time?
  Is it a particular event taking place?
  Is it because one party failed to perform?
  Is the contract renewable either automatically or by notice?
  Are there specific conditions under which a party can terminate the contract?
  Can you terminate early by paying a penalty?

- Be knowledgeable about how amendments can be made to the contract.

- What happens if either party fails to perform?

- Depending on the nature of the contract, here are some other important items to think about:

> Is there a refund policy and/or early termination fee?
> Is arbitration required or mediation?
> Is the contract automatically terminated if a defined event occurs? If so, what are the consequences?
> What happens to your health club membership, apartment rent, or car lease if you move away from the area?
> What happens if you leave your job? Can you work for a competitor? Can you get a better deal if charges are automatically made to your credit card or your checking account?

Always ask yourself whether it makes sense to investigate the other party before entering into a contract to verify reputation, claims made, or financial standing?

Certain factors may **void the entire contract** or just a certain part of the contract. Such factors may include:

- Fraud
- Misrepresentation
- Mental incompetence
- Duress including violence or coercion

If resolution of the contract occurs in a court of law, the court may issue a **judgment** when the parties are unable to settle. The judgment states how much money must be paid or what action must be taken on behalf of a damaged party. Judgments become a matter of **public record** and may be reflected in a person's **credit report**, especially when money is owed.

Depending on various state laws, judgments may give injured parties additional ways to collect money, including legal access to checking and savings accounts, garnishing wages, or even posting a law enforcement officer next to a business' cash register to intercept incoming cash.

Make sure all blanks are filled in so that changes cannot be made without your knowing about them. If changes are made to the contract, be sure all parties initial and date them.

Do not be pressured into signing a contract.

Take time to read it. Get professional help or help from someone you trust. Some types of contracts require the signature be authenticated by a **notary public** who is a public officer constituted by law to **witness the execution** of certain classes of non- contentious documents, including contracts such as mortgage documents, wills, trusts, deeds, durable power of attorney, power of attorney for healthcare, tenancy-in-common agreements, and administering of oaths. Some types of contracts require at least one or more creditable witnesses, such as a marriage certificate.

Do not agree on a handshake or a promise.

Get it in writing or at least have a creditable witness or two. If you end up in court or arbitration, the written word or a creditable witness can be very important. Otherwise, it may be your word against theirs.

Always **get a copy** of the contract you sign. There may be state laws that require a **cooling-off period**, frequently three days, for certain types of contracts. A cooling-off period allows you to legally reject the contract without penalty within that time frame. Sometimes, wording about a cooling-off period is in the contract. Regardless, always know your rights, or contact your attorney, your state attorney general's office or a consumer protection agency for help.

There is a second type of contract which bears mentioning, called a **unilateral contract.** In a unilateral contract only **one party makes a promise** or expresses an offer based upon another party's performance. An example might be where a governmental agency promises a reward for information leading to the arrest and conviction of a criminal, or a private party posts a reward for finding their dog. If you help the authorities catch the criminal, or you find the dog, you are entitled to the money, even though you never made a promise yourself or signed a contract to perform.

The best protection is always to make sure the underlying objectives are well thought out.

Make sure the contract is drawn up correctly to reflect the understanding of the parties so that issues can be resolved based upon its terms and condition. The best time to get legal advice is before a contract is signed.

When a contract is contested, I always recommend getting legal assistance. In many cases it may be possible to arrange a settlement between the parties. Considering the cost of a lawsuit, settling may be your best option.

Notes and Updates

CHAPTER 6

SOCIAL SECURITY AND MEDICARE

The Trend is Not Your Friend

The Federal Insurance Contribution Act, "FICA" is more commonly known as Social Security. You will find FICA on your paycheck stub in a little box showing you how much money has been taken out of your paycheck for Social Security. You will find another deduction on your paycheck stub for Medicare.

Social Security and Medicare are two huge government programs in serious trouble.

Social Security

Social Security is **a massive program**. Nearly 60 million Americans and legal immigrants receive monthly benefit checks totaling over $865 billion a year. That is about one out of every six people living in the United States. Some 200,000 visit its field offices each day, and it handles 450,000 phone calls a day. Although complicated, it is a good thing that this program exists because 50% of the workforce has no private pension coverage, and 35% has no savings set aside for retirement.

Why worry about Social Security (FICA) and Medicare at a young age? **Because you will be paying for it,** and **most people pay more in FICA and Medicare taxes than they do in federal income tax.**

Why have these programs become so large and indebted? **Because these programs were not designed for the demographics of today's workforce.**

Social Security became a law in 1935 under President Roosevelt. The designated retirement age of 65 was based upon the 1930 census when the average life expectancy for a male was 60, mainly due to smoking, driving, and work stress. The government set the "retirement" age at 65 realizing that, by that age, most men were probably dead. The average life expectancy for a female was 73 years, mainly because most stayed home, did not smoke, drive, or have the same work stress.

The first person to receive a Social Security check was Ida Mae Fuller. She paid $24.75 into the system and received $22,888.92 before dying at age 100 – a good deal for her but we cannot afford many more like that!

In 1935, 40 workers put into the system for each person that received a Social Security benefit. Since then, while life expectancy has been increasing, the birth rate has been declining, leaving fewer young people to work, contribute to the system, and care for an increasing number of senior citizens. Currently, about three workers put into the system for each person that receives a Social Security benefit. By 2030, it may be down to 2.5 workers putting in for each person receiving a benefit. Ironically, if all undocumented workers went home, we would be in bigger trouble because many of them are young, working, and paying into the system.

Now, life expectancies are longer and far more people are reaching the age of eligibility. The gender gap has narrowed and by 2030 it is estimated that 20% of the population will be over 65. On average, seniors take out about six times what they individually put into Social Security and Medicare.

Not only are there more elders taking from the program and fewer young workers contributing to the program, but also many senior unemployed workers are deciding to take Social Security retirement benefits sooner than planned out of necessity, increasing overall benefit payments. Some between the ages of 62 and 66 are unemployed, have exhausted their unemployment benefits, have little or no other source of income, and are desperate. Due largely to the Great Recession, the IRS estimates half of all those age 61 plan to start taking sharply reduced Social Security retirement benefits at age 62, despite the fact that such benefits might be further reduced if they earn more than a modest amount of income due to a complicated earnings test.

Overall, this adds up to the fact that **over 42% of all the money the federal government currently budgets are for senior citizens** including Social Security, Medicare, Medicaid for seniors, veterans' pensions and health care, federal employee pensions, and other benefits.

Under Social Security, the amount you pay into the system and the number of quarters you work largely determine the US dollar benefit you receive. In **2018**, to be eligible for benefits you need 40 quarters of employment, equal to 10 years, earning at least $1,320 per quarter. Dollar amounts tend to rise each year.

As structured today, the employer and the employee share equally in contributions to the program. Whereas the employers' contributions to Social Security are tax deductible, those made by an employee are not.

Years ago, the FICA contribution rate was 1% of the first $3,000 earned, or $30. In 2018, for Social Security, **the total rate of tax is 12.4% of all earned income** up to a maximum annual "salary cap" of $128,400. The cost is shared equally. 6.2% is paid by the employer and 6.2% is paid by the employee. For many years, the percentage rate has stayed the same, but the wage base or **cap has increased almost every year due to cost of living adjustments.**

The maximum annual contribution in 2018 is $15,921, divided equally between the employer and the employee. If you earn the current salary cap of $128,400 or more it works out to $7,960 for the employer and $7,960 for the employee. Earned income above the cap is not taxed for Social Security. The wage base cap in 2020 is projected to exceed $135,000, with the percentage rates continuing at 12.4%, split 50% to 50% between the employee and the employer. However, there are no guarantees.

At this time, you do not pay Social Security taxes on unearned income such as interest, dividends, or capital gains. This may change in the future and could lead to a surtax on high-income earners, similar to that already applied by Medicare to high-income earners.

Social Security is an **entitlement program** with only a few basic requirements to receive retirement benefits as listed hereunder:

- Age
- The required number of quarters you have paid into the system
- A minimal amount of income earned over those quarters
- You must be a citizen or lawful alien to receive benefits

The maximum monthly retirement benefit under Social Security is now about $2,800, though the **average** monthly retirement benefit is about $1,400.

Those who delay benefits until age 70 1/2 may have a current maximum benefit of about $3,500. A change in the method of calculating benefits is currently under discussion, the purpose being too slow or limit the rate of future benefit increases.

Besides benefits for workers, Social Security also offers spousal, widow, orphan, disability, and death benefits.

Divorcees are entitled to the higher of their own benefit or half of their ex- spouse's benefit, whichever is greater, but only if they were married for 10 years or more. If married for less than 10 years, that option is not available. As a result, there are spouses who have never worked but were married to high-income earners for more than 10 years who are receiving a larger monthly benefit than some low-income workers who have worked all their lives and contributed to the system for years.

Currently, seniors can take full benefits at age 66 and 4 months, or reduced benefits at age 62 subject to certain income restrictions. By taking early retirement at age 62, the monthly retirement benefit is reduced by 25%. Also, if one applies for early retirement and is still working, Social Security deducts $1 from the benefit payment for every $2 earned above an annual limit, which is currently set at $17,040, and tends to rise each year. Upon reaching full retirement age, qualified seniors will receive their full benefits **regardless of income**.

Without major changes to the program, for those born in 1960 or later, their full retirement age is expected to reach 67, and their early retirement monthly benefit will probably be reduced by 30%. The next steps might be to increase the full retirement age to 69, increase the age of early retirement, and make deeper cuts in benefits, especially for those who have other sources of income.

Further, 85% of **Social Security benefits are currently taxable** to the individual, however, lower-income people are able to exclude more of their benefits from federal taxes. Benefits are usually adjusted each year for inflation as calculated by the government. A new method of calculation is now being used to slow the rate of inflation and the growth of future benefits.

Social Security was never intended to be a nationwide, federally funded pension plan for everyone. It was designed only to **supplement a person's own pension plan and lifetime savings.** This fact has apparently been lost on most people today, many of whom believe Social Security is their pension plan and will adequately support them.

Under current law, even Bill Gates will one day be eligible for Social Security.

There is currently **no means test** for Social Security. You do not have to be poor to receive a benefit. Even very rich people can and do collect Social Security. If there were a means test, people with higher levels of income or assets might receive little or no benefits until such time as their income and assets were depleted to a stipulated amount. In your lifetime, there will likely be a means test applicable to your receiving retirement benefits. As a financially independent person, you need to be prepared to support yourself in case you are not eligible to receive much from Social Security when you retire.

Social Security is a **pay-as-you-go plan** so as costs rise taxes must also rise. Social Security did run a surplus for many years which ended up in the US Treasury's general fund. The government literally borrowed all the excess funds and left behind US Treasury Notes. Now, those notes are being sold to raise money to pay for rising benefits. The result is that the surplus is being sharply reduced each year.

The good news about Social Security is, if you end up nearly broke you will probably collect enough money to keep you going month-to-month. The bad news is, as a middle-to-high income earner, you will probably pay a lot of money for benefits you may never qualify to receive.

Politicians find it difficult to take action. Senior citizens vote in large numbers and fear reductions in their benefits. For most, Social Security and Medicare are their lifelines and they cannot afford a cut in benefits or an increase in cost.

With 78 million "boomers" heading toward retirement, Social Security is spending more than it takes in. It's ahead of previous deficit estimates. Its reserves will likely be gone by 2030. When politicians will deal with reality is unknown.

Do not count on it!

Like the Federal government, many other employers, both public and private, can no longer afford the pensions and health care retirement benefits promised to their employees. Many people may not get what they counted on. Among these are airline employees, auto workers, and city workers who were victims of bankruptcy. How would you feel if you worked for 40 years and found out that your promised pension was not going to materialize?

The Pension **Benefit Guarantee Corporation (PBGC)** is an agency of the federal government which takes over certain **private pension plan** payments when businesses go into bankruptcy and their retirement plans fail. Employees of **government agencies and nonprofit organizations are not covered** by the PBGC. In 2018, the maximum annual payout for a 65-year-old retiree is $65,040, regardless of what had originally been promised.

Social Security Disability Insurance

Social Security Disability Insurance (SSDI) is a disability program which was created in 1957. Its Disability Trust Fund is designed to pay benefits to eligible Americans who are unable to work due to a disability which has been or is expected to last at least 12 months. "Disability" is narrowly defined as **total disability**, not partial or temporary disability. "Unable to work" includes the work a person was doing, as well as their ability to adjust to other work because of a medical condition. Disability continues until the person is able to work again on a regular basis.

During the Great Recession, participation in the program soared as many additional people of all ages applied for disability coverage because they needed money to live on and their unemployment benefits expired. The application process was full of unintended consequences. Judges were appointed in each state and Puerto Rico to screen and approve applicants, but there was no consistent standard of acceptance. Puerto Rico had the highest acceptance rate which was over seven times greater than the acceptance rate in Massachusetts.

There are now more than 10 million people receiving disability benefits that currently average about $1,170 per month, with a maximum monthly benefit of $2,687. Since many recipients remain in the program for life, the average lifetime cost per person is about $300,000. After two years on disability, the recipient qualifies for Medicare **regardless of age.** The Disability Trust Fund relies upon Congressional funding to supplement contributions by employers to meet current obligations. Its ability to continue benefits at current levels is questionable.

For additional information and updates on Social Security, please visit www.ssa.gov.

But Social Security is only part of the problem.

Medicare

Medicare came into being in 1965 during the Johnson administration. Like Social Security, according to its trustees, Medicare too is spending far more than it takes in. We all know that **medical costs are skyrocketing.** New **high-tech treatments** are expensive. **Consumption per person** is rising rapidly due to the cost of new drugs, treatments, and procedures such as magnetic resonance imaging (MRIs), chemotherapy, replacement of hips and knees, and bypass surgery. Alzheimer disease, obesity, diabetes, and end-of-life expenses will be even greater as the boomers begin to reach retirement age in ever greater numbers. There seem to be few effective controls on cost although that will have to change.

Not only is the per person cost of treatment rapidly rising, but **fraud** is extensive. In addition, large court awards for bad outcomes have increased **malpractice insurance costs** to extreme levels. As we go to print, a large newly insured population is being served as a "highlight" of the Health Care Reform Act. whose very existence at present levels is being politically challenged. What the future holds is unclear, but you can expect major changes in the availability and cost of medical care and insurance coverage. As people live longer, their assets are being depleted, reducing their ability to pay medical bills even further.

Like Social Security, Medicare taxes are shared 50% to 50% between employer and employee. However, under the Health Care Reform Act, Medicare taxes paid by high-income earners are substantially increased along with a new Medicare tax on their **unearned** income. These tax increases apply only to the employee's contribution, not to that of the employer.

Medicare is a three-part health care entitlement program available to most people at age 65, unless they are covered by some other plan. Many aspects of Medicare are in transition and will continue to be impacted by the Health Care Reform Act in terms of revenue, coverage, and costs. Actions by Congress, the Oval Office, and the Supreme Court could substantially alter the program. However, due to the recent slowdown in the rate of rising medical costs, Medicare is now expected by some to be solvent beyond 2025. Eventually, action will be required to raise more revenue or cut benefits, subject to unforeseen changes. (See Chapter 24 for additional details on the Health Care Reform Act.

Part A of Medicare is currently free to seniors who apply, and is financed by a 2.9% payroll tax on **all earned income** paid by all workers with **no salary "cap."** In effect, 1.45% is paid by the employer and 1.45% by the employee.

- Benefits cover major items such as hospital, skilled nursing, home health care, hospice, and blood transfusions, though **not at 100%.**

- The current Part A payroll tax has been increased for high-income earners under the Health Care Reform Act by an additional 0.9% on income (AGI) over $200,000 for singles and $250,000 for couples. It applies only to the employee.

Part B of Medicare is optional and means tested. It is financed by monthly premiums paid by the insured, which currently range from about $134 to $428 per month, based on a person's prior year's adjusted gross income. It is paid directly or deducted from Social Security checks. **Parts A, B and D have deductibles.**

- Benefits are the same regardless of what you pay per month.

- Eligible benefits include the doctor, outpatient medical services, lab work, outpatient hospital services, physical exams, and cardiovascular and diabetes screening.

- Recipients are responsible for monthly premiums, copayments, and deductibles and costs not eligible for Medicare.

- Many seniors purchase **supplemental** insurance from private carriers to cover items not covered by Medicare. Without this additional coverage, retirement savings for many could be wiped out by costly medical bills. This insurance is highly recommended.

- To help pay for Medicare, an additional **3.8% surtax** now applies to the investment income of these same high-income earners. It is not certain what will happen should the Affordable Care Act cease to exist as we know it.

Part D of Medicare is optional and means tested. It is a **prescription drug plan currently** provided only by private insurance companies, and financed 25% by monthly premiums from the insured and 75% by taxes.

- Monthly premiums vary widely depending on the coverage and may be different in every state. Some states have many different plans just for residents of that state.

- Those with an adjusted gross income (AGI) exceeding about $85,000 pay a monthly surcharge in addition to their insurance cost to Medicare just for the right to purchase Part D coverage. The monthly **surcharge** ranges from about $14 to $77 per month in addition to the cost of the insurance.

However, a low-income subsidy program is available to those who qualify.

- Part D covers prescription drugs only. It currently includes a standard deductible and a 25% coinsurance payment by the beneficiary and has a gap in coverage, called a "donut hole," which adjusts annually.

- Not all plans cover the same drugs or have the same copays. It is a confusing program that needs to be reviewed annually.

Today, Medicare provides medical coverage to over 47 million people. At the rate it is growing, by 2030 it is estimated that the number will rise to 80 million and the federal government will be paying 70% of all the medical bills. Medical bills can virtually wipe out an estate.

The reality is that you are expected to pay for a system that may not be there for you when you become a senior citizen, perhaps 30, 40, or 50 years from now. You need to prepare to meet that obligation as one who pays into the system, yet may receive few, if any, benefits.

The most logical conclusion is you must increase your savings and investment returns or be willing to risk accepting a lower standard of living and medical care as a "senior citizen" supported in large part by the government.

Notes and Updates

CHAPTER 7

GOVERNMENT REVENUE AND EXPENSES

Taxes, Taxes, and More Taxes

The government uses the tax code not only to collect money, but to influence the way we live our lives.

Most likely, over your lifetime, the biggest expense you will have is taxes. Just add them up: federal income tax, state income tax, Social Security tax, Medicare tax, sales tax, property tax, estate tax, fuel tax, automobile registration tax, airfare tax, hotel tax, entertainment tax, liquor tax, tobacco tax, marijuana tax, fishing gear tax, archery equipment tax, etc. **Add it all up** and it tells you a lot about where the federal government gets its tax revenues. Here's an approximate breakdown:

- Individual income taxes   46%
- Social Security/Medicare taxes   34%
- Corporate income taxes   11%
- Excise and other taxes/fees   8%
- Estate taxes   1%

Social Security and Medicare taxes are shared about evenly between the employer and the employee at approximately 17% each. In total, well over two-thirds of all the taxes collected by the federal government are paid directly by individuals.

Since over your lifetime taxes are probably your biggest single expense, as an individual taxpayer you need to have a basic understanding of how the federal, state, and local tax laws work and how they will impact many of the decisions you make. The objectives are:

- Conserve as much income as you can by paying only the taxes you are required to pay.

- Take advantage of special tax subsidies that may exist for such items as home ownership, retirement savings, medical care, child care, college expenses, electric cars, solar systems, or windmill farms.

- Better manage your investments of stocks, bonds, real estate, or a business venture.

The Internal Revenue Service offers all forms, schedules, and instruction booklets that you may need for free, both online at **www.irs.gov** and in print. There are also toll free numbers to call and local IRS offices you can visit to get information.

Be aware that over the years the IRS budget has been cut by billions of dollars and thousands of employees. The resulting staff shortage means half of the incoming calls may not be answered. However, there are software packages easily available to help you file your return. You may also want to seek professional help from a tax preparation firm like H & R Block, Jackson Hewitt, or a qualified tax accountant or attorney.

The federal income tax is a pay-as-you-go system. Governments want their money as soon as possible so they expect us to pay most of it as we go through the year. There are two ways in which the pay-as-you-go system operates:

- Your employer is required to withhold and pay to the Treasury, on your behalf, a tax based upon your **filing status** (single, married filing jointly, or head of household; and your **payroll amount.**

- You may be required to pay an additional **quarterly estimated tax** based upon income for which no tax has been withheld such as fees, commissions, and income from dividends, interest, capital gains, rents, and royalties.

If you do not pay enough in withholding and estimated taxes throughout the year, you may be subjected to a penalty from the IRS.

Filling out **Form W-4** is one of the first things an employer will have you do when you start a job. The purpose of the W-4 form is to let your employer know how much it is required by law to deduct or withhold from each paycheck for your personal income taxes, both federal and state. These income tax deductions are in addition to Social Security and Medicare deductions.

The IRS has revised Form W-4 so the withholding calculator now reflects the increase in the standard deduction and changes in tax rates and brackets.

The IRS anticipates further changes will be made in calculating withholding, so do your best to avoid over and under withholding surprises as laws, rules and regulations are adopted.

Some people have trouble saving money every month and prefer their employer withhold more money out of their paychecks than required so they don't spend it and will have less to pay at the end of the year, or even get a refund.

Others want less money withheld to maximize their take-home pay so they have more money to spend or pay off debts, and hope that by April they have enough money to cover any tax shortfall.

When it comes to withholding I've always liked having my employer withhold a larger amount than required. This has been a cushion which has helped me cover taxes due on interest, dividends, capital gains or other unexpected income producing items. And if I still end up with a refund, it's fun taking the family on a special outing or paying for some other project.

In a two-income family you might spend a little time doing a few calculations in advance to determine earned income, unearned income, and various tax deductions and credits. If the Health Care Reform Act is still in place, high-income earners may want or need to increase their withholdings to meet increased tax obligations stemming from the Medicare surtaxes.

The IRS expects you to be able to pay all your taxes due for the prior year by **April 15**. In fact, it is such an important date that preprinted and electronic calendars in the United States mark April 15 as "Tax Day," just like many "holidays."

Tax basics you should know

The Tax Cut and Jobs Act ("H.R.1" or the "law") was passed by Congress, signed by the President in December, 2017, and became effective on January 1, 2018. It was the first major change in tax law since 1986. Following is a summary of major items which you should be familiar with. This discussion focuses on your personal finances, not the laws that are more applicable to business enterprises, charitable organizations, etc.

As always, you should **seek professional advice** from reliable sources for the laws, rules, and regulations currently in force. Tax lawyers, accountants, and lobbyists will be busy for many years advising clients on ways to optimize their tax filings, which may include strategies for avoiding taxes (legal), but not strategies for evading taxes (illegal). Changes and interpretations regarding these rules and regulations can happen at any time.

Filing Status

There are five basic categories: (1) single, (2) married filing jointly, (3) married filing separately, (4) head of household, and (5) widow(er) with dependent child. Your status determines the tax brackets that apply to your income. The IRS now recognizes same-sex marriages regardless of which state the couple lives in.

Earned Income

Includes wages, salary, bonuses, commissions, royalties, tips, and other money you have received for your personal services. These are evidenced by a W-2 form from each employer to be filed with your tax return. If you are self-employed you will report your income on a separate IRS form according to the instructions.

Total Income

This is earned income **plus unearned income** such as taxable interest, ordinary and qualified dividends, business profits or losses, capital gains or losses on investments, pension receipts, certain tax refunds, Social Security benefits, unemployment compensation, individual retirement account distributions, real estate activities, and partnership income.

- **Qualified stock** dividends are **currently** taxed at a **maximum rate of 20%** for singles with taxable income in excess of $425,800, or couples above $479,000 if the stock has been **held for at least 61 days**. A maximum **15% rate** applies to those with incomes below these amounts. However, filers with less than $38,600 (single) or $77,200 (married) may benefit from a **0% tax rate**. These numbers may change from year to year so be sure to double check the brackets each year.

- **Nonqualified dividends** are those received from stocks **held less than 61 days,** dividends from Real Estate Investment Trusts and certain other dividends which are called **"ordinary dividends."** These are reported on Form 1040 and are **taxed as ordinary incom**e at your individual tax rate. The year-end statement from your investment broker will itemize which are qualified or nonqualified dividends for tax purposes.

- **Taxes on interest received,** including interest from savings accounts, CDs, money market funds; and corporate, treasury, and certain other bonds (except certain municipal bonds), are reported on the appropriate schedule and taxed as ordinary income.

Adjusted Gross Income

To determine your adjusted gross income **subtract from total income** specific deductions such as contributions paid into retirement plans, student loan interest, tuition and fees, health savings accounts, flexible savings accounts, one half of the self-employment tax, and certain other qualified items.

The term **"modified"** adjusted gross income (AGI) occasionally appears. It means adding back to AGI items such as tax exempt interest, foreign income, student loan deductions, and portions of Social Security benefits. When included in a calculation, you will need to consult the specific IRS instructions.

Capital Gains Tax

The capital gains tax is reported on the designated Form 1040 schedule. This is a tax on the profit (or loss) from the sale of an asset, which is something you own. It includes capital gains or losses from the sale of stocks, bonds, real estate, art collections, and other assets. This does not include taxes on profits from the sale of a house which is reported elsewhere and taxed differently. (See Chapter 14, "Purchasing a Home.")

There are two types of capital gains and losses based on how long you have owned the asset. They are taxed differently.

- **Short term capital gains:** For assets owned 12 months or less, the profit is added to your income and is taxed at your individual tax rate with a current maximum of 37%.

- **Long term capital gains:** For an asset owned **over 12 months**, the profit is subject to a maximum tax of 20% for singles with taxable income in excess of $425,800, or married above $479,000. For filers with incomes below these amounts, the maximum tax is 15%. However, if your income is less than $38,800 for singles or $77,200 for married joint filers, you may be eligible for a 0% capital gains tax rate. The numbers may change from year to year so be sure to double check the brackets each year.

Capital losses can usually be used to offset capital gains for tax purposes. First apply short-term losses against short-term gains. Then, long-term losses against long-term gains. Excess losses can be applied to either type of gain.

For example, if in the same tax year you had a short-term gain of $2,000 upon the sale of a stock, and a $1,000 short-term loss from the sale of another stock, you would report both transactions and end up with a $1,000 net short term capital gain for tax purposes.

Capital losses in excess of gains in any one year can be used to reduce taxable ordinary income **up to $3,000 per year**, and any remaining losses beyond $3,000 can be carried forward to offset future years' capital gains and/or ordinary income until the loss is exhausted.

Selling shares of the same security: Investors may specifically identify which shares of a security are being sold for tax purposes.

Pass-through deduction: This is **a brand new 20% tax deduction of business income** from a proprietorship, partnership, limited liability corporation (LLC), or S-Corporation. Only the remaining 80% of the income is taxed at the taxpayer's marginal rate (up to 37%). It is available even if the filer does not itemize deductions.

For those earning more than $157,500 (single) or $315,000 (married) this deduction is phased out or eliminated entirely if they are in certain "**specified service businesses**" such as medical, legal, and consulting practices. For these and other service professionals that rely on their own labor or reputation for income, the pass-through fully phases out if they earn more than $207,500 (single) or $415,000 (married). However, larger phaseouts of income are available to real estate investors who own tangible, depreciable property such as hotels.

As we go to print, there will be ongoing changes in IRS rulings and regulations applicable to this new way of taxing income from these business structures. As a result, some business enterprises may change their structure in order to lower their taxes. For example, a proprietor may decide it would be beneficial to convert to an LLC. I recommend you seek professional advice if the pass-through deduction might apply to you.

Individual losses from businesses: Losses from a proprietorship, partnership, LLC, or S- Corporation which exceed $250,000 (single) or $500,000 (married) are **not tax deductible** but may be carried forward to offset future profits. (See Chapter 9 for information on business structures.)

Real estate investing has different tax laws. (See Chapter 20, "Real Estate Investing")

Wash Sale Rule

For tax purposes, you cannot declare a loss on a security if you purchase the identical security within 30 days before or after the sale. For example, this would prevent someone selling a stock at a loss on Monday and buying it back on Tuesday just to create a loss for tax purposes. It remains a loss; but it's **not a tax deductible loss.**

Other Deductions Before Adjusted Gross Income (These may change over time.)

Educator Expenses for K-12 teacher's classroom supplies up to $250.

Student Loan Interest deduction up to $2,500.

Health (HSA) and flexible (FSA) healthcare savings account contributions.

Self-employed health insurance deductions.

IRA, 401(k) and 403(b) retirement account contributions.

Self-employed contributions to SEP, Simple, and other retirement plans.

Personal moving expense deduction only for eligible military personnel.

Self-employment tax deduction related to Social Security payments.

Alimony: Alimony payments made under **pre-2019** divorce agreements **remain tax deductible** to the payer, and taxable income for the recipient. In other words, these agreements are grandfathered.

Effective, **January 1, 2019**, alimony payments required under divorce or separation instruments executed or modified after December 31,2018 **are not tax deductible** to the payer. Those who receive alimony will no longer report that money as taxable income. This change in the law **applies only to divorces finalized after December, 31, 2018**.

Tax Deductions

These are the expenses you are permitted to **subtract from your taxable income** to reduce your taxes.

- **Standard deduction:** A no-questions asked deduction to income before calculating your tax. You need no records or proof to take this deduction.

> If you are single, the standard deduction is $12,000.
> If you are married and filing jointly, it is $24,000.

Higher amounts are available for the elderly or blind.

- **Itemized deductions:** If you believe your eligible deductions are more than the standard deduction you can itemize them on the designated schedule of Form 1040 and deduct them before calculating your tax. It is important you maintain records because proof may be required b y the IRS.

Examples of Eligible Deductions Include:

Medical Expense Deductions: Available for eligible **uninsured medical expenses** in excess of 7.5% of adjusted gross income (AGI) in 2018, after which the threshold rate increases to 10%.

State and Local Taxes: State and local taxes **plus** your residential property tax when added together are deductible up to a combined total annual amount of **$10,000**

Home Mortgage Interest: Individuals are allowed an itemized deduction for mortgage interest on their primary residence and a second residence up to a **combined mortgage total of $750,000**. However, this **does not apply to** mortgages taken out prior to December 16, 2017, which are grandfathered, in which case the loan status can be maintained even during a refinancing to upgrade the home if the refinanced amount does not exceed the prior loan's balance or $1,000,000.

Interest on a home equity loan ("HELOC") is not tax deductible, and that applies to both old and new equity loans. However, you may be able to deduct the interest if the loan is used to "substantially" improve the home.

Charitable Deductions: Gifts to qualified public charities are tax deductible as long as they do not exceed 60% of the taxpayer's AGI.

- For deductions made by check, use the date mailed or handed over.
- For deductions by credit card, use the date charged not paid. The charity will legally receive only the amount after transaction fees have been deducted, but it seldom is of any concern.
- For deductions using a retail store credit card, deduct in the year paid.
- For deductions made by contributing shares of stock with a short-term gain, you may only deduct the cost basis of the shares.

- For deductions made by contributing shares of stock with a long-term gain, you can deduct 100% of the value at the time of the donation.

Casualty and Theft Loss Deduction: The itemized deduction for personal casualty and theft losses applies only to an official **presidentially declared major disaster** such as a forest fire, hurricane or flood. As a result, someone who loses their house in a huge wildfire may be eligible for relief. But if they were the victim of a random house fire they would not have an eligible deduction.

Tax Credits

These are for **special situations** and the eligible amounts are directly subtracted from your tax liability. **Tax credits are worth more than tax deductions.** Tax deductions reduce taxable income. Tax credits reduce the amount of tax you owe dollar for dollar. **Caution**! Tax credits can be very important, but they do tend to change over time. Check to see that you're not overlooking any.

Some of the more **current tax credits** are:

- **Dependent tax credit**: A $500 temporary credit for non-child dependents such as elderly parents, children 17 or older (including college students) or adult children with a disability.

- **Child tax credit: For** each child under 17 years of age.

  Child and dependent care credit: Tax credits for children under 13.

- **Alternative energy credit:** electric cars, solar, wind, etc.

- **Earned income credit** for lower-income earners.

- **Education credits:** American Opportunity credit; Lifetime learning credit; Hope Scholarship credit.

Tax rates and brackets: The current maximum federal individual income tax rate is **37%** of taxable income.

- There are different tax brackets for single, married filing jointly, married filing separately, head of household and widow(er) with a dependent child.

- There are currently seven tax brackets for each category: 10%, 12%, 22%, 24%, 32%, 35%, and 37%, with the ranges and dollar amounts based upon filing status. The maximum tax rate of 37% applies only to taxable income over $500,000 for a single person and $600,000 for married filing jointly. However, income brackets are reviewed and adjusted annually for inflation.

The Marriage Tax Penalty

The marriage tax penalty refers to the fact that for those who are married there may be additional taxes due if their combined income exceeds $400,000. The way the code is currently written, singles living together can **each deduct** up to $10,000 in state and local taxes, whereas a married couple would be limited to a combined $10,000 maximum. Again, these thresholds can change over time.

In some cases the penalty or additional tax would be increased more if their combined AGI would also subject them to the Health Care Reform Act's additional Medicare tax surcharges.

Gift Tax

This tax is designed to prevent people from avoiding estate taxes by giving away their assets anticipating death. Everyone has a lifetime gift tax exemption of $1 million. Taxable gifts above that amount will be subject to the gift tax. Any unused portion of the lifetime gift tax can be used as a deduction to the estate tax. The gift tax is paid by the giver.

Currently, you can give up to **$15,000** to as many people as you like **free of gift tax**. A married couple can each give $15,000 to the same person for a total of $30,000. The recipient need not be related. This is in addition to the lifetime exemption of $1 million.

You can also pay any medical bills or school tuition free of gift tax as long as the amount is paid directly to the medical provider or institution for the benefit of a student.

The highest gift tax rate is usually the same as the highest estate tax rate, which is currently 40%.

Federal Estate Tax

This tax was originally designed to discourage (1) the formation of an aristocracy whereby total wealth was passed from generation to generation upon death, and (2) as a means to collect additional taxes from wealthy individuals and families.

Surprisingly, over half of adults do not have a will. In such cases, each state will determine according to "intestacy laws" how the estate is distributed. Usually, the state's laws call for dividing the proceeds among a surviving spouse, children, or next of kin.

Furthermore, in settling an estate, claims of improper distributions may be contested. Some of these stressful and complicated situations among potential heirs may need to be resolved in a court of law. Such situations will become a matter of public record unless they are settled out of court.

To avoid complications, maintain privacy, and reduce court costs, both single and married couples are establishing trusts, both revocable and irrevocable, to govern the distribution and allocation of their estates. I strongly recommend this be done in consultation with an **estate planning expert**.

The maximum individual federal estate tax, gift tax, and generation-skipping tax exemptions, when combined, is $11.2 million per person with a maximum tax rate of 40% applied to amounts above $11.2 million. The exemption is portable, so a surviving spouse could have up to a $22.4 million estate tax exemption. The exemption is indexed annually for inflation.

In addition to the federal estate tax, about **20 states** also have some form of estate or **inheritance tax**. The estate tax is paid out of the estate before distribution. The inheritance tax is paid by the heirs. Therefore, it is quite possible that some estates may be exempt from the federal estate tax, but still be liable for state estate or inheritance taxes. Historically, very few estates ever owe any estate or inheritance taxes.

As of the date of death, the value of the deceased's estate is calculated on a **"stepped-up" basis** which, for future tax purposes, establishes a **new cost basis for the heirs**.

Excise Tax

This is a tax on purchases of specific products or certain activities. Often excise taxes are included in the price of the product or activity. Excise taxes used to be just a luxury tax on expensive items such as furs, jewelry, and yachts. Currently there are excise taxes on wagering, highway use, fuels, airline tickets, archery equipment and many other items.

Alternative Minimum Tax

For over 30 years, the individual tax code has consisted of two parallel tax systems: the regular individual tax summarized above, and an alternative minimum tax ("AMT"). The AMT was designed to impose taxes on high-income people who were paying little or no income tax by taking advantage of tax loopholes. The AMT ignores certain tax deductions otherwise allowed individuals in the regular tax code, and applies special tax rates.

For many years the AMT affected less than 1% of taxpayers. But because it was not indexed for inflation, over the years as payrolls increased millions more were required to pay the higher AMT.

The AMT forces you to recalculate your taxes by adding back many of the normal deductions allowed on your federal tax return such as state income and property taxes, tax free interest on certain state and local bonds and gains on certain stock options.

If your **taxable income** is over $70,300 for a single filer, or $109,400 married, you must recalculate your tax using the AMT and pay the **higher** of the regular tax or the AMT, which is currently 26% to 28%. In the future, the AMT exemption level will be adjusted for inflation using the consumer price index. Married couples filing jointly may be affected by the AMT when their incomes are combined. If the IRS has to calculate the AMT for you and you owe money, they will bill you for the tax you owe and may include an interest charge and a penalty. Tax credits may be used to offset the AMT.

Quarterly Estimated Taxes

The IRS and many states require those who have a significant amount of income which is not subject to adequate withholding for tax purposes to file and pay quarterly estimates of additional federal taxes owed. The estimates are due April 15, June15, September 15, and January 15 for the previous quarter. Such income might come from the sale of a house, business or other asset, dividends, interest, capital gains, a sole proprietorship, Social Security and pension payments or some other source. Other items you might consider which could cause you to recalculate your withholding or the need to file quarterly tax estimates might include bonuses, rents, fees, commissions, tips and any other source from which withholding was not made.

If you cannot pay your taxes, there are no good options. But there are some things you can consider:

- **Always file a return.**

- Consider borrowing money or selling assets to raise cash.

- You may be able to arrange for late installment payments by filing Form 9465.

- Consider using your credit card. The interest and "convenience" fee you must pay on the card may be lower than the interest and penalties you owe or would owe to the IRS. You might even get miles or cash back on the credit card.

- Few people know that the IRS has a **First-Time-Abate** program for those who file or pay late, enabling it to waive first-time late filing and payment penalties. At this time you would not even find it in the 1040 Instruction Booklet. It must be requested by the taxpayer.

- The IRS has a contact phone number (1-800-829-1040) to plead your case. You can discuss with them your problems and some payment options and they will let you know what they are willing to do. I doubt you will be too happy with the outcome, but it is an option. Always be polite and stay cool. Prepare in advance to state your case and have your information available.

- As a last resort you can file an **Offer in Compromise** with the IRS, but those are rarely accepted.

Kiddie Tax: Congress has enacted a Kiddie Tax to restrict the ability of parents and grandparents to shift investment income from themselves to their children and grandchildren to avoid higher tax brackets. The tax applies only to gifts of cash, stocks, real estate, and other assets that generate unearned income.

> The result is the **unearned income** of children under 19 (or age 24 if a full-time student) **is taxed** the same as if it were ordinary income or a capital gain in a trust or an estate. Only income more than $2,100 is taxed, at rates from 10% to 37%.

> The Kiddie Tax **does not apply** to a child's earned income. It does not apply to a child's investment income if the child provides more than half of his or her support and files their own tax return. For details check with Form 1040 Instructions or seek professional assistance.

529 Accounts: What was originally designed as a savings account for attending college, has now been **expanded** to include contributions for "a public, private, or religious elementary or secondary school" education. Contributions to 529 plans are not tax deductible at the federal level but may be deductible for state tax purposes. Assets grow free of taxes. And **withdrawals** for eligible expenses are **tax free**. Annual distributions up to $10,000 per student are now available for elementary and secondary education. Be sure to check the most recent details.

College tuition deduction: Up to $4,000 of college tuition may be **tax deductible** above-the-line (before AGI). **Graduate student** tuition waivers are not treated as taxable income.

Inflation indexing: Annual inflation adjustments impacting Social Security benefits, tax brackets and a host of other items are calculated by the Chained Consumer Price Index. This usually generates a lower rate of inflation than the Consumer Price Index. By reducing the rate of inflation, future Social Security benefits will increase at a lower rate than if the CPI were used.

IRS Audits: The IRS has the power to **audit** or review tax returns for accuracy, avoidance, fraud, or other issues. About 1% of returns are reviewed, although 8% of those with higher incomes can expect to be audited. About 80% of audits are conducted just by mail. Those with higher incomes or unusual, large or highlighted deductions are audited more frequently. Examples of the reasons for audit are:

> Failure to sign the tax return
> Mathematical errors
> Failure to report all taxable income
> Declaring larger than average deductions
> Deducting excessive business expenses
> Claiming a home office deduction
> Declaring a hobby as a business for loss purposes
> Claiming 100% business use of a vehicle
> Declaring losses from rental property
> Failure to disclose a foreign account

If you are audited:

- Always ask yourself first if professional help is necessary.

- In some cases the IRS will give you a phone number to call if you have a question. It is OK to call and give them your file number if necessary.

- Check first to see if the "mistake" is yours or that of the IRS. They make mistakes too.

- If the problem is a math error, a misplaced or omitted number, or a return not signed or filled out correctly, you may feel comfortable making the correction.

- Whether by mail, over the phone, or in person, address **only** the matter that has been raised. The more you say or write the more issues that are likely to be raised.

- Have available the thought process and documents you used to support your position.

- Treat the IRS agent with respect. They have a tough job to do. You can disagree, but anger, yelling and profanity probably will not help your cause.

- If you do owe more tax try to at least get the interest and penalty waived.

- Finally, reconsider if you need professional help, and if so, get it. Certain tax preparers, such as H&R Block and Jackson Hewitt may be willing to attend the audit with you without charge if they prepared your return.

Caution! When sending checks to the IRS always make them out to "**US Treasury**". The IRS **contacts taxpayers only by mail**, never by phone or email. "Scammers" are calling and emailing people claiming they owe taxes and threatening them with penalties or jail if they do not pay, usually by wire transfer or a prepaid card. This is known as **phishing**. Do not be fooled.

Corporate Tax Rate

Corporations spend billions of dollars on accountants, lawyers, and lobbyists to reduce their taxes, while federal, state, and local governments promote tax incentives for specific activities. The current **corporate tax rate is 21%**. There is no alternative minimum tax for corporations. Losses can be used to offset taxes on future profits. The corporate tax code is massive and complicated. Many large corporations legally pay no taxes or substantially less than the 21% tax rate.

Disclaimer: The information herein provides preliminary guidelines to an analysis of **current tax laws** compiled from various sources considered reliable. However, all such laws, rules, and regulations dealing with taxes, entitlement programs, investments, interest, education, medical care, retirement programs, etc. are always **subject to interpretation** by the IRS, Congress, and the judicial system.

This just cannot go on forever!

The federal government is currently spending substantially more than it is collecting. This has created a huge federal debt which can be expressed as **more than $200,000 for a family of four. The federal budget, the annual budget deficit, and the total federal debt** are now defined in terms of trillions of dollars, an amount that is hard for us to even imagine and impossible for my calculator to handle.

National governments typically fund their deficits a number of ways, none of which are particularly appealing:

- Raising taxes and fees

- Cutting benefits and expenses

- Borrowing lots of money which drives up interest rates and devalues the currency

- Selling assets such as bandwidth, timber, oil, or mineral rights

- Printing money and risking inflation

Regardless of what the federal government does, you need to **keep up with the tax rules that impact your life**, including ordinary income tax rates; individual tax deductions, expenses, and credits that can affect you; alternative minimum tax rules; capital gains rates, short vs long term tax rates on dividends, tax exempt interest, and the impact of taxes on your retirement plans.

Your best resource when it comes to taxes is www.irs.gov.

Notes and Updates

CHAPTER 8

BEGINNING TO SAVE

"I Get Paid First"

There is something very valuable to learn from the "boomer generation" which has spent too much, saved too little, and is living too long. First, you need to shift your focus from spending money to saving money. Second, you need to start saving as early as possible. Some people are already doing that. For everyone else, there's no better time to start than now. You are never too late.

**Saving needs to become a priority.
Investing is the other half of the story.**

It is important to save, but equally important to know what to do with the money you save. It is very difficult to accumulate wealth based solely on salary or wages. You need to invest wisely so that your assets can generate interest, dividends, and capital gains.

Investing has an inherent risk. But **not** investing does too. Cash sitting in a savings account or a certificate of deposit earning less interest than the rate of inflation means you are losing ground by losing purchasing power. If the rate of inflation is 3%, for every $50,000 you spend this year for goods and services, next year they will cost you $51,500.

Bill Gates said it best: "If you're born poor, it's not your mistake. But if you die poor, it is your mistake."

Let's start now developing your saving strategy. The more you do now, the less chance you will need to make painful decisions later in life. Every time you add to your savings think of it as **a gift** you're giving yourself; a gift you will really appreciate sometime in the future.

**The key is to save something each month and to have
a plan for what to do with these savings.**

We begin with "The Rule of Fred"......four magic words that are the key to saving money. Memorize these four words and remember them **every payday**.

"I GET PAID FIRST"

The first person you should pay every payday is you. Save something from each paycheck. Otherwise, you are nothing more than a conduit between your employer's payroll department and the merchants you choose to support. You did not **make** this money. The only people who make money work at the mint. You **earned** this money. And you deserve to have something to show for your effort.

Just because you have money does not mean you have to spend it. Credit cards, charge accounts, checking accounts, and poor planning make getting into debt a lot easier than getting out of debt. When you **save before you spend**, you do not have to pay interest, fees, and penalties.

Don't forget every dollar you borrow can cost you nearly two dollars of earned income, or wages, to pay it back. If you borrow the money on a credit card, you will also be paying on your balance a high rate of interest and possible fees. You also need to factor in that for every dollar you earn you will need to subtract federal income taxes, state income taxes, various other state payroll taxes, Social Security tax, Medicare tax, and contributions to your medical insurance, and retirement plans before you can begin to pay back your debt. On top of that, you're losing the opportunity to use your money to generate income for yourself. It's not difficult to see why it is so hard to pay off one's debts.

Spend a dollar and it is gone. Save and invest a dollar and it can start working for you generating more dollars which you can invest to earn more dollars even while you are at work, asleep, or on vacation. Now, you're starting down the road to financial independence.

Frugality is the cornerstone of saving money. It's different than being cheap. Cheap is buying only based on the lowest price without regard to quality or value, or not buying at all. Frugal means not spending freely or unnecessarily, but considering quality, value, needs and benefits along with price.

Budgeting will help you establish your priorities, live within your means, and set financial goals. A budget enables you to **manage your money** instead of letting your money manage you.

Creating a budget or spending plan is the first step in saving money. The budget tracks, estimates, and adjusts one's income and expenses over months or years and compares your projected income to your estimated expenses. The goal is to ensure there is something left over which we call **savings**. Budgeting is **financial**

planning, and a budget will enable even those earning average incomes to become "millionaires" and achieve financial independence.

Budget formats are available at websites such as www.mint.com; www.kiplinger.com; and betterbudgeting.com, and you can find others by searching "household budget worksheet." Start by preparing your budget worksheet monthly for a period of several months, but no longer than one year.

Following are some useful tips for starting to prepare your personal budget, or what I'd rather call a "spending plan".

- List and **total all your sources of income** on a monthly basis. Wages and other forms of earned income should be **after all payroll deductions.**

  Lump sums that you receive should be divided into monthly amounts.

  Items such as loans, family support, grants, and scholarships should be included in your monthly income.

  Other income items, such as interest, dividends, and capital gains should not be included. These are to be reinvested as part of your plan to create wealth.

  Review your pay stubs, bank, and brokerage statements and other deposit accounts to make sure you capture all your sources of income.

- List and **total all the expense categories** you want to track, also on a monthly basis.

  Itemize basic categories such as mortgage or rent payments, utilities (phone, cable, electricity, etc.), food, clothing, transportation, entertainment, medical expenses, insurance, tuition, medical expenses, taxes, and loan payments.

  Review all bills, credit card and bank statements, other payment platforms, and your checkbook register to make sure you capture all of your expenses.

- After a couple of months a pattern will emerge. Budgeting and tracking expenses shows you where your money goes and how seemingly inconsequential daily expenditures can add up over time. It may be time for some radical rethinking or cutting back at least temporarily in some categories such as rent, car and transportation expenses, parking fees, credit card interest and fees, and entertainment.

The Magic of Compounding

Albert Einstein described **compound interest as the greatest invention of mankind**. And we all know Albert was one smart guy......relativity speaking. Compound interest occurs when interest is paid on **both** the principal and accumulated interest.

Let us look at how compounding works. There are two basic methods of calculating interest:

- **Simple interest** is calculated as a percentage of your initial investment on an annual basis.

    Example:
    4% of $1,000 would earn $40 of interest each year.

- **Compound interest** is calculated as interest on your initial investment **plus** interest on the interest you earned in prior years. The difference between simple and compound interest may not seem like much at first, but the result of compounding over a long period of time is **astounding.**

    Example:
    If you earn 4% on $1,000 the first year, you end the year with $1,040. But by compounding the second year, you earn 4% on $1,040, and end with approximately $1,083, and so on, year after year.

Here's how it works. Let's say your grandmother gave you $2,000 to invest and you invested it at 8%, never touching it. This is what compounding can do.

Example:

After 5 years	$2,939
After 10 years	$4,318
After 20 years	$9,322
After 43 years	$54,733

So, if she gave it to you when you graduated college at 22, by the time you turn 65 that $2,000 would grow to $54,733. And if you still leave it there, by the time you are 75 you will have **$118,165.** Thanks, grandma!

Now let us assume you are working and able to save $2,000 **every year** on your own, in a tax-sheltered account. Not counting grandma's gift, let's see what happens to the money you're putting away **each year** at the same rate of 8%.

Example:

Starting at age 22:	At age 65	$713,000	(43 years)
Starting at age 25:	At age 65	$518,113	(40 years)
Starting at age 35:	At age 65	$291,546	(30 years)

This is an example of why it is so important to start saving as early as possible. The difference between starting at 22 and waiting until you are 35 is a difference of $421,454 in what you will have saved at age 65. That is why we call it "**the magic of compounding.**"

You may be wondering how these numbers are calculated but that is the easy part. There are compounding calculators readily available at bankrate.com; investor.gov; math.com, and many other online sites. Look and play with the numbers yourself. I guarantee it will get you excited.

But sometimes you need to make a quick calculation or estimate in your head or on the fly. There is a simple mathematical calculation called the **Rule of 72**, which can be used to estimate how long it will take for a sum of money to double at a given interest rate, assuming interest is compounded annually. You can use the Rule of 72 a couple of ways:

- **Calculation #1:** Divide 72 by the interest rate or the expected rate of return. The result is the number of years it will take to double your money. At 8% compounded it will take 9 years to double your money.

- **Calculation #2:** Divide 72 by the number of years it would take to double your money and it will tell you the interest rate you will need to earn. To double your money in 10 years you need to earn 7.2% compounded.

The key to using the Rule of 72 is to realize that, at 8%, money will double every 9 years. It might take 34 years to get to $350,000, but at 8% compounded, it will take only another 9 years to double that again to over **$700,000 at age 65**.

There are some useful ways to use **compounding and the Rule of 72** in your everyday life. For example,

> **The danger of inflation:** If inflation averages 3% per year compounded, using the Rule of 72, in 24 years the prices of goods and services, on average, will double.

> **The time value of money:** Receiving $1 today is better than receiving $1 tomorrow. Getting a lump sum today and putting it to work with compound interest is usually better than receiving installment payments over a number of years. This is why lottery winners take the lump sum, pay the taxes, and get the money working for them using compounding.

Begin to save NOW!

When it comes to formulating a plan of saving money and creating wealth, compounding is one of the most powerful tools you have. But to compound your money, the first step is to accumulate money to work with. For most of us, that means beginning to save, which means spending less than you receive and learning how to live below your means.

> Bill, **age 22**, puts $2,000 every year into his retirement account for nine years, to age 30, for a total of $18,000 at 6% and STOPS. He contributes no more money to the account. At age 65, he has **$579,000**.

> Jim likes to party and waits until **age 31** to begin putting $2,000 every year into his retirement account for 35 years, to age 65, for a total of $70,000, also at 6%. At age 65, he has **$470,000**.

Bill put in $52,000 **less** than Jim, and ends up at age 65 with $109,000 **more** than Jim. It turns out those were expensive parties for Jim. That is the benefit of time! That is why **starting as soon as possible** is so important.

Compounding is a two-way street.

But compounding **can work against you** when you borrow money instead of saving it. Lenders of money, such as banks and credit card issuers, know all about compounding and use it to their advantage. They know by calculating compound interest more frequently on the money you borrow, rather than using the stated or simple rate of interest, the cost to you increases.

Example:
Suppose you are borrowing money at a stated rate of 5% interest. The more frequently the compounding takes place, the higher the effective rate of interest.

Compounded annually	5.00%
Compounded semiannually	5.06%
Compounded quarterly	5.09%
Compounded monthly	5.12%
Compounded daily	5.13%

Now, you understand why interest on credit card balances is calculated daily. You pay more on your borrowing. **The lender earns more** on its loan.

Pay yourself first!

Remember the Rule of Fred. Each time you receive a paycheck, it's **"I get paid first."** Begin by saving 5% to 10% of your **earned income** in your early years. Move that, as soon as possible (ASAP), up to 15%, including amounts contributed by your employer, which you should always take advantage of. For very simple investing, CDs or a money market deposit account may earn you a higher rate of interest than a savings account.

Before you tell me that you do not make enough money to start saving, take a look at this:

Example:
Saving just $100 per month at 8% compounded:

Starting at age 22:	At age 65	$450,000
Starting at age 32:	At age 65	$195,000

For $12,000 more in contributions, the early starter earned $255,000 more. Not bad! Now don't you think you can find an extra $100 per month to save? Keep in mind you're doing this for yourself and those closest to you. Do not be discouraged if you don't have a lot to save initially. Develop a budget, set spending and saving goals, and use time to your advantage. **You can do it!**

While saving, I always recommend establishing an emergency fund to cover at least 3 to 6 months of living expenses in the event of illness, job loss, or other emergency. One never knows when something comes up that requires immediate cash. The emergency fund might keep you from sliding back into debt.

Save more, spend less.

It's okay to bargain to get the most for your money. Americans are typically poor negotiators, but you should not be shy about bargaining. If you don't ask, you don't get! Think in advance how you might ask for a better price. Try phrases like: "Is it going on sale soon?" "That's more than I can pay," "Give me your best price," "I think I can get a better price elsewhere," or "I need you to waive that charge."

With the aid of the internet, do your homework so you know what is available and the prices. Look for sales and coupons. I'm amazed by the bargains you can find online.

If you're dealing face-to-face with a merchant take printed prices with you to the merchant as evidence of what's out there. Make it known that this is a competitive situation, whether it is or not. Try to have a few details ready as to what the competition is offering in the way of features or enticements. Usually, the higher the price, the greater the opportunity to bargain.

Don't be a quitter. Expect the initial response to be negative. If it's not, keep going lower. Ask about discounts for students, AAA members, Costco members, state employees, etc. Be patient, practical, pleasant, but persistent. Be willing to be flexible, to give and to take if necessary. Being unreasonable usually does not work.

Don't be afraid to walk away. Let them know that is what you are going to do in a nice way. "I'm going to look around some more." They might change their mind. Leave them your card or point of contact in case they later change their mind about your offer.

When **selecting a bank or credit union**, consider both convenience and cost. Know what the fees are for such things as making multiple deposits, maintaining minimum balance requirements, using a live teller, using ATMs in the USA or in foreign countries, making account inquiries by phone, closing the account, stopping payment of a check, taking cash advances, using overdraft protection, doing online banking and bill payment, and exchanging currency.

Even after you have selected a bank, there are things you can do to keep bank charges to a minimum. Some ideas include the following:

- Make sure to reconcile your checking account and review credit card statements monthly to catch mistakes early and avoid additional charges.
- Avoid out-of-network ATM charges.
- Eliminate late charges on credit cards.
- Switch your credit card to a new issuer with a zero balance transfer fee, a low or zero introductory interest rate, and/or a higher credit limit.

You can negotiate with banks, too. They may be willing to waive certain charges in return for your beginning a new relationship with them or for giving them a bigger share of your banking business.

There are lots of excuses for not saving money. Now that you understand the importance of saving and compounding, I hope you realize how reckless they can be. Some examples I have heard:

- "I don't make enough."   No one ever does. Pay yourself first.
- "I'll get around to it later." Wrong! Make compounding work for you now.
- "This purchase will pay for itself." Not if it's a vacation to Fiji.
- "I deserve a little luxury in my life." It's OK after you save 15%.
- "Someone else will take care of me."… Don't bet on it.

A spouse?	Don't forget there is a 50% divorce rate.
An inheritance?	Not with today's life expectancy.
Win the lottery?	Good luck with that!

More hints for saving

Do not become a victim of advertising. Do not shop on impulse. **Shop on line.** Do not use shopping as a form of recreation. Look for sales and special offers. Shop at outlet and discount stores. It does not take any special brains to pay full retail! Do not go overboard on holiday spending. Be creative. Use the internet for consumer information and comparison shopping. Try saving toward large purchases instead of purchasing on credit.

A penny saved is a penny earned . . . . no, really!

- Shop for life insurance. Rates are getting lower. Compare at www. accuquote.com.

- Shop for auto insurance. There are a lot of competitors out there like Geico, State Farm, and AAA. Look for free roadside assistance. Raise your auto insurance deductibles.

- Raise the deductible on a renter's or homeowner's policy.

- Review your health insurance annually as to coverage and deductible.

- Use cash-back cards if you are tired of getting airline miles you don't use.

- Shop around for your internet, smart phone, and television cable plans.

- Combine with one provider if seems to be advantageous.

- Refinance a home mortgage.

- Save on drugs by buying generics.

- Pay tickets and fines on time.

- Save for vacations. Don't charge everything on a credit card and pay later with interest, fees, and penalties.

Notes and Updates

CHAPTER 9

INVESTMENT VEHICLES

Get in the Game!

As if saving money were not difficult enough, once the money is saved you need to know what to do with it. It's very difficult to become financially independent just by saving earned income. You need to invest it wisely to make it grow. In today's complex financial world there are many potential investment vehicles to choose from. Sure, each has some level of risk. But so does keeping cash stashed in a savings account as it loses value each year because the interest you earn is less than the rate of inflation.

Remember, you build wealth by investing savings that generate income, which you use to acquire assets, which generate income, enabling you to buy more assets to generate even more income. Add to that the magic of compounding and you are on your way.

In a way, you're forming your own start-up company whose goal is to enable you to be part of that wonderful 5% who are free to follow their passions in life without being controlled by some financial institution. These are the people who are financially independent, able to take care of themselves for their entire adult life without assistance from government agencies. These are the people we call "21st century millionaires."

Business Structures

We begin the search for investments by looking at various types of business structures and organizations. Some of these are entities that you might form someday yourself to conduct a business of your own, full time or part time, maybe even working out of your residence.

Sole Proprietorship
A sole proprietorship is usually the simplest type of business to form. It's a business owned solely by one person. The proprietor may need to obtain a business license along with other permits. Maybe it is a food truck, a franchise, or a part-time business helping people file their tax returns. In a sole proprietorship,

if the owner dies, the business dies. It is estimated there are over 20 million such businesses in the United States with annual sales over $1 trillion.

In a sole proprietorship, the owner is the boss and owns it all. He or she is responsible for everything. The proprietor has **unlimited personal liability and** may need to purchase liability insurance to protect his or her assets. Sole proprietors have limited ability to raise money.

Sole Proprietors have a separate Schedule to file along with their individual Form 1040 tax return to report their profit or loss from the business to the IRS for tax purposes. One thing the IRS looks for is that the proprietor is operating it as a real business, not a hobby. Profits are taxed at ordinary individual tax rates. Losses may be used to reduce taxable income.

Partnership
A partnership is an enterprise jointly owned by two or more entities, which may have a very large number of partners. It is estimated there are over 1.8 million partnerships nationally, with sales exceeding $1 trillion. More skills, talent, and capital are usually available to a partnership than to a sole proprietorship.

There are two types of partners. A **general partner** manages and runs the partner-ship. The general partner has unlimited liability and would likely purchase insurance to cover the liability risk. **Limited partners** invest in the business and have limited liability, limited only to **the amount of their investment**. Some limited partnerships have tens of thousands of limited partners. So, both limited and unlimited partners can exist in the same partnership. The enterprise survives the death of a partner.

One of the things that makes a partnership unique is the partnership **does not pay federal income taxes**. That becomes the obligation of each individual partner for his or her share of the total profits or losses. Individual partners are allocated their proportional share of the profits and losses, and they pay any taxes due or claim eligible losses on their individual tax returns.

Partnerships may or may not make annual cash distributions to the partners even if there are profits. That is the general partner's decision to make. For example, the general partner may decide not to make a distribution but instead reinvest all the profits back into the business. Profitability of the partnership, not the amount of a distribution, determines each partner's tax obligation.

The result is that even if the partnership makes no distribution or only a partial distribution of profits, **each partner is still responsible for reporting their share of any profits (or losses) on their individual tax return.** Usually the partnership will distribute enough cash to at least reimburse most partners for their tax obligations, but the partners will have to pay their taxes regardless.

At the end of the year, each partner will receive from the partnership a **Form K-1** which states the financial information required to be filed with the partner's individual tax return. That same information is **provided to the IRS** for checking. If you are involved in a partnership you may need to seek professional advice to understand your tax obligation.

Corporations

Most large businesses are corporations. There are more than 5 million corporations in the United States with sales estimated to be far in excess of $20 trillion. **American corporations are chartered by the state.** They have the greatest ability to raise large amounts of money and provide limited liability to the owners/shareholders. Corporations file their own tax returns. The corporation survives the death of any shareholder.

Dividends are that part of the earnings of a corporation which are distributed to its shareholders. Dividends are declared by the corporation's board of directors and paid out of the corporation's **after-tax profits**. They are usually distributed quarterly to the shareholders. Dividends are taxed again to the shareholder. Therefore, **dividends are taxed twice**, once at the corporate level and again at the shareholder's level. Not all corporations pay dividends. Some very profitable corporations do not pay dividends but prefer to keep their cash to reinvest back into the business.

There are a few different types of corporate structures including:

- **Charter Corporation ("C-Corp"):** A C-Corp is chartered by a state, or in some cases, by a foreign country. It is owned by shareholders who purchase shares and have the right to vote on certain issues and receive a portion of profits, called dividends. C-Corps file their own tax returns and the corporation pays taxes at the corporate rate. The vast majority of giant enterprises are C-Corps (Home Depot, IBM, Amazon, Apple, etc.).

  Shareholders are not responsible for taxes on the profits of the corporation. Shareholders are responsible for personal taxes on any dividends received plus the capital gain or loss upon the sale of their shares. Shareholders have limited liability and upon death their shares become part of their estate.

- **Subchapter S Corporation ("S-Corp"):** An S-Corp is chartered by a state. It is owned by its shareholders. Shareholders have limited liability. S- Corps pay no dividends. Profits and losses are passed through to the shareholders and reported on their individual tax returns, similar to a partnership. The main objectives are limited liability and lower taxes.

- **Limited Liability Corporation ("LLC"):** An LLC is chartered by a state. Shareholders have limited liability. LLCs do not pay dividends. Profits and losses are passed through to the owners individually and accounted for on their individual tax returns. This corporate structure is well suited to companies with a **single owner**, but there are also some very large enterprises that are structured as an LLC. It is considered to be a way for a "proprietor" to have limited liability and possibly some tax benefits.

If you are forming an enterprise, you should **seek legal counsel and accounting advice** as to which type of business structure would work best for you, your investors, your employees, and your customers.

Investment Instruments

Common stock is a share of ownership in a corporation which entitles its owner to all the risks and rewards of the enterprise. Once you have paid for the stock, its value may go up or down. Your liability is limited. You cannot lose more than you invested.

The first time a corporation sells stock to the public it's called an **initial public offering or "IPO."** Thereafter, those shares will be bought and sold in the open market. After the IPO, corporations may issue and sell more shares to raise more money, known as a **secondary offering.** These new shares are priced at or about the current price of the stock in the marketplace, which may be higher or lower than the prior IPO.

Corporations may pay a **dividend to their shareholders.** If so, they are usually paid quarterly. Dividends are paid out of **after-tax** net income. The decision to pay or not pay a dividend is decided by the **Board of Directors**, which is elected by the shareholders. Dividends are not a tax deductible expense to the corporation. However, once paid, dividends are taxable income to the shareholder. **Therefore, dividends are said to be taxed twice, (1) once to the corporation via the corporate income tax and (2) once again to the shareholder as income.**

Corporations sometimes use their shares to buy other companies or parts of other businesses. They may also use excess cash to repurchase their own shares as a way to **increase profits per share** and hopefully the value of each share of stock in the open market.

In the event of a **liquidation or bankruptcy**, the common stockholders are usually the last to get paid. Many times, they get little or nothing.

Bonds are like loans that obligate the issuer to pay a specified amount of interest for a specified period of time, usually several years, and then repay the bond holder the face amount of the bond. Interest is usually paid twice a year. Bonds are typically sold with a face or printed value of $1,000. Simply put, to issue or sell a bond is just **another way to borrow money** and pay interest for the time you expect to need it.

Bonds issued by corporations are **secured** by corporate assets. Bondholders have a legal claim on those assets. If interest is not paid according to the bond agreement, or the issuer is unable to repay the principal on the maturity date, there is a **default** in which case the bondholders are entitled to those assets in satisfaction of the debt.

Interest paid on corporate bonds is **tax deductible to the corporation as an expense, but taxable to the bondholder as ordinary income.** Some corporate bonds may be convertible into common stock. These bonds allow the holder the choice of holding the bond and collecting interest or exchanging it for an agreed upon number of shares.

Bonds issued by state and local government agencies are called **municipal bonds** or **"muni"** bonds. They are secured by assets, taxes, revenue, or assessments. Many, such as school bonds, need to be approved by voters in advance. For the bondholder, **interest from municipal bonds issued by state and local governments is free from federal income tax. In some states, if you reside in the state of issue, the interest may also be free from state income tax.** (California and New York are among those states.) Interest may or may not be subject to the AMT. Ask your broker before making a purchase.

When considering a muni bond, know the **equivalent yield,** which is a comparison between taxable interest vs. nontaxable interest as it pertains to your tax bracket. This will help you answer the question as to whether you are better off owning a bond with taxable interest of 7%, or a bond of equal quality with tax-free interest of 5%. The answer will depend on your tax bracket. If you are in a 37% bracket you are probably better off with 5% tax-free interest. If you are in a 24% bracket, earning 7% and paying the tax is better. Just do the math.

Bonds and notes issued by the US Treasury are guaranteed by the federal government. They are, therefore, generally considered the safest investment in the world. Issuing bonds is one way the federal government raises money when it spends more than it takes in to cover the deficit. Bonds are issued with a fixed rate of interest and a fixed term. Interest on treasury bonds is free from state and local taxes, but **subject to federal income tax.**

Bond prices are hugely impacted by changes in interest rates. **When interest rates rise, existing bonds decline in market value. When interest rates fall, existing bonds rise in market value.** If the next major move in interest rates is up, the prices of existing bonds will drop, unless they are nearing maturity. Bond prices and yields can change dramatically when the bond quality rating, or level of default risk, is deemed to have increased or decreased.

Mutual funds are professionally managed portfolios which may consist of stocks, bonds, or other investments divided into shares. Each fund must have a defined investment **strategy**; for example, growth, income, domestic, global, or emerging markets. The minimum purchase may be less than $500. **Net asset value (NAV)** of each share is the total value of the fund's holdings (including cash) divided by the number of the fund's shares outstanding at that time. The NAV is posted once a day after the market closes.

There are two basic types of mutual funds:

- **Open-end funds** are pooled investment portfolios open to any investor with the money to make a minimum initial purchase. The fund issues new shares to accommodate new purchases, and redeems (purchases) outstanding shares when they are sold, **all based upon NAV.** Open-end funds have various kinds of sales fees, management fees, and administrative expenses.

  Open-end funds must be sold with a **prospectus,** a document of disclosure which details the fund's investment policy, strategy, expenses, and past performance. It is important to read the prospectus. The fees of open-end funds are considered to be relatively high, which is why their popularity has dwindled in recent years.

- **Closed-end funds** are pooled investment portfolios which raise money by issuing and selling a set number of shares in an initial public offering. Thereafter, the shares are listed on an exchange and publicly traded. The NAV is published daily even though the shares may actually trade at a higher or lower price, based upon **supply and demand**. Management fees and expenses tend to be much lower than those of open-end funds. You may pay broker's commissions, not sales fees, when buying or selling the shares.

Mutual funds pay out the dividends and interest they receive, less all expenses, to their shareholders each year. Mutual funds also make year-end distributions to their shareholders resulting from net capital gains made on investments during the year. These dividends and distributions are taxable to the individual investor.

You do not want to buy mutual fund shares in December until **after the year-end distribution for capital gains** has been made if it would require you to pay tax on the distribution. After all, why would you want to invest your money and have the fund give you some of the money right back in the form of a taxable distribution?

Suppose the NAV of the shares is $20 and you buy 1,000 shares for $20,000 and the very next day they pay a $1.00 per share distribution. The NAV then drops to $19 per share because cash distributions lower the NAV of the shares. Had you waited just one more day your $20,000 would have purchased 1,053 shares at $19 and you have no tax to pay on the distribution.

I prefer closed-end mutual funds and index funds over open-end mutual funds because they have lower fees and expenses. You may want to get help from a professional advisor. Keep in mind that mutual funds and index funds with the highest past records of performance do not necessarily repeat that performance year after year.

Exchange Traded Funds (ETFs) are securities that track an index, but trade on an exchange like a stock. They are frequently referred to as "index funds." ETFs typically consist of a bundle of stocks identical to those that comprise a specific index, **providing instant diversification** within an industry, geographic area, or other specified category. During trading hours, the ETF electronically buys and sells the same investments in the same ratio as the index itself, so that it tracks the prices of those stocks and mimics the ups and downs of that particular index.

Another benefit of ETFs includes **low expenses** because the investment is run by a computer program which automatically does the tracking by continuously buying and selling the individual shares during market hours. ETFs usually pay quarterly dividends which are taxable. ETFs have the same holding period as stocks for tax purposes.

As an example, one popular index is the Standard & Poor's 500 (S&P 500), which tracks the stock prices of 500 of America's largest and most successful companies in various industries. The symbol is "SPY." It is set up electronically to buy and sell the stocks that comprise the index throughout the day. Because ETFs trade on the major exchanges, their prices fluctuate throughout the day. They can be purchased directly through major investment and brokerage firms.

Recently, Wall Street has created some ETFs that are actively managed. The idea is to try to identify the "best" and the "worst" individual investments within the index and to allocate capital to those that are expected to have the best future performance. Investors will have to decide whether the higher fees charged for active management will be justified by better performance.

Other Wall Street "twists" on ETFs are (1) use the ETF's assets to borrow additional funds from lenders with which to make larger investments and (2) use the money to invest or trade commodities such as wheat, corn, and copper. I recommend avoiding both because of the additional risk caused by their use of leverage or borrowed funds.

Sector funds are similar to, and sometimes referred to as ETFs, except instead of tracking an index, they track stocks in a **specific industry** (such as energy, utilities, or biotech); **geography** (such as India, Japan, China, or Latin America); **emerging economy** (such as Vietnam, Poland, or Columbia); or some other specific category.

For example, there are ten categories of sector funds, called **SPDRs** (pronounced "spiders") that are made up of stocks found only in the S&P 500 index. They are Consumer discretionary "XLY," Financial "XLF," Health care "XLV," Consumer services "XLP," Industrial "XLI," Energy "XLE," Materials "XLB," Technology "XLK," Real Estate "XLRE," and Utilities "XLU."

Shares of sector funds trade on exchanges in the open-end market just like stocks. Always consider **commissions and fees** when evaluating the purchase of openend mutual funds, closed-end mutual funds, exchange traded funds, and sector funds. Although fees and expenses do not always correlate with performance, open-end mutual funds tend to charge the most, and exchange and sector funds the least. Also consider brokerage commissions for trading closed-end funds, exchange traded funds, and sector funds.

Bank certificates of deposit (CDs) are interest-earning deposits placed with a Federal Deposit Insurance Corporation (FDIC) member bank. Interest rates, length of deposit or term, and early withdrawal penalties will vary from bank to bank. Terms are usually three months to five years. Interest rates are usually higher for longer-term commitments and larger deposits.

The **FDIC** is an independent agency of the federal government which **insures and guarantees** the safety of the money held in various accounts of its member banks.

The insurance provides coverage up to $250,000 per account. These accounts include CD, checking accounts, and savings accounts. Since all member banks are equally insured, it pays to shop for rates and other features.

The FDIC also insures individual retirement accounts (IRA) and certain other retirement and trust accounts up to $250,000 per account or up to $250,000 per beneficiary if there is more than one beneficiary. I recommend doing business only with member banks.

Money market funds (MMF) are like mutual funds which invest in short-term corporate, government, or municipal debt. They pass the interest received on to their shareholders. Some MMFs may invest only in treasury notes or corporate "paper," others in municipal debt, or commercial notes or bonds. Your selection may be based on your tax bracket or your comfort with the risk.

> MMFs are offered by brokerage firms. They represent a way to earn current market interest. Interest rates are not fixed as in a bond, but will rise and fall with short-term market interest rates. If short-term interest rates rise, the MMF interest rate will follow over time. There is no term or maturity date. You can buy or sell the units at any time without penalty.
>
> **The FDIC does not insure or guarantee MMFs,** but the government does have rules regarding their allowed investments. **The government is considering major changes in the structure of money market funds.** I recommend you seek professional advice before investing in them.

Money market accounts (MMAs) and money market deposit accounts (MMDAs) are not MMFs. MMDAs are offered by banks and credit unions and are designed to compete with MMFs offered by brokerage firms. They tend to pay higher rates of interest than savings accounts and are insured by the FDIC up to $250,000 per account. A minimum balance, usually $1,000 to $5,000, is required to earn interest or avoid monthly fees. They are similar to a checking account except that only a limited number of checks may be written, and withdrawals made each month.

Credit unions are nonprofit organizations, owned by their member depositors. They provide services similar to banks, such as saving and checking accounts, home loans, personal loans, car loans, and credit cards. Because they are nonprofit organizations, surplus earnings of credit unions are returned to their members in the form of higher saving rates and lower borrowing rates. That is why they have earned the reputation of being very competitive.

Most credit union deposits are insured by the National Credit Union Share Insurance Fund which is guaranteed by the full faith and credit of the US government, up to a maximum of $250,000 per account. I strongly recommend you only do business with credit unions who are members of NCUSI.

Where it all happens

Stock exchanges are places where investors buy or sell shares. There are exchanges all over the world, some of the largest being the New York Stock Exchange, the London Stock Exchange, and the Tokyo Stock Exchange. Results are public. Liquidity is provided. Members of the exchanges and specialists match buyers and sellers and help to maintain an orderly market. The vast number of trades now take place electronically through registered dealers.

NASDAQ/Over-the-counter (OTC) is an electronic exchange conducted by some 500 private market making firms that provide quotes, and transact the trading of shares. These firms operate all over the world, providing a virtual 24/7 marketplace for securities trading.

Commodity exchanges are physical places where commodity futures contracts trade. It is an auction market with high leverage, high volatility, and high risk. Oil, wheat, corn, soybeans, cotton, cattle, hogs, gold, silver, sugar, and coffee are a few of the commodities that trade. I do not advise individual investors either trade or invest in commodity futures. Contracts are highly leveraged and far too risky for investors. As with stocks, more and more trading of commodities is being done electronically.

How to buy and sell

There are a number of common terms used in the placing of orders to buy or sell shares of stock or other investments. It is helpful to know a few of them before you begin investing.

- **Last:** The last price at which a stock actually traded. This can change in a fraction of a second. It occurs when both the buyer and the seller of a stock have agreed on a price and the number of shares.

- **Bid:** The highest price a buyer is willing to pay at that very instant in time.

- **Ask** or **offer:** The lowest price a seller is willing to sell at that very instant in time.

- **Market order:** The best available price at that instant in time for an immediate execution or filling of an order.

  If you place a **market order to buy**, expect to buy at the ask price. If you place a **market order to sell**, expect to sell at the bid price.

- **Limit order:** The specific price you set at which you are willing to either buy or sell a stock, no more/no less. A limit order does not limit losses.

If you place a **limit order to buy**, you set the highest price you are willing to buy. If you place a **limit order to sell**, you set the lowest price you are willing to sell.

I usually recommend using limit orders for all trades, whether you are using a broker or placing a trade yourself to avoid getting caught up in unexpected volatility.

I do not recommend individual investors sell shares "short", or use "stop orders". **Selling short** means you are hoping the price of the shares will decline. It also involves the potential risk of absorbing losses to infinity if you are wrong. In today's market with its emphasis on electronic trading and the frequency of increased volatility, **stop orders** can lead to unexpected losses caused by electronic malfunctions or the unexpected volatility in a stock's price. So, defining either type of order in greater detail will not be done here. Do not use them!

As an investor, you are not likely to be sitting in front of computer screen trading stocks all day long. Do not mistake the risk of investing with the risk of day trading stocks for a nickel here or a dime there. They are not the same thing. So, let's focus now on **investing in stocks**.

Notes and Updates

CHAPTER 10

INVESTING IN STOCKS

Not a Big Mystery

In *The Intelligent Investor*, Ben Graham defines investing:

> **"An investment operation is one which, upon thorough analysis, promises safety of principal and an adequate return."**

Stocks claim to have historically been the best hedge against inflation. Stocks can be used to invest in a wide range of assets such as owning part of a company; purchasing an exchange traded fund, sector fund, or mutual fund; or investing in real estate. Understanding stock ownership and how stocks are valued, bought, and sold, could play an important role in your financial future.

When you are young, you can take advantage of time and compounding to build your investment portfolio. Stocks can be volatile, and when almost everything goes down in value at the same time, you can expect to sustain losses. The good news is you can afford to take intelligent risks because you have time to recover from the periodic downturns in the market.

Gerald Loeb was known as the "Wizard of Wall Street." Many years ago, he authored the first book on investing in stocks that reportedly sold over one million copies, *The Battle for Investment Survival*. We worked at the same firm and lunched together several times in his later years. My most memorable takeaway was that bad days in the market are not just days when your investments decline in value but are frequently the days when the best buying opportunities present themselves. These are the days when stocks go on sale. I liken this to the days when shoes go on sale at Nordstrom.

> **The value of an investment is a function of your common sense, your analysis, the price you pay, and the goal you seek to achieve.**

To achieve better than average results, the investor should follow the most tested and successful investment strategies, and not just follow Wall Street's latest craze.

That means not looking at the stock market as a casino where quick profits are made. Active trading, borrowing money to invest, and financial products which involve greater leverage, risk and so-called "sophistication," generate fees, commissions, and bonuses for Wall Street, while just buying stocks and holding on to them does not. It's no mystery why Wall Street prefers speculation and active trading, and downplays investing.

When you buy a stock, you are not buying a piece of paper. You are actually buying a piece of a business, even if you own it only for a short time. Simply put, you want to sell the stock in the future for more than you paid. At the same time, deliberately, in a disciplined way, you want to protect yourself against serious losses. You should seek adequate returns with reasonable risk, not extraordinary performance with a high degree of risk.

If a stock's price is such that it can reasonably meet your investment goal by giving you future growth, you should consider owning it. But be aware that most of the money made in the market is made by being in the right asset class at the right time. **The key is spotting trends.** Be observant. If you find a business that is doing well and expanding with a great idea, research the company, and if it meets your criteria consider buying its shares. You might beat Wall Street to the punch.

There are three basic categories of investors. Which are you?

Growth Investor
This is an investor looking for strong companies to grow their sales and earnings, which usually means sales and/or earnings could grow **15% or more** from one year to the next. But in times like the Great Recession or a slow growth economy, even modest single digit growth can be exciting.

The best time to buy a growth stock is when it is not as popular as you think it will become over the next 6 to 18 months. These are often smaller companies with new and exciting ideas, and to that extent they might entail more risk. Consider **what makes the company unique.** Perhaps it's terrific management, a lasting competitive edge, a brand name, great marketing, or its history of research and developing exciting new products or services.

These stocks may be out of phase, not popular, or too small to catch Wall Street's attention at a particular point in time. In a declining market these stocks tend go "on sale" quickly. In a rising market, one worries about getting in too late, losing money, and feeling foolish. It can be emotionally difficult to buy, and there is always risk involved. Over time you will gain more confidence in your decision-making ability.

Value Investor

This is an investor looking for stocks which have stumbled and whose shares are at "bargain" prices. In down markets there may be many stocks that fall into this category. Sometimes stocks have been beaten down due to temporary problems you think will be fixed. These are **broken stocks, not broken companies**. You need to figure out why the stock sells at such a low price, and what would cause the price to rise over the next 6-18 months.

Value investments may be more difficult to identify and research. A serious value investor does not need day-to-day changes in the price of a stock to feel better or worse. They understand success may take a while, but they watch for milestones along the way.

Dividend Investor

This is an investor wanting **income** more than growth. The focus is on stocks that pay above average dividends. As a starting point, a "good" dividend is one that provides a current yield greater than the interest rate on a 10-year treasury bond. Look for companies with a **history of raising dividends** each year. Look for companies with available cash with which to pay a dividend. Look for companies that earn substantially more after taxes than they pay out in dividends. Also, look for some potential appreciation in the value of the shares.

In declining or volatile markets, stocks that pay a reliable dividend will tend to hold their value better because of the dividend. At least you're getting paid while waiting for the stock or the market to recover. Be skeptical of stocks that are paying very high dividends. Many times, these are companies that may be about to cut their dividend payments which is not what you're looking for.

No strategy works all the time. You might decide your portfolio should include all three types of investments at the same time: some growth, some value, and some dividend stocks. There is nothing wrong with that. In fact, it may be a comfortable way to balance risk while the portfolio generates dividends and appreciation. As time passes, you might decide to lean in one direction more than another.

However, the focus for young investors should probably be on growth companies, growth industries, and growth or emerging economies via ETFs, sector funds, mutual funds, or individual stocks. Growth is important because you want the stock to be worth more in the future than when it was purchased. History is not the best judge. Look to the future. You have time on your side. Do not overlook dividends. They can account for a meaningful percentage of your total return on investment. If your stock pays a dividend of 3%, it only need increase 5% in value over a year to get you to an 8% return.

Be disciplined when buying stocks!

When buying or selling stocks, discipline is more important than emotion. Let's identify some of the major disciplines which, if you follow them, should greatly increase your odds of success as an investor in stocks. As difficult as it might be, setting your emotions and your hunches aside is hard to do. Even experienced traders fall into this trap now and then. Do not beat yourself up if it happens. Just stick with these disciplines for the best results.

Discipline: **NEVER borrow money to buy stocks** or invest in the stock market. I made that mistake early in my career thinking I had a sure thing investment. It wasn't! It was tough losing the money and still having to pay back the debt. Even worse, I had borrowed the money from a family member. Don't you do it! Not from a family member, your credit card company, or your broker.

Discipline: **Market timing.** There is never a right time or wrong time to invest in stocks. Trying to "time" the market is extraordinarily difficult to do with any degree of certainty. Not even the most experienced investor can do it except occasionally, and often by chance. So, don't think you can do it either.

Discipline: It is best to **invest in stocks with money you will not need for five years.** If you are saving money for a specific purpose within the next few years, for example to start a business, make a down payment on a house, or for graduate school, that money should probably not be in stocks. You certainly don't want to be forced to sell good stocks if the market happens to be down. And you certainly do not want to risk putting off such goals.

Discipline: **Identify trends.** Jim Jubak, in his book, *The Jubak Pics*, believes that a majority of the money made in the stock market will result from "…..being in the right class of asset at the right time." And once you identify these trends and classes, you can focus on finding the best stock or fund in that category. I could not agree more.

In the book, Jubak identifies some future areas of growth such as energy, mining, agriculture, clean water, and the environment. He also looks at social trends such as the aging of the world's population and the impact of emerging economies on world trade, all of which create investment opportunities. Keep in mind the book was first published in 2008, and his trends might not be the ones you would pick today. But the important thing is his focus on trends. It certainly has worked well for him and his followers over the years.

Discipline: **Dollar-cost averaging** is investing a set amount of money in shares of a stock on a regular time schedule, **regardless of the price** of the shares at the time. By doing this, mathematically you will buy **more shares at lower prices** than at higher prices. Dollar-cost averaging is essential to a successful long-term investment program regardless of what happens to stock prices. Dollar-cost averaging of ETFs, sector funds, mutual funds, and individual stocks is a good way to start investing and not worrying each day about the market. Combined with diversification and reinvesting dividends, this is an effective way to build a portfolio. Make sure you keep accurate records of all trades for tax purposes.

Discipline: **Diversify.** As "mad money" man Jim Cramer says, "The only 'free' lunch in investing is to diversify." Diversification substantially **lowers your risk.** Spread your investments over different industries or sectors, different areas of the world with different risks and growth rates, and different size companies. Find different ETFs, sector funds, mutual funds, or individual stocks, and make sure they do not overlap, thus creating unexpected concentration.

How many individual stocks does it take to diversify? At least five stocks in five very different industries. Or five mutual funds or ETFs in five different categories. Or just a few individual stocks combined with some mutual fund shares or ETFs. No more than 20% of your portfolio should be in any single stock for a prolonged period of time. Those with larger portfolios might set the limit at 10%.

> **Life cycle funds:** One investment twist is to automatically balance and diversify the ratio of stocks to bonds in a professionally managed fund based primarily on the age of the investor. The emphasis with younger people is to own mostly stocks, and for those approaching retirement to own mostly bonds. The ratio will adjust toward bonds as the investor ages, the goal being to provide more security and income later in life.
>
> I am not a big proponent of this approach. For example, if interest rates are exceedingly low, why would one want to be in fixed income securities when there are quality stocks with higher dividends, especially since those dividends can increase over the years and the stock may appreciate? Why would one want to own bonds at any age during a period of high inflation?

Discipline: Try not buy your entire stock position at one time. **Stage and stagger your purchases.** When taking a position in a stock, consider buying it in 2 or 3 stages to get the best average price either by the number of shares or by dollar amount. You cannot count on getting the absolute lowest price, but if the stock drops a bit the second purchase will be at a lower price. And if the price has risen, you are already making money. That is not too bad either.

Discipline: Allocation of assets or rebalancing. At least once a year, review the allocation of assets in your portfolio. For example, let us say you started the year investing 20% of your money in each of five stocks. By year's end, suppose stock A now represents 30% of your portfolio. Proper allocation suggests you take some profit by selling enough shares of stock A so it once again represents 20% of your portfolio. This forces you to take some profits and gives you some additional cash to invest in another opportunity.

Perhaps stock B declined from 20% to 10% of your total investment. You now have to decide whether to take the loss, purchase more shares at the lower price, or look for a new investment. Keep in mind you can also use that loss to offset the profit in stock A for tax purposes. Rebalancing your portfolio encourages you to review your strategy for the future, something we all should do at least once a year.

Discipline: The market usually attempts to forecast the sales and earnings attributable to an individual share of stock over the next 24 months. I recommend a **range of 6 to 18 months**, because I am not a short-term trader, and estimates beyond 18 months become more unpredictable. I also prefer to own a stock for at least a year to take advantage of reduced long-term capital gains tax rates but taxes alone do not dictate final decisions. You might want to do the same when researching your investments and planning your strategy.

Discipline: Do your homework! Do not blindly trust someone else with your money, even a professional. It is your money, not theirs. There are no "hot tips." One way to approach investing is to do some of your own research and manage or at least oversee your own portfolio, whether or not you enter your own orders or work with a broker. Check out these websites for information about companies and their stocks:

- Yahoo Finance: This is one of the best websites for gathering basic information on a company and its stock. I usually turn to it first for information. www.finance.yahoo.com.

- Moneyshow.com: A website to read and listen to securities analysts discussing the global economy and specific stocks and industries. www.moneyshow.com.

- Bloomberg and CNBC: Excellent economic, business, and market coverage found on radio, Sirius, and television. Also, many interesting and informative interviews. Check their websites and your local radio and TV listings.

- Kiplinger: Independent business resource including its website and its various publications. www.kiplinger.com.

- Marketwatch: Up-to-date information on news items related to the economy and the marketplace. You can create and track your own portfolio of stocks or put together a watch list of stocks that are of interest to you. www.marketwatch.com.

- Go to a company's own website and find the annual report and 10-K or 10-Q reports filed with the Securities and Exchange Commission. Read the description of the company and its business, and carefully read the rest of the report, including the **footnotes,** which are where they may disclose some things in "smaller print." Read the section on **risk factors**. Think about the company's future prospects. You can usually listen to a taped replay of investor conference calls. In most cases you can call the company's investor relations department and ask for reports or additional information.

Jim Cramer's rule is to spend 1 hour per week for each stock or fund your own. I would include in this the time spent looking at magazines, newspapers, television, and websites having to do with global economic, social, and financial issues and trends. You might even start with some of the merchants you deal with, whose products and services impress you so much you'd like to own some of their stock.

Discipline: Keep it simple and stay informed. Many investors are not able to beat the overall stock market by choosing individual stocks, so don't bother trying unless you are willing to do some homework and pay attention to the marketplace. If you are not interested enough or do not have the time, stick to investing in ETFs and sector funds which are publicly traded, not actively managed, have low expenses, and provide diversification. Consider doing that along with a strategy of dollar-cost averaging.

Regardless of your investing strategy, it is still important that you keep up-to-date with what is going on in the world and looking for trends that could be important to your financial success. Some readily available sources include the *Wall Street Journal, NY Times, Bloomberg Business Week, USA Today, The Financial Times,* "Money Line" on PBS, "Mad Money" with Jim Cramer on CNBC, and Bloomberg Network on television, radio, and online.

If you follow these disciplines and are right a majority of the time, you can do well and make very good money. However, no matter how good or how diligent you are, you will sometimes make mistakes. Don't let it get to you. A mistake is a lesson to be learned. In this business, nobody is right 100% of the time no matter what they say at a cocktail party. If you save and invest regularly and can average 6% to 8% per year or more compounded over your earning years, you can become financially independent.

Decision Time

There are a number of things to think about as you consider investing in a business.

- What does the company do? Is it operating in a growth sector or an emerging economy?
- Is the company or sector profitable and will its profits grow?
- How do the company's operating margins compare to others in their industry?
- Who is the competition and what is the company's unique advantage?
- What is the latest news?
- Do they own patents? Are they developing new products or services?
- Is there merger and acquisition activity in their sector and are they likely to participate?
- Have they been increasing dividends or buying back their own shares?
- Are they involved in any major lawsuits or government regulatory issues?
- **Maybe the most important of all – is management doing a good job?**

These are some of the questions that can be answered by doing your research. If I think I may be interested in a particular company, I often start with Yahoo Finance to get key information on its summary, profile, headline news, key statistics, analysts' estimates, and recent events, often from objective third party sources.

If it still looks interesting I go to the company's own website, and if I continue to see potential, it's time to do some calculations. Do not be intimidated as some simple math will give you very good insights into **whether and at what price** to buy the stock.

Sharpen Your Pencil

Market cap is the total value investors are placing on the company at a moment in time. It is calculated by multiplying the market **price of a single share** of stock by the **total number of shares** outstanding. Common categories are as shown in the following:

Mega cap	Market cap over $200 billion
Large cap	Market cap from $10 billion to $200 billion
Mid-cap	Market cap from $2 billion to $10 billion
Small cap	Market cap from $300 million to $2 billion
Microcap	Market cap from $50 million to $300
billion Nanocap	Market cap less than $50 million

Some investors and portfolio managers prefer investing in the stocks of larger cap companies with more shares outstanding for greater liquidity. These are the ones that tend to get the most attention. Others may prefer smaller-cap companies which might offer greater growth potential, even though they might be considered more risky.

Earnings, and specifically the prospect of future earnings, are the **single most important factor** in determining whether investors will pay more for a stock in the future. Companies may use earnings to reinvest and grow the business, to acquire other companies, to reduce debts, to buy back their own shares, and to pay dividends. There are a number of earnings-related definitions that you should understand and be able to use:

- Earnings are expressed as **earnings per share** or **"EPS."** Investors want to know the profit or loss attributable to each share.

- Comparing the market price of a share to its earnings per share is called the **price/earnings ratio**, or **"P/E ratio."** It is the price "P" of a single share divided by the earnings "E" of a share that determines the P/E ratio. If the price is 10 times the earnings, the P/E ratio is 10. It may also be expressed as shares selling at a "multiple of 10."

- **The P/E ratio tells you what the market is currently paying for each dollar of earnings.** You may think that is too low or too high, but that is how the market is valuing those shares at this point in time.

- **Growth** is determined by calculating the percentage rate of increase of earnings over a period of time, usually a quarter or a year, past or current, to the same period of time in the future. We are looking to calculate the **rate of growth.**

  > Example: If a company's EPS for last year was $1.00, and the estimate for this year's EPS is $1.15, the annual "growth rate" would be 15%. Stated differently, earnings are expected to increase 15%.

  > Example: Many times we compare the EPS of a company's current quarter to the same quarter a year ago. If the quarter's EPS a year ago was $0.20 per share, and the earnings for the same quarter this year are $0.22, the rate of growth is 10%.

- **"PEG rate"** is a tool frequently used to try to decide if a stock is in a "buy" range or a "sell" range. It compares how much investors are currently willing to pay for each dollar of earnings, to the expected growth rate of future earnings. Specifically, the PEG rate compares the current price/earnings ratio (P/E) to the growth rate of earnings (G) to determine whether the company's anticipated growth rate is being reflected in the current price.

When calculating the growth rate, you may want to add to it a "secure" dividend rate as a bonus. For example, if the earnings are growing by 12% and the stock's dividend is 3%, the growth rate may be considered as 15%, especially if you intend to reinvest the dividend or compound by purchasing additional shares.

  > Example: If each share of a stock is currently selling for 10 times what that share earns, and the earnings are projected to grow by 15%, the calculation of the PEG rate would be:

  > PE/G = 10/15 = 0.67, which is the PEG rate.

If the PEG rate is about 1.0, the assumption is that the current market price may not be reflecting the stock's future growth potential. PEG rate is only a tool, and no tool works all the time. Do not use the PEG rate as your sole criteria for buying or selling stocks.

Following is an exercise that might help you better understand the purpose and the application of the PEG rate:

Let us look at the value investors are currently paying for the stock of company A (the price/earnings ratio). Then let us compare that to the estimated rate of earnings growth (as a percentage) over the next 12 months. This can help us decide if the stock is in a buying range and likely to be worth more in the future.

Assume company A has just reported earnings (profits) after taxes last year of $15,000,000. Company A has 10,000,000 shares of stock outstanding. The shares are currently trading in the open market for $22.50 per share. Since the most important factor is earnings, let's base this exercise on the annual growth rate of the earnings from last year to our estimate of the earnings for this current year which has just begun.

Step 1: Earnings are usually stated as EPS, which is calculated by dividing the company's earnings after taxes by the number of common stock shares outstanding.

Earnings/Shares = $15,000,000/10,000,000 = $1.50 EPS

Step 2: If this were a public company you might go to "Yahoo Finance," enter the stock symbol to find the "analysts' estimates" and calculate the growth rate between last year's EPS and this year's forecast EPS. Note that analysts' estimates may vary widely and in no way should be considered 100% accurate. This is why Yahoo uses the average of their estimates for this model. Assume the average estimated earnings of company A for this current year are
$1.80 per share, up from $1.50 last year.

Growth rate = $1.80 – $1.50 = $0.30
$0.30/$1.50 = 20%

Step 3: Divide the current market price of a share of company A ("P") by the EPS and you will get the price to earnings ratio of the stock.

Price per share/EPS = P/E ratio
P/E = $22.50/$1.50 = 15x

This tells us that the market is currently valuing these shares at 15 times what a single share earned in profits the prior year. The question is, how does this P/E compare to other companies in the same business? Still in Yahoo Finance, you could go to competitive companies and see how it compares to similar companies' P/E ratios.

Conversely, you can multiply the EPS by the P/E and you will get the current price of the stock.

$$\text{Share price} = \$1.50 \text{ (EPS)} \times 15 \text{ (P/E)} = \$22.50$$

Step 4: To calculate the PEG rate, just relate the price/earnings ratio of the stock to the projected year-to-year growth rate of company A's earnings.

$$\text{PEG} = 15 \text{ (P/E)}/20\% \text{ (growth rate)} = 0.75$$

Some investors believe a PEG rate of about 1.0 indicates an attractive buying range because the growth rate is increasing at a faster rate than the market is currently valuing the stock.

Some investors believe you should not buy or continue to own a stock whose PEG ratio is more than 2.0 or 2 times its growth rate. They would say that a stock whose PEG ratio is two or more times its estimated growth rate is priced at a level beyond its ability to expand its growth and sustain its price. For example, consider a stock currently priced at 25 times its earnings, but whose projected growth rate is only 10%. Is this stock in a "buy" or "sell" range?

$$\text{PEG} = 25 \text{ (P/E)}/10\% \text{ (Growth Rate)} = 2.5$$

Be a skeptic. There is no sure way to determine the future price of a particular stock.

P/E ratios, earnings estimates, and PEG rates are just tools like so many other factors. I do not recommend estimating future earnings per share beyond two years. Longer than that, the margin of error is too high. You should also consider the risks involved when considering any investment. Even when you buy a house you have to consider fires, floods, broken pipes, and termites. Consider how much risk you are willing to take if the shares decline.

An often overlooked source of information is to **listen to the quarterly or annual conference call** for analysts given by the company's senior management via the internet or telephone. These are recorded for replay if you can't make the live presentation. Check the website or call the company's investor relations department for details. Some investors will not buy a stock without listening or reading the transcript of these calls as they can be extremely informative.

Always be wary of initial public offerings ("IPO") which are often done in a rising or "hot" market and are timed and priced mainly for **the benefit of the seller** rather than the benefit of the investor. Sometimes, IPOs are referred to as:

"It's Probably Overpriced"

"Imaginary Profits Only"

In some cases, an IPO is a good way for a corporation to raise capital to expand its business. New shares are sold, and the cash goes directly into the company. In other instances, however, it is done so that insiders can sell their stock and take their profits. In this case, the cash would not go to the company. Insiders likely know more about the company than you do so be sure you know why they are selling.

IPO shares are mainly sold to institutional investors, not individuals. Individuals can usually buy them on the first day of trading after some initial investors decide to sell their shares and quickly take their profits. In that case, as a retail investor you are not getting in on the IPO but are actually buying shares in the open market and are probably paying more than the IPO price. In general, if an IPO is available to retail investors, there is probably a reason why, and you might consider staying away!

More disciplines, this time for selling.

Discipline: Establish your sell price when you buy a stock. Review and adjust it as you update information. True investors are not forced to sell their stocks due to daily or weekly market declines unless the market price actually indicates a change in the company's prospects or its industry, or the economy's fundamentals.

The toughest thing for most investors to do is to sell a stock or a fund. Do not let your emotions get the best of you. A common saying in the trade is, "Sell your losers and let your winners run." Reasons to sell might include:

- Falling revenues and/or profits

- Accounting problems or lawsuits

- Poor management, high turnover, or abrupt unexplained management changes

- Over expansion, poor acquisitions, and obsolescence

- Competition in the marketplace

Discipline: Be smart about **tax strategies**. Do not worry too much about paying taxes. Gains are fleeting, so take them, especially as you rebalance your portfolio. To optimize for tax purposes, make sure you buy stocks in the right account. Gains, losses, interest, and dividends in a regular account are taxed differently than those in retirement accounts.

Be aware, too, of the 1-year rule when a short-term gain becomes a long-term gain. You may not want to take a profit on day 360 and pay the higher-tax rate when you could wait another week and get the lower-tax rate. Losses taken in a regular account within one year of purchase may be worth more than losses taken after one year. The difference between short- and long-term capital losses is that short-term losses can be used more effectively to offset income, which is subject to higher ordinary tax rates.

Discipline: Sell if the **reason you bought the stock or fund no longer exists**. So many times, I have seen people hold on to stocks long after bad news has surfaced or expected results failed to occur. It's like refusing to admit times and events have changed. In reality it is a wakeup call that money would be better invested elsewhere.

Discipline: Sell if the stock **declines by a preset percentage,** such as 10% to 15%. Consider selling in stages. For example, if the stock declines 10% you might sell 25% of your position. If it drops another 5% you might sell 50%. This way you are limiting your losses, and if the stock rallies in the meantime you are still in the game by owning at least some of the shares.

Remember, if you sell a stock for a loss and buy the same stock back within 30 days, you may not use that loss for a tax loss. This is a **wash sale.**

Buying more of a stock that you already own at a loss, and then selling the original shares within 30 days to create a tax loss is also a wash sale.

Discipline: **Do not panic out of either winners or losers.**
When selling a position, consider selling it in 1 or 2 stages or pieces to get the best average price either by the number of shares or by dollar amount. An exception might be if something dramatic has happened and you have a good reason to sell it all at once. Always keep accurate records for tax purposes.

Discipline: Be **cautious of companies that buy back large amounts of their own stock**. They may view it as a good investment and a way to increase shareholder value. However, in some cases, they may just be trying to increase earnings per share and the stock's price by reducing the number of shares outstanding. Executive bonuses are sometimes influenced by the gain in price of the company's shares. If buying back shares results in a higher stock price, bonus payments may increase. Is this the best use of the company's cash? Is it better than reinvesting in the business or increasing dividends?

As a general rule of investing, expect a stock will go down right after you buy it and go up right after you sell it. Do not get discouraged. It happens to me all the time. As much as you would like, you cannot expect to buy at the low or sell at the high. Just do your homework, take profits when appropriate, and limit your losses by adhering to these disciplines.

The cash you receive from dividends is just as good as any other cash you receive. Don't forget to count your dividends along with capital appreciation when figuring the return on your investments. If your stock has a current dividend of 3%, a 5% appreciation of the shares in a year's time amounts to an 8% total return. To determine the dividend yield or percentage, divide the annual dividend by the current share price.

The Trend is Your Friend.

Looking for trends may be the most important thing you do in investing. Look ahead for 6 to 18 months. Once you identify the trend and the right kind of asset, the odds are your investment, be it a stock, ETF, sector fund, or mutual fund, will outperform the market averages.

Here are some examples of trends you might find helpful as you form your own opinions over time. **Keep your eyes open for new trends.**

> **Trend: Emerging market growth.** Recognize the accelerating growth rate of emerging economies, and the slowing growth rate of many developed

economies. These economies are creating jobs, consumer demand, and a need for raw materials, infrastructure, and certain food products. Some of these economies are seeking direct foreign investment, not only via private funds, but from sovereign controlled funds, and international consortiums. Many of these economies are dealing with major issues such as human rights, rule of law, civil unrest, and maintaining political control.

Trend: Rising inflation and rising interest rates. This includes the prospect of inflation in commodity prices, food costs, drugs, manufactured goods, college expenses, and retirement costs. Inflation may even be a way some countries will try to pay off their massive debts. With inflation come higher-interest rates. As interest rates rise the market price of existing bonds will decline. Some investors seeking income will sell stocks with low dividends to reinvest the proceeds in bonds with higher- interest rates and less risk.

Trend: The world is getting older. Birth rates are declining. That means there will be fewer young people to support the needs of elders. It also means an increasing demand for medical care; senior housing, recreation, and social services for the elderly, along with financial services.

Trend: Raw materials are in more remote and hard to reach areas. Many are in politically unstable areas. Many need major infrastructure construction to get them to market. Major projects need financing. Silicon, lithium, and rare earths are in short supply.

Trend: More people have higher incomes. They want more protein found in beef, poultry, and pork. This means huge increases in grain, soybeans, and corn for feeding. It requires more arable land and potable water of which there is a shortage. It requires more fertilizer, tractors, transportation, fuel, etc.

Trend: Environmental needs. This means clean water for drinking, industry, and irrigation. It means converting the use of coal to natural gas and renewable sources. It includes protecting populations from nuclear disasters, pollution, and possibly rising sea levels.

The opportunities for careers and investments presented by these trends are staggering. New products, services, applications, and technologies are needed in virtually every sector. The opportunities are endless in energy, processing, logistics, communication retailing, medicine, agriculture, construction, and financial services. Look for trends and let them be your guidelines for successful investing and exciting careers.

How and where to actually invest

One way to invest is to seek professional advice by establishing a relationship with a licensed investment firm or individual, professionally trained to provide financial assistance. If this is your choice you should contact different firms, seek recommendations from others, and meet with the individual who would be handling your account. That person needs to know about you and your investment goals. You need to know about that person, the areas in which they specialize, and how they work with clients.

Registered investment advisers may be found in a brokerage firm, bank, or insurance office. They are compensated by fees which are a percentage of your assets, usually in the range of 0.5% to 1.5% per year, but in some cases may be more. They should not be financially incentivized to sell you one product over another, but to pursue what is called "**fiduciary duty**" in their recommendations.

The "fiduciary duty" standard for financial advisors who are registered with the Securities and Exchange Commission requires that they **put the best interest of their clients first,** rather than just making recommendations that are deemed "suitable."

On the other hand, commissioned brokers are allowed to recommend investment products that are "**suitable,**" a lower standard, which gives them far more latitude to suggest products that provide them with the biggest payouts such as those found in actively managed funds.

Currently, the standard of "suitability" for brokers is to "know your customer" and give advice accordingly by recommending only investments that reflect the investor's financial objectives, risk tolerance, age, and means. That is not to say that commissioned brokers are not doing a good job for their clients. Many have been performing at the fiduciary level of their own volition, helping their clients, and maintaining high standards throughout their careers.

It is very good news that attention is now being focused on giving increased protection to individual investors when giving financial advice and recommending investments.

An advisor should "help" you invest, not just do it without direction. You should know enough to have some input. If you do not understand an investment, I recommend you don't buy it. And keep in mind the costs and expenses of professionally managed investments and brokerage fees will impact total returns on your investment. The higher the expenses the lower the returns on your investment will be and, due to compounding, it can make a big difference over a long period of time. Professional services are not free but be alert for excessive management fees and brokerage commissions.

However, if you intend to invest only in large publically traded ETFs and sector funds with very low expenses, you may be better off using a discount broker to handle orders rather than a full service investment advisor or broker.

There are two basic types of brokers you may want to consider when opening an account. Services, commissions, and fees may change frequently; so, check them out carefully:

- **Discount brokers**: Discount brokerage firms can help you buy and sell securities at low cost due primarily to electronic trading. Some clients may choose to do their own research and place their own orders over the internet without even using the services of an individual broker. Orders can be placed by phone for about $30 per trade or entered online for $7 or less per trade.

  Some of these firms offer ETFs, sector funds, and mutual funds with little or no commissions. They may also provide full investment services as an adjunct to their basic business.

- **Full service firms:** Full service brokers provide a wide range of personal financial services for their clients. These include placing trades, independent research, financial guidance and advice, and, with your written approval, full discretion over your account.

  You are usually assigned a registered representative who handles your account. Annual fees are typically in the range of 1.0% to 2.0% of the assets in the account. But others may also charge commissions on individual trades. Most full-service firms are not geared toward small investors and many have high minimum investment requirements.

The Securities Investor Protection Corporation ("SIPC") is a federally mandated, nonprofit corporation funded by its members which protects securities investors from certain types of financial consequences if a member broker–dealer firm goes bankrupt or if securities are misappropriated, stolen, or never purchased.

In the event of bankruptcy, the SIPC will liquidate a firm's assets and organize the distribution of cash and securities to customers. If cash and securities are not available or are insufficient to cover the losses, the SIPC will compensate customers for their losses up to a current maximum of $500,000 of their equity, including up to $250,000 in cash. The SIPC will also cover customers from unauthorized trades based on documented details.

The SIPC does not cover losses or potential losses from investing activities. Certain types of losses are not covered at all including commodity futures contracts. **Only do business with SIPC member firms.** SIPC rules and regulations are substantially different than those of the FDIC.

Securities law now requires stock brokerage firms to send each account a year- end form 1099-B showing the proceeds, cost basis, and selling price of investments sold during the year; short and long term gains and losses; wash sales; qualified and nonqualified dividends; interest; and foreign transactions. This information is very helpful in filing individual tax returns. The IRS also gets a copy of your 1099-B.

You need to have a strategy!

To prepare for longevity you need to have a **long-term horizon**. Getting started or increasing your effort is often difficult, and may require you to overcome the most common errors in starting to invest such as:

- Not getting started, thus reducing the magic of compounding.
- Not having a coherent and workable investment plan or strategy.
- Not taking time to be informed.
- Not checking up on your broker, advisor, or money management group.
- Investing money in stocks which should go elsewhere, such as paying off high interest credit card debt.
- Buying on hot tips and rumors. Tips are for waiters, not investors.
- Becoming emotionally attached to a company or a stock.
- Thinking a low-priced stock will make you more money or have a greater percentage gain than a high-priced stock. This is not true. **Focus on the percentage gain or loss.**

So let's get started. . .

This is a good time for you to plan or review your investment strategy based upon the principals we have discussed, your individual financial goals, and the many investment options available to you.

We begin the plan with the Rule of Fred…….."I get paid first."

If you are not already doing so, start **saving 15% of your earned income** as soon as possible. Pay off any high interest credit card balances and other debts with 12% to 25% annual interest rates. That is a better use of funds than trying to earn 8% to 10% through investments.

Establish a 3-6-month **emergency fund**. This money might be in a savings account, certificate of deposit, or a money market deposit fund where you can get to it quickly if needed.

Contribute the most you can to an **employer sponsored retirement plan** to get the biggest possible employer contribution. This is **free money**, and free is good. You can **count any employer contribution** toward your 15% savings goal.

To get started investing if you do not already have an account, open a cash account at a bank, brokerage, or money management firm, and deposit funds. Again, I recommend you never borrow money to buy stocks. If practical, ask to have your dividends reinvested to begin compounding.

Working with your account representative, discuss your financial goals, and your level of risk tolerance. Determine the balance between being a growth, value, or dividend investor. Invest the first $10,000 to $20,000 in ETFs, sector funds, and mutual funds. Be patient. **You shouldn't invest it all at once.** This is the base from which you begin to grow.

Consider investing in individual stocks if you intend to devote the time necessary to manage your investments. Otherwise, you may decide to continue on with ETFs, sector funds, and mutual funds.

Decide what percent of your money goes into your retirement accounts, and what percent goes into your own investment accounts. If you want to speculate, go ahead. It is okay and can be fun, but it should be limited to no more than 5% of your portfolio.

Use diversification, allocation of assets, dollar-cost averaging, and all the other disciplines we covered in your plan. Keep in mind your goal in investing in stocks is to **earn an above average annual rate of return of 8% to 10% or more, including dividends, and to compound that rate of return over time.** As you do so, consider the tax consequences of short-term vs. long term capital gains, ability to offset losses against gains (and income up to $3,000), and tax-sheltered retirement accounts. This is true whether or not you use professional management.

Remember, **no strategy will work all the time**, and unless you are working in the securities industry or have nothing else to occupy your time, you are probably not going to sit in front of a computer monitor trading stocks all day. That brings us back to fact that the majority of the money made is by being in the right kind of asset at the right time. This is why we look for trends.

Notes and Updates

CHAPTER 11

INVESTING IN BONDS

Not Even a Small Mystery

Fixed Income Investing

Bonds

Bonds are an interest-bearing security obligating the issuer of the bond to pay the bondholder a specified amount of interest for a specified period of time, and then repay the bondholder the face amount of the bond, usually $1,000 per bond, on the termination date according to its terms and conditions.

Bonds are debts that must be repaid. They are often issued as an alternative to bank loans. Usually, the issuer of the bond is one of the following:

- US government
- Agencies of the federal government
- States, counties, cities
- Municipalities such as school, water, and transit districts
- Corporations
- Nonprofit organizations such as universities and hospitals
- Similar entities in foreign countries

A key difference between stocks and bonds is that stocks make no promise to pay a dividend or guarantee the principal. Issuers of bonds guarantee to pay a set amount of interest each year in return for use of the money and to pay back the loan, in full, on a specific date which is called the date of "maturity".

Bonds are **rated as to quality** (AAA, AA, A, BBB, BB, etc.) by independent rating agencies assessing the risk of default or failure to meet the terms of the bond. Defaults are the result of the nonpayment of interest or the inability to repay the bond when due. The lower the quality, the higher the interest rate must be to attract investors. Those with ratings of AAA through BBB– are considered **"investment grade"**, and those with ratings of BB+ or lower are referred to as **"high yield"** or "junk" bonds.

Moody's, Fitch, and Standard & Poor's are considered the three major rating agencies investors rely on most. Ratings are not investment recommendations but judgment calls or opinions about the creditworthiness of an issuer or the credit quality of a specific debt security. Rating agencies are not perfect. The failure of these agencies to recognize and downgrade the risky and speculative issues which they were rating as AAA was a major factor in causing the Great Recession. Many believe these agencies have an inherent conflict of interest in that the agency that is rating the bond is actually hired and paid by the entity that is issuing the bond.

Why do individual investors buy investment grade bonds? They want to receive a reliable source of periodic income along with safety of principal.

Why do individual investors buy speculative grade bonds? They want to be paid a higher rate of interest and are willing to accept a higher risk of default.

When a bond is issued its **face value** or **principal** amount, called **par**, is usually $1,000. The issuer promises to pay a predetermined rate of annual interest, called a **coupon**. Interest is usually paid twice a year in equal amounts, but when bought or sold bond interest is calculated precisely as of the day of the transaction. When a bond is purchased, regardless of the price paid, the issuer still promises to pay back the face value on a specific date to whoever owns the bond. That date is the **maturity date.**

Let's say you buy a bond with a $1,000 face value, a 6% coupon, and a 10-year maturity date. You would receive $60 of interest in each of the next 10 years. And on the maturity date you would be paid $1,000 which is the face value of the bond.

Once issued, bonds may be bought and sold in the open market for more or less than the face value. There are times in the "business cycle" when bonds can be very profitable investments, not only for their high rates of interest, but for potential appreciation as well. That is why it is important to understand some of the terms used in describing bonds.

> **Bond premium:** This is the amount **above face value** the bond is valued at in the marketplace ($1,050 market price vs. $1,000 face value = $50 or a 5% premium). Part of the premium you pay can be **deducted each year** that you own the bond for tax purposes since the amount you will receive on the maturity date will be lower than your cost and create a loss.

Bond discount: This is the amount **below face value** the bond is valued at in the marketplace ($1,000 face value vs. $950 market price = $50 or a 5% discount). Part of the discount is reportable as taxable **income for each year** you own the bond until the maturity date since the amount you will receive on the maturity date will be higher than your cost and create a profit.

But why would the market price of a bond with a face value of $1,000 be worth either $1,050 or $950 in the open market? The first reason is **interest rates.** If you are holding a bond that pays 6%, but market interest rates have moved down, and new bonds of equal quality are being issued for 5%, your bond becomes more valuable. After all, someone would rather have your bond at 6% than the new one at 5% and they would pay more to get it. This is your premium, or capital gain. **Conversely**, if new bonds are now paying 7%, or $70, your 6% bond, paying $60, is suddenly less attractive and no one is likely to buy it unless you give them a discount in price.

The second reason is **credit quality.** If your 6% bond was rated AA when you bought it, but the bond's rating has been downgraded to BB, or if investors just do not feel the credit quality of the issuer is as good as it was, there is deemed to be more risk in the investment and, therefore, those who might buy it will want a higher return for the added risk. The coupon is fixed at 6% so the only way to get a higher return is to buy the bond at a cheaper price. To get someone to buy it from you, you will have to give them a discount from par. **Conversely**, if a bond is upgraded to a higher credit rating but still paying 6%, it has become more valuable and someone would pay you more for it. This becomes your premium.

Usually, investors do not buy bonds and hold them until they mature. They typically buy and sell them in the open market before they reach maturity. Therefore, a bond in the marketplace may sell for more or less than the face value, depending on changes in interest rates and credit quality.

Yield refers to the return earned by an investment in bonds. There are three basic kinds of yield:

Coupon yield (or "nominal" yield): This is the fixed percentage rate of interest based upon the par value of the bond. The coupon rate does not vary with the price of the bond. A bond with a coupon rate of 4%, pays $40 a year to the owner. That does not change.

Current yield: This is the annual interest payment divided by the market price of the bond. The coupon (or interest paid) stays the same, but **changes in the market price** of the bond will change the current yield either up or down. If you purchase a bond you will want to know the current yield.

If the coupon yield is 4% and the bond is priced at $950, the current yield is 4.21% ($40 divided by $950 = 4.21%).

Yield to maturity: This tells you how much you will receive in the future if you **hold the bond to maturity**. It is **the sum of all cash flows** from both coupon payments and repayment of the face value ($1,000). If the bond was purchased at a discount (less than face value), the yield to maturity will be higher than the coupon. If the bond was purchased for a premium (more than face value) the yield to maturity will be lower than the coupon. The yield to maturity is expressed as an annual percentage rate without accounting for any taxes to be paid by the holder of the bond.

Here is an example of how it might all work. If a $1,000 bond with a coupon of 6% is purchased for $800, the new owner receives $60 per year in interest, which is a current yield of 7.5% ($60 divided by $800.) If that person holds the bond for 20 more years, to maturity, he/she will receive $1,000. Allocate the extra $200 cash flow over the 20 years until maturity and the yield to maturity rises to 8.75%.

Remember this Relationship. It is not Intuitive!

When interest rates rise, bonds which were previously issued decline in value. When interest rates decline, previously issued bonds increase in value. They go in opposite directions.

US Government bonds are bonds issued by the federal government and backed by the full faith and credit of the US government.

- US treasury **bills** mature (or come due) in 90 days to 1 year. No actual interest is paid because the government sells the bills at a discount and they mature at face value.

  For example, if the government sells a treasury bill for $950 and it matures in 1 year at $1,000 the return to the owner is 5.26% ($50 divided by $950 = 5.26%).

- US treasury notes usually have 2, 5, and 7-year maturities. Interest is paid twice a year.

- US treasury **bonds** mature in 10 to 30 years. Interest is paid twice a year.

Interest on US government bonds is **exempt from state and local taxes**, but not from federal income taxes. Bonds can be purchased from a broker or directly from the federal government.

Proceeds are used by the government for many reasons, including paying off previously issued bonds that are maturing, funding budget deficits, financing wars, and stimulus packages. US bonds are very popular with foreign governments and investors who buy US bonds, which help us fund our deficit.

Federal agency bonds are those issued by federal agencies to help fund projects relevant to public policy.

They are designed to provide low interest rate financing to support sectors of the economy that might otherwise not be able to borrow at such low interest rates. These include the following well-known agencies:

- Federal National Mortgage Association (Fannie Mae)
- Federal Home Loan Mortgage Assoc. (Freddie Mac)
- Small Business Administration (SBA)
- Student Loan Program (Sallie Mae)

Federal agency bonds are **not guaranteed by the US government**, but held in high regard, since they are issued by government agencies.

Municipal bonds also called "muni" bonds, are bonds issued by state and local governmental agencies. Muni bonds are used to finance schools, roads, and other public projects. Interest and principal are paid to investors from taxes on income, sales, and property; and revenues from tolls and various fees.

Muni bonds **are exempt from federal income taxes and may even be free from some state income taxes,** if owned by residents of the state in which they are issued, such as California, New York, and others. This feature enables these entities to raise money at a lower cost of capital because of the tax advantages afforded investors.

Your "after-tax" net return depends on your tax bracket, so always bear this in mind when comparing the return on muni bonds to that of higher interest rate taxable bonds. Is it better to own a 7% taxable bond or a 5% tax-free municipal bond? Do the math using your tax bracket. Muni bonds are probably not the best deal if you are in a low-tax bracket.

However, the **interest from some municipal bonds may not be exempt from the alternative minimum tax,** so always ask your broker about this before you invest.

Corporate bonds are bonds that represent loans to corporations. These bonds are considered "safe" when issued by strong companies, but "junk" when issued by weak companies. Weak companies pay the highest rates of interest. Interest on corporate bonds is **fully taxable**, both state and federal. They are typically issued in maturities up to 30 years, and generally pay interest twice per year. For diversification, there are a multitude of bond funds available.

Bonds are fixed income securities. By far, the greatest **dangers for bond investors are rising interest rates and inflation**. As you have learned, when **interest rates go up**, the value of bonds being held goes down. When **inflation is high**, you will receive the full-face value of a bond at maturity, but the dollars you receive will likely have less purchasing power.

The Federal Reserve Board plays a major role in determining interest rates. It is worth paying attention to their meetings and public comments as they signal their intentions. If it is anticipated that rates will rise, investors will predictably sell bonds to avoid losses.

Bond Ratings

Standard & Poor's	Moody's	Fitch	Creditworthiness
Investment Grade			
AAA	Aaa	AAA	Highest quality. Extremely strong ability to meet financial commitments.
AA+	Aa1	AA+	Very strong ability to meet financial commitments.
AA	Aa2	AA	
AA-	Aa3	AA-	
A+	A1	A+	Strong capacity to meet commitments but somewhat susceptible to changes in circumstances or economic conditions.
A	A2	A	
A-	A3	A-	
BBB+	Baa1	BBB+	Adequate capacity to meet commitments but more likely to be weakened by adverse circumstances or economic conditions.
BBB	Baa2	BBB	
BBB-	Baa3	BBB-	
Noninvestment Grade			
BB+	Ba1	BB+	Somewhat speculative. Vulnerable over the long term to major ongoing uncertainties or adverse business, financial, or economic conditions.
BB	Ba2	BB	
BB-	Ba3	BB-	
B+	B1	B+	Speculative. Has the capacity to meet commitments, but adverse business, financial, or economic conditions will likely impact ability or willingness to meet obligations.
B	B2	B	
B-	B3	B-	
CCC	Caa	CCC	Poor quality. Currently vulnerable and dependent on favorable conditions to meet obligations.
CC	Ca	CC	Most speculative. Currently highly vulnerable.
C	C	C	Highly vulnerable to nonpayment. Bankruptcy petition may have been filed.
D	C	D	Has failed to pay one or more obligations when due.

Notes and Updates

CHAPTER 12

STOCK OPTIONS AND GRANTS

The Modern Day Gold Rush?

Stock options give one a **right, but not an obligation**, to buy a stock at a set price within a specified period of time. Options are designed to attract, retain and reward employees, and make them stakeholders, incentivized as part owners of the enterprise. If the stock increases in price, the options have value and are **in the money**. If the stock decreases in price, they have no value and are **out of the money**. If the options are not exercised by the **expiration date**, they terminate.

During the dot-com craze of the 1990s, stock options were commonly used in lieu of cash by start-up companies to attract employees. The intent was to align the interests of employees with shareholders, the common goal being a rise in stock price. The ultimate hope was the company would go public and both the employees and shareholders could sell their shares and make a lot of money.

Being attracted by the prospect of becoming rich, employees were willing to accept lower pay. But start-up companies benefitted too as they were usually underfunded and used stock options instead of cash as part of their compensation packages. There were also some accounting benefits to companies that used options instead of cash, giving them higher reported net income. And, ultimately, if successful, the company would actually receive some cash in the future when the employees paid to exercise their options.

Employees were **given the stock options for free.** But some companies issued so many options that if all the options were exercised, the employees might own 20% or more of the company, diluting the ownership of all the other shareholders.

And the incentives did not always work so well either. If the company went public, some employees became "rich" and quit. If the company did not do well, the options might be worthless, so some employees quit anyway, leaving the shareholders holding the bag. There were some successes, but most hoped-for fortunes never materialized as the hot initial public offering market collapsed.

Stock options are **granted by the board of directors**. The board of directors also **sets the price** at which the employee can purchase shares of stock sometime in the future. When granted, the options are free and there is no taxable event as long as the options are not exercised (converted to stock).

Here's an example of how options work: Suppose an employee has an option to purchase 10,000 shares of stock at $5 per share any time over the next 10 years, when the option will expire if not exercised. However, five years later the stock is at $30 per share and is **"in the money."** The employee can exercise the options by arranging to put up $50,000 and in return receive 10,000 shares of the stock with a market value of $300,000, which can immediately be sold.

However, if the stock is trading at $4, the option is probably worthless, or **"out of the money."** Why would someone pay $5 for a stock if they could buy it in the open market for $4? They wouldn't!

But here is where the tricky part comes in......taxes! When the options are **exercised**, the employee pays the required price per share to the company ($5/share = $50,000), and is issued the shares. When the option is exercised, there is **ordinary income tax** due immediately based upon the difference between the exercise price and the market price at the time of exercise ($30–$5 = $25/share = $250,000). On top of that, the profit of $250,000 resulting from exercising the options may be considered compensation by the Internal Revenue Service and subject to Social Security, Medicare, withholding, and other payroll deductions, as well as potentially being subject to the alternative minimum tax (AMT).

Finally, when the shares are eventually **sold** there may be a capital gain tax to pay and depending on how long you held the shares after they were exercised, the gain may be taxed either as a **long term capital gain or a short term capital gain**. For example, if you ultimately sell the shares for $40, you have an additional $100,000 capital gain ($40–$30 = $10/share = $100,000.) If you ultimately sell the shares and the sale price is below the exercise price there could be a capital loss for tax purposes.

Many of those who exercised options in the past believed the stock's price would never go down but always continue to increase. They decided to hold on to their shares regardless of the risk. If they were right, and the stock did increase in price, it may have been a good decision as they could sell some shares to raise money for the taxes and still come out ahead.

But if the shares declined in price after exercising the option, the result was not so good. Employees lost money in the shares from the time when they were acquired, **but still owed the taxes on income created when they exercised the option** in the first place. In addition, they became subject to the alternative minimum tax which increased their taxes on all their income. Many found themselves selling shares at a loss just to pay taxes owed for exercising the options. In other words, they ended up paying taxes on income they never got! This can happen if you're not familiar with the tax laws on options. This is why getting professional **tax advice before you exercise** is so important.

This is why in most cases I recommend exercising the options and selling the shares immediately. Then, upon expert advice, immediately set aside the funds needed to pay any and all taxes. And remember, these taxes are probably due by the next quarterly estimated tax date or it could get even more expensive.

Stock grants are gifts of stock. Many companies have now replaced stock options with grants of the company's stock. Most grants are made to executives and managers. Grants may either be free to the employee or require purchasing the shares at bargain prices. Additionally, certain conditions must be met such as length of service or profitability before the shares are actually transferred to you.

Granted shares may or may not be **restricted or vested**. In cases where the stock is restricted, if you have not qualified by length of service or meeting profitability goals, or your employment is terminated, it means the shares are not yours and you cannot take them with you. If the shares are vested it means that all the restrictions have been met and if your job is terminated, whether you are fired, retired, or quit, you can take those shares with you. If not vested, the shares are not yours when you leave.

Again, there are instances when if the stock is vested and received, it is reported as compensation equal to the value of the stock on the date of the grant or award, whether or not you sell the shares. Such compensation is subject to payroll deductions, withholding and ordinary income tax rates. To cover the cash required for withholding, the company will usually sell enough of your shares to pay the required withholding tax, unless you want to put up the cash yourself.

When the shares which remain after the withholding are ultimately sold, there will be a capital gain or loss depending on how long the shares were held and the difference between the sale price and the value of the stock on the day any restrictions terminated. The AMT may also enter into the picture.

In some cases, if the employee holds the shares for one year after the option exercise date, or two years after the date of being granted shares, any profit on sale will be taxed as a long term capital gain. But this strategy requires the holder to take on additional risk by holding the shares for a longer period of time to take advantage of a potential tax benefit.

Again, all options and grants are not the same. I repeat, always check with a tax advisor well in advance when dealing with stock options and grants for the up-to-date tax ramifications of your specific situation.

It is a complex tax code out there and mistakes can be very costly.

Notes and Updates

CHAPTER 13

LOVE AND MONEY

"With this Debt I Thee Wed"

Couples talk about a lot of things when they are planning to get married or move in together. But there is one topic that often feels too personal to talk about, and that is "money." And, according to money.com, "70% of married couples argue about money ahead of fights about household chores, togetherness, sex, snoring, and what's for dinner."

Today's families seem to be functioning under more **stress over money**. Only 30% feel financially secure. The traditional family, with a mom, dad, two kids, and a dog is just about over. The demographics now include blended families, single parents, cohabitating households, married gay couples, and grandparents raising children.

Just the stress of making a living and paying everyday bills, mortgages, student loans, credit cards, and taxes puts pressure on a relationship. That is why almost 80% of households have two people working. That is what it takes to support most families these days.

Financial stress can exist when the combined income is too low; when there is a significant gap in earnings between the parties; when there are financial obligations outside of the relationship such as alimony, child support, or a business; and even when the combined income in a marriage pushes some couples into a higher-tax bracket. It can also exist for no good reason, simply a question of who makes the decisions and how.

It's not surprising that one of the major causes of divorce is financial conflict. The answer is seldom just one person changing their financial habits. The best case is when both partners agree to work as a team.

A lasting relationship requires financial intimacy.

Financial intimacy means coming up with a shared approach to spending, saving, and investing. It is a clear sign of how much you truly love, respect, and trust one another. Money decisions are with you every day of every week for the rest of your life. If you are not in sync with your partner you could have constant stress in your relationship. Will you be financially compatible and trustworthy?

Relationships normally begin with dating, a world which has changed dramatically over the years. Certain questions which usually were not asked when first meeting a "person of interest" are now quite common, making the first few dates more like an interview:

> "Are you in a relationship now?"
> "Have you been married before?"
> "Do you have children?"
> "Do you want children?"
> "What is your credit score?"
> "How much student loan debt do you have?"

There are two basic types of personalities, **consumers and savers**. One of the patterns you might observe is which category a person falls under. To some people, spending is an addiction. The signals might be:

> Driving a "too expensive" car.
> Owning lots of new clothes.
> Making impulse purchases.
> Living in expensive digs.
> Always ordering the most expensive thing on the menu.

To some, saving, or not spending, is an obsession. Possible signals are:

> Taking mustard and ketchup packets home from McDonalds.
> Walking into hotel lobbies looking for a bowl of free apples.
> Driving 10 miles to save 3 cents on a gallon of gas.
> Having fun is too expensive.
> Always ordering the cheapest thing on the menu.

And then there is the financial "judge," who says, "You manage the money and make the investment decisions. Afterward I'll tell you if you were right or wrong."

Understanding a person's financial habits can be easier if you know something about their **money history**. In some homes money was given freely, like an allowance, and college was paid for. In some homes money was scarce and children had to "earn" money by doing chores. In some homes, money was scarce, and everyone pitched in. Some want to follow their parent's pattern; others may want the opposite. If the saver is miserly and the spender is irresponsible, compromise may be your only hope.

The consumption of alcohol and drugs, and the addiction to gambling, are serious flaws which can kill a relationship financially as well as emotionally. Usually the process of dating exposes these troubling patterns, but some people seem willing to overlook them, at least for a time. But they can have disastrous consequences; physical, mental, and financial. In today's world, as unromantic as it may sound, it is not unheard of for someone perhaps a little older and with significant assets to seek a background check as a relationship begins to get serious.

One thing is certain. **If you do not talk about money before you get married or move in together, you are just delaying inevitable problems**. In the rush and excitement to become married, domestic partners, or significant others, couples often think that love will overcome disagreements about money. It doesn't seem to work that way. People do not change readily. Even among the most compatible couples, the prewedding vow of personal financial silence can lead to frustration, fights, power struggles, and separation or divorce. More than 50% of divorces are estimated to be over money, but many articles that discuss love, marriage and divorce don't even mention finances. Maybe discussing it doesn't sell as many magazines.

Talking about money does not mean fighting about money.

NOT talking about money is where the problem begins. Whether you're 20 years old and marrying for the first time, or 50 and planning partner number four, **you need to talk.**

How to start a conversation about spending habits by a spouse or partner is something most people have not thought about. Pick a relaxed time and do not start with accusations. Discuss your own stress and worry about your financials. Try opening lines like these:

> "I really want to talk to you about this without either of us getting angry or yelling."
> "How do you think we got this way?"
> "How do you think we can better control our finances?"

141

It is possible to find true and lasting financial harmony with your mate, but it takes time, effort, honesty, respect, and trust. Just like in every other aspect of your relationship, both parties need to be patient and understanding. Throwing things is bad. Physical abuse should never be tolerated. Discuss financial matters in a calm moment, not during a crisis. You want to negotiate.

What role will money play in the relationship? Usually one person is more interested or inclined to manage the money than the other. Usually one person is more interested or inclined to spend the money, and if it is the same person who manages and spends, there is the potential for a problem.

Surveys have shown that about half of all couples admit that they have committed **financial infidelity** – lying to a partner about money. According to a CreditCards.com report, one in five Americans admits to having spent $500 or more on a purchase without their partner's knowledge. Some even have a bank or credit card account hidden from their spouse or partner.

Couples should share certain financial information when committing to live together in a loving relationship, especially where legal obligations or contracts come into play. What are your financial assets and liabilities? How much do you earn? How much debt do you have in credit cards, student loans, medical bills, and car payments? Whose name is on the apartment lease, phone, and utilities? What expenses are coming up that need to be planned for? These numbers will not stay hidden for long. They will surface the first time you try to rent an apartment, lease a car, or buy a house together.

Couples and partners should also discuss their financial future. What are each persons' financial goals and aspirations? What are each of your career and work expectations? Will you both be working? How long? What will we do if a job or promotion means moving? If we have a child, will one of us stay home?

How will we share financial duties and responsibilities? How many checking accounts? One, two, or three? Yours, mine, or ours? Who pays bills, balances statements? Who takes care of insurance, investments, medical bills, and retirement planning?

One way to share expenses when both parties work is to do so based on income. Remember, it is equal shares, not necessarily equal dollars. Is the money yours, mine, or ours?

Managing cash flow is where couples experience financial flare-ups. Telling your mate how to spend every dime can lead to a bad outcome. Each person should have some **discretionary money to spend**, and some "fun" money too. Couples need to work out a day-to-day money management system that works for both individuals.

Finding your partner has a hidden debt or a hidden bank account can be a big turnoff. Alimony and child support obligations can be a nasty surprise. The kind of debt one has may tell you something about that person. For example, there is a big difference between student loan debts and gambling debts.

Don't let money become a proxy for love, sex, and power. One of you may earn a lot more than the other. **Many women today earn more than men**. It's okay. One may be getting a large inheritance. Family finances work best when both parties know what is going on with the money. After all, relationships can easily last over 50 years given today's advances in healthcare.

8 million cohabitating households in America!

Before discussing prenuptial agreements and the possibility of divorce, let's address the fact that there are over 8 million cohabitating households in America. Many include minor children. If you are not married to your partner, the benefits of joint property, inheritance, Social Security, or other retirement benefits may not be available to you. For example, if you or your partner becomes ill or disabled without some form of cohabitation agreement, next of kin may disallow visiting rights and decision-making to the person you most trust. And if one of you dies, who will inherit their belongings?

Surprisingly, the fastest growing segment in cohabitation involves those over age 50, including many senior citizens. Why are so many older couples choosing to live together outside of marriage? It's usually related to financial planning. There may be concerns over pensions and Social Security benefits, healthcare costs, debts, estate planning, taxes, control over assets, loss of alimony, and helping children and grandchildren with their student loans, marriages, and home buying.

Every cohabitating party should have a will or trust designating beneficiaries of assets, a durable power of attorney and nomination of a conservator, and a power of attorney for healthcare. Each party should also regularly review their beneficiary designations on various retirement accounts and insurance policies. An agreement should also address what happens if the couple chooses to separate.

Many still do get married.

That brings us to marriage. **Separately owned property may be retained** after marriage by the spouse who owns the property. **Individual inheritances and gifts may also be retained** as separate property even after marriage as long as they have not been co-mingled. Each partner may want to make a list and keep a record of the fair market value of the assets and liabilities acquired before the marriage. Equally important, **when you marry you do not legally take on the debt your partner amassed before you wed.**

Property is either owned separately or together, the latter called **community property.** California and several other states have community property laws. Typically, everything you or your spouse accumulate during the marriage in a community property state is community property and is a **joint responsibility**. This includes all earnings during marriage and everything acquired with those earnings, as well as most debts incurred during the marriage, **joint and several**. As stated above, it does not include inheritances and gifts provided they are not co-mingled and are kept in a separate beneficiary labeled account.

The Internal Revenue Service has ruled that all same-sex married couples are now treated as married for federal tax purposes regardless of the state in which they reside. However, state tax laws may be different and may require professional advice.

And if you are changing your name, remember to change it on your Social Security, driver's license, passport and other forms of ID; your will and other estate-planning documents; bank, savings, investment and retirement accounts; credit and debit cards; life insurance policies; beneficiary designations; and healthcare documents.

Do we need a **prenuptial agreement?** This may be an explosive question. To many it may imply mistrust or a lack of faith or commitment in the relationship lasting, but prenuptial agreements have now become quite common, with 50% of marriages having them in place. To some extent the growth in prenuptial agreements is due to the fact that people are marrying later in life when many have careers and assets they want to protect. And it might surprise you to know that the biggest reason is not divorce, it's death.

There may be good reasons for a prenuptial agreement. One person may want to segregate certain assets to take care of a special-needs sibling, a parent, or child from a previous marriage. Or, perhaps someone is giving up a career or losing out on a pension or inheritance. One person may have a lot more assets than the other and want to protect them. One may have an established and successful business. If you just cannot bring up the subject ask your financial planner, accountant, or lawyer to do so.

State laws govern but will usually not allow one person a financial incentive for divorcing the other. Incorporate your agreement into a written contract at least 60 to 90 days before the wedding to **avoid the appearance of duress** and to clarify issues. Be reasonable. You cannot stipulate how much weight your partner gains as a violation of the marriage contract, or who gets the cat as part of the separation.

But it does not always work out as planned.

What to do if divorce is imminent? Each state has its own divorce laws and at least one of you must be a resident of the state in which you file. Establishing residency is not the same in every state. Understand the divorce laws of that state well before filing. Always seek legal assistance. However, there are some specific actions that will help you through the process:

- If you do not already have them, privately open checking and savings accounts in your own name. Fund them with as much money as you can. You may need this money for rent and food during the divorce process.

- Make sure you have a credit card in your own name to establish your own good credit.

- Gather as much information as possible before divorce is even discussed.

- Make copies of bank and credit card statements, tax returns, and information on investments.

- Store copies in a safe place. Consider getting a post-office box for private mail.

- In the case of divorce if you ultimately change your name, remember to change it on all of the documents mentioned above.

Remember, in a community property state everything you spend before announcing or filing for divorce is spent with community property, the split being roughly 50% and 50%.

Divorce also means dividing or uncoupling on some basis checking, saving and credit card accounts, debts, investments, including a house, and all other assets and liabilities. It may cause a change in health insurance for at least one party and will probably add to expenses the cost of maintaining two households.

In many cases there is alimony to be paid. This is a legal obligation to provide financial support to one's spouse or ex-spouse after separation or divorce. Alimony payments made under pre-2019 divorce agreements remain tax deductible to the payer and taxable income for the recipient.

Effective January 1, 2019 all new divorce or separation instruments executed or modified requiring alimony payments will not be tax deductible to the payer and will not be taxable income to the recipient.

When children are involved, there is likely to be child support. This is a payment made by a parent typically following divorce or separation to a custodial parent or guardian for the care and support of a child. Child support is not tax deductible or taxable income.

Most judges and family law attorneys will use a software package into which the value of the assets and liabilities and other factors are entered to calculate the division of property according to the laws of that state. Alimony and child support are typically determined the same way. Some negotiation and trade-offs are then negotiated, for example, who gets the dog? How do we split a pension? Who keeps the airline miles? Who gets legal custody of the children for any tax purposes? Keep in mind that alimony, child support, and most student loans are not protected from bankruptcy. So that's not an "easy way out". Garnishing a paycheck by court order may be the unpleasant solution.

Relationships can be complicated, but there are ways to reduce the stress that comes with the financial aspects of a marriage or partnership. Separation and divorce are complicated, emotional, and expensive. Learn to work as a team. Negotiate and compromise.

And do not forget the advice my grandfather gave me.
"A happy wife makes for a good life."

Notes and Updates

CHAPTER 14

PURCHASING A HOME

To Buy or Not to Buy? That is the Question

Purchasing a home is probably the biggest financial commitment most people will make in their lifetime. Usually it is done by taking out a large home loan payable monthly over many years during which individual circumstances and the market value of the property may change dramatically. In other words, we are taking on a financial obligation that may last 10, 15, 20, or 30 years.

Things Change.
Mistakes along the way can be very costly.

Years ago, when I bought my first house, the document signing process took 15 minutes. The last time we refinanced our current home loan the document signing took an hour and a half with a notary public at our dining room table to witness our signatures. We were surprised by the number of documents since all we were doing was refinancing with the same lender who already had all our information from our last refinancing.....eight months earlier. But interest rates were falling, and we were about to reduce our payment by $235 a month over the next 120 months. Not a bad hour and a half after all.

It was difficult understanding all that was in that stack of documents. We did our best, took our time, and even had the notary call the lender twice to make sure we understood some key points. If you ever find yourself in the same situation, don't be afraid to ask questions or get professional help from the lender, a real estate agent, banker, lawyer, or accountant. Buying a house is a big deal. It's a major commitment. So, let's go over the terminology.

Mortgage: This is a legal document which pledges a piece of property to a lender as security for repayment of the loan by the borrower. Repayments are comprised of principal and interest.

Collateral: This is property you pledge as a guarantee you will repay the loan. If you default and do not repay the loan, the lender can legally take possession of the property and sell it to get its money back; or when you sell the property you must simultaneously pay back the unpaid balance of the loan.

First mortgage: This is the mortgage that has first claim on the property in the event of a default or the sale of the property.

Second mortgage: This is an additional loan taken against the same property which is considered riskier than a first mortgage since the first mortgage must be paid off first in the event of a default or sale of the property before the second mortgage is repaid. The second mortgage usually has a higher rate of interest and a shorter term of 3 to 5 years.

Equity: This is the difference between the current market value of the property, less what is owed on the mortgage(s) and any other debts against the property. Equity represents the value of what you would receive if the property were sold and all debts against the property were repaid. You may be able to borrow against the equity in your house by taking out a home equity loan or establishing a home equity line of credit.

Home equity loan: A one-time **lump sum loan** secured by the property, with a fixed rate of interest, to be paid off with equal monthly payments over several years. The interest is probably not tax deductible unless the loan is used to "substantially improve" the home.

Home equity line of credit ("HELOC"): A revolving line of credit to reborrow funds up to a maximum amount, like a credit card. However, unlike a credit card which is unsecured debt, a HELOC is secured by the property.

In recent years, many homeowners used home equity loans and HELOC's like a personal piggy bank. As soaring home prices created additional equity in the property, it allowed them to borrow more money. However, because they are secured by the property, home equity loans and HELOC must be paid back to the lender upon default or sale of the property. In some cases, as loans came due, borrowers no longer had the cash to repay them. Hopefully, in the future, homeowners will use such borrowings for more appropriate things as originally intended, such as remodeling or renovating the property to add value, rather than funding vacations or luxury items.

Private mortgage insurance ("PMI"): When buying a house, if your down payment is less than 20% of the purchase price, the lender may charge a higher rate of interest and **require you to purchase** private mortgage insurance. Private mortgage insurance protects the lender from loss in the event of a default for the amount of the loan in excess of 80%. Currently, the cost of PMI is about 1.0% and is tax deductible as if it were additional mortgage interest. I suggest you check this out annually since it has been treated tax wise quite differently in recent years

Once the loan accounts for 80% or less of the appraised value of the property, which means the equity is now 20% or more, the PMI is eligible for termination. This occurs when either the property has increased in value, or the owner has reduced the principal amount of the loan by monthly or additional payments.

Short sale: A short sale is what happens if the value of the house declines to the point where the amount of the loan(s) is greater than the market value of the house. So even if the house is sold the proceeds will not be enough to repay the loan(s). It would be a "short sale."

Banks realize they tend to lose less on a short sale than a repossession which may be very expensive in legal fees and court costs, and take months or years to process, while property taxes and maintenance costs continue. If a short sale does not occur, the house will likely go into foreclosure.

Foreclosure: A foreclosure is when a bank or other secured lender legally repossesses a house after the owner has failed to comply with the loan agreement. The lender can then sell the property and keep the proceeds to apply toward its loan and its legal costs and to satisfy any liens on the property such as overdue property taxes. They will then distribute anything that might be left to the borrower.

Lien: This is a process whereby the property becomes security for the payment of a debt, but unlike a mortgage, the filer of the lien does not have the power to force the sale or take possession of the property. This commonly occurs when contractors or subcontractors make improvements or repairs, or when the owner fails to pay all property taxes and assessments. When a lien is paid, it is important to make sure a lien release is signed as proof of payment. Title to the property may not be transferred until all liens are paid.

Second lien: These liens include second mortgages, home equity loans, and home equity lines of credit whose holders **must approve any transaction** to sell a house for less than the amount owed on it (a short sale) since they will undoubtedly be taking losses. In some cases, second lien holders may try to extract payments in return for approving a short sale.

Refinancing a mortgage: Refinancing refers to replacing an existing mortgage with a new mortgage, either by negotiating with your existing lender for a new loan or moving to a new lender and paying off the existing loan. There are many reasons you might want to refinance a mortgage but it usually relates to lowering the interest rate or monthly payment or changing the term of the loan.

Other reasons to refinance may be to consolidate first and second mortgages; to borrow money using your equity in the house to fund remodeling, education, a business venture or other need; or simply to take money out of an otherwise illiquid asset.

Refinancing is not always as easy as it sounds. Interest rates and market values change over time. That's why it's so important that your home loan payments (including property taxes and insurance) are within your budget. If interest rates decline, refinancing can lower your monthly payments. If they increase, your existing loan protects you from higher rates.

Prepayment penalty: In some mortgage contracts there may be a clause which states that if the borrower prepays the mortgage prior to a specific date, a penalty will be assessed. Usually the penalty is equal to a certain number of months of interest, or a percentage of the outstanding loan. Try to avoid borrowing from a lender demanding a prepayment penalty since if interest rates decline you may want to refinance your loan and would not want to pay a penalty to do so.

Like people, mortgages come in many sizes and shapes.

Over the years, housing prices have usually appreciated, typically at a rate above the rate of inflation. In addition, inflation has enabled homeowners to pay off their loans with cheaper dollars. Taking on a mortgage seemed like a natural and easy thing to do. That changed during the Great Recession when the American dream to own a home became a nightmare for many. Millions lost their homes. The big culprit was rising **interest rates**.

Fixed rate mortgage: A fixed-rate mortgage enables you to **lock in your interest rate for the entire life of the loan**. Therefore, your monthly payment of principal and interest remains constant. That portion of your monthly payment going to principal grows monthly over time, and that portion going to interest will decline. For the first several years, over 90% of your monthly payment may be going toward interest.

A 30-year fixed rate mortgage with 20% down is still the benchmark against which other loans are compared. Terms of 10 or 15 years are also common. Think about coinciding the term of the loan with your expected year of retirement. Entering your nonworking years with no monthly house payment can be a major bonus. Down payments are frequently quoted at 20%, but you may find a lender willing to offer you a mortgage for less, even 0%. Be careful. There may be fees, a higher rate of interest, and PMI to pay.

Adjustable rate mortgage (ARM): These loans start with a set rate of interest for a defined period of time, usually 1 to 5 years, after which **the rate is "adjusted."** This adjustment **changes your monthly payment.** Low introductory "teaser" rates are designed as an inducement to get the buyer into a house. But do not be tempted. The risk is that the new payment amount, after being adjusted, may be far more than you anticipated or can afford. Rate increases are normally limited to a maximum percentage increase each adjustment period, subject to a maximum total interest rate cap that cannot be exceeded during the life of the loan.

Interest-only loan: As the name implies, with these loans you pay interest only, with no part of the payment going toward principal. The benefit is that your monthly payment is reduced. It may be available for periods up to five years. The problem is because you are not paying principal, your loan never gets smaller. When the "interest only" period expires, and the loan converts to a fixed rate mortgage, the monthly payment may be unaffordable, not only because the interest rate may be higher but also because the entire principal must now be paid over a shorter period of time.

Some interest only loans may require the borrower to pay only the interest on the loan for a period of time, with the entire loan due at the end of the term. This is called a "balloon payment" and might be in as few as 2 to 5 years. This type of loan is not recommended because, if affordable refinancing is not available, the property might be lost.

Negative amortization loan: With a negative amortization loan the homeowner sends in monthly payments, but instead of the loan decreasing, **the loan amount is actually increasing.** This occurs when below market teaser interest rates are used to entice people to buy a house. These low rates are not free. The difference between the low teaser rate and the market rate of interest at the time the loan is made is added to the amount of the loan. When the teaser rate ends in two or three years, the interest rate increases to the prevailing market rate, sometimes **doubling or tripling the monthly payment**. Now the owner has a much higher interest rate on a larger loan to be paid over a shorter period of time. Lack of understanding about negative amortization forced millions of people to lose their homes. My recommendation is…..**Don't even think about it!**

Conforming loan: A conforming loan is defined as a loan under a certain size. Today, in most areas the current maximum size for a conforming loan is $424,100. However, in certain very high cost areas it may be upward of $636,150. Conforming loans generally have **lower interest rates** because they represent a smaller risk. They may also have substantially **lower down payment loans** of only 3% to 5%.

Another reason conforming loans are attractive is that public government sponsored secondary market buyers such as **Fannie Mae and Freddy Mac** will purchase these loans under certain circumstances from the lender. This secondary market activity is important because, by purchasing loans which meet their guidelines, these agencies provide banks and other financial institutions with new money to make new loans for more home purchases.

To qualify, the loans currently must meet certain conditions:

No negative amortization.
Points and fees cannot exceed 3% of the loan. (1 point is equal to 1% of the loan amount and is tax deductible as interest.)
The term of the loan cannot be longer than 30 years.
The annual percentage rate cannot exceed 1.5% of the prime offer rate.
Special low down payment loans may be available if at least one of the borrowers is a first-time buyer.

Fannie Mae has developed a homeownership education and housing counseling program for **"HomeReady"** transactions. In most cases, at least one borrower on each HomeReady transaction must complete the Framework Online Education Program. The cost is currently $75, and it takes about 4 hours. It is meant to be taken after their loan application is completed, but it **must be completed** by the closing.

Jumbo loan: Jumbos are larger loans which do not **conform** to the size maximum set by Fannie Mae and Freddie Mac, so they may not be eligible for purchase by government agencies in the secondary market. These loans are typically made by financial institutions and investors such as banks and pension funds. As a result they usually carry higher rates of interest and may require larger down payments. You should check the size parameters of a conforming loan and a jumbo loan, as the maximum amounts may change periodically.

As you can see, there are many types of mortgages available in the marketplace. When discussing loan alternatives with your lender, make sure they are offering you terms and conditions that will work for you. One of my favorites is to ask the lender to accept biweekly payments equal to one-half of the standard monthly payment. Because you will be making 26 "half-monthly payments" a year, instead of the normal 12 "whole monthly" payments, this feature alone can shorten a 30- year loan to about 27.5 years and, on a $500,000 loan at 5.5%, you would save approximately $107,000 in interest. For more examples, see the mortgage loan calculator at www.bankrate.com.

Leverage is created by the use of borrowed funds to buy a house. The goal is to use other people's money to help you make money. Here is how it works: If the property increases in value, the loan amount does not change, and the entire gain goes to your equity. On the flip side, if the house goes down in value, the loan amount still does not change, and the losses will come out of your equity. Therefore, leverage magnifies both increases and decreases in the owner's equity.

Before the Great Recession, small down payments and large mortgages had become the norm because people had assumed that houses only go up in value. Some people did not understand the consequences of leverage in a down market where the equity is wiped out first and the owner, for various reasons, cannot or will not continue making monthly mortgage payments.

Loan-to-value ratio (LTV) This is the amount of the loan divided by the market value of the property. However, 80% LTV means the amount of the loan is 80% of the market or appraised value of the house. A higher LTV (bigger loan) may result in a higher interest rate because the lender is putting up more of the purchase price and has greater risk if the property value declines.

Some federal agencies, like the Federal Housing Authority (FHA) and Veteran's Administration (VA), will insure or guarantee certain loans if they qualify, but they require extra paperwork and appraisals that can cause delays. If you qualify, FHA or VA may guarantee your loan and you may need little or no down payment.

For first-time buyers one of the most difficult things is to make the down payment needed to qualify for a mortgage. Typically, lenders ask for 20% of the purchase price as a down payment. However, if this is out of reach and other programs such as FHA or VA are not available to you, try these low down payment approaches:

- Lenders or investors in certain "hot" markets may finance 100% of the price with a combination of a first mortgage, a second mortgage, and mortgage insurance.

- Ask the seller to "take back a second" mortgage or a note to cover the shortfall in the down payment. Some will do this to facilitate a sale.

- Consider a family loan or gift to help with the down payment.

If none of these options are possible, look for a smaller, less expensive home or one that needs remodeling so you can make improvements as your finances permit.

What can you really afford?

When assessing the cost of home ownership, consider not only the **down payment, mortgage payments, closing costs, moving costs, property taxes, insurance,** and **tax benefits,** but other costs of ownership. These include **maintenance and repairs**; **the opportunity cost** of not being able to use your money to invest in other areas that may be increasing in value faster than your house; and lost liquidity and flexibility. Remember that selling a house is not like selling a share of stock. It takes time and may require fees and a sales commission.

Be prepared. It's best to begin the process of buying a home by reviewing your financial situation and preparing a budget. First of all, check your credit report/ FICO score several months before applying for a loan. You may need time to correct any errors.

Rapid rescore is a technique available only through mortgage lenders and brokers. It enables borrowers to pay down debt or correct errors and **get accurate information updated** in their credit files in just a few days rather than months. Keep in mind, the lowest interest rates are reserved for those able to afford a down payment of 20% or more with a credit score of at least 750. The fee for this service may be worth it as it may result in your qualifying for a loan with a lower interest rate.

Consider your needs for a down payment. A 20% down payment has been the standard or benchmark, but 10%, 5%, or 0% may be available. The less cash you put toward a down payment, the less cash you will need at closing, but you can expect a higher interest rate and higher monthly payments, and you may need to provide PMI. With less down, you may also benefit from greater leverage, but be aware that if market values decline slightly you might quickly find your equity is zero and your loan "under water."

With a 20% or larger down payment, the reverse is true. You will need more cash at closing, but your monthly payments will be less, the interest rate lower, no PMI expense, less leverage, and it would take a very sharp slump in market values to wipe out your equity.

Pre-qualify with a lender by contacting a bank, credit union, mortgage lender or savings and loan. You need not be an existing customer. Get bids from at least three lenders, either in person, by phone or online, and make sure they include the costs of all fees and expenses. Bids should be provided free of charge. Market conditions in real estate do change over time. So do interest rates and other factors. Just as a **guideline**, most lenders would believe you can afford:

- A mortgage amount up to about three times your annual gross income.
- A monthly mortgage payment, **including** principal, interest, insurance, and property taxes, not to exceed about 28% of your gross monthly income.
- Total debt payments not to exceed about 43% of gross income. Assume a house is for sale for $375,000. Let's do the math:

Assumptions

Gross annual income	$100,000
Gross monthly income	$8,333
Appraised home value	$375,000

Loan Qualification Amount

Down payment	20% × $375,000	$75,000
Loan-to-value	80% of $375,000	$300,000
Mortgage maximum	3 × $100,000	$300,000
House payment	28% of $8,333	$2,333
Total max debt payment	43% of $8,333	$3,583

Check credit scores: FICO scores and "Rapid Rescoring Service."

Verify: Tax returns, pay stubs, employment, etc.

The lender may help you prepare a personal balance sheet and cash flow. You may also need to show the lender three years' tax returns, salary stubs, and monthly worksheets. The lender will usually get **three credit reports on each buyer** and review them carefully. The rate of interest quoted will be based on the **lowest credit score**. If you are applying jointly, both incomes and debts will be combined in determining your qualifications. A good credit score can earn you a lower rate of interest and reduce the time to get a loan approval, ultimately saving tens of thousands of dollars in interest over the life of the loan.

Interest rates are quoted and advertised as **annual rate** and **annual percentage rate (APR)**. Sometimes you will hear or see ads that quote an annual interest rate of 3%........APR 3.3%. The difference between these two amounts is that the APR includes the fees that you are required to pay. The 3% is to get your attention. 3.3% is what you actually pay. Listen carefully and read the fine print.

If you are in **financial distress** and foresee a **problem making your mortgage payments**, ask your lender for help, including refinancing. If you have already missed payments, see if you can strike a deal with your lender that brings your account up to date. The lender may be willing to reduce your payments for a few months or work out an arrangement for making the payments you missed at another time in another way. **Seek help** from a counseling agency approved by the Dept. of Housing and Urban Development at www.hud.gov. If you are worried about foreclosure, contact the Homeownership Preservation Foundation at www.995hope. org or call 888-995-4673.

You are now ready to begin the process.

Home sellers usually enlist the help of a professional real estate agent or broker to represent their interests. Sometimes sellers try to sell the property themselves to avoid paying a large commission. You may want to retain a real estate lawyer to represent you in completing the documents. Be careful! Make certain the proposed seller actually has clear title to the property.

In a typical real estate transaction, the seller signs an exclusive agreement with a licensed real estate agent or broker to **represent the seller**. The selling agent usually lists the property on a **multiple listing service** (MLS) online for all to see. When the property sells, it is usually the seller, not the buyer that pays the commission. Historically, the commission has been approximately 6% of the sales price. Today, it is common to negotiate the commission lower, especially on higher-priced homes. The seller's agent splits the commission with the buyer's agent upon closing of the transaction.

As a buyer, make certain your agent is not also playing the role of the listing or seller's agent, as that could create a conflict of interest by trying to represent both parties to earn the entire commission. This is known as **dual agency** which is illegal unless it is properly disclosed to both buyer and seller. Sometimes, when dealing with a large realtor, you may be asked to sign a waiver permitting your agent to deal with another agent from the same firm representing the other side of the transaction. This should be okay.

Since agents only get paid if a transaction closes, the pressure is usually on the seller to lower the price and the buyer to raise the price so that a transaction can get done and the agents' commissions are earned. Sometimes the agents will agree to reduce their commissions to help close the gap. Buying or selling property is a negotiation.

Interview your prospective agents for **knowledge of the area** in which you want to buy, the price ranges they usually operate in, and whether you think you can get along with them. Get references. This is a big transaction so get the best professional help you can.

Now that you have an agent, you are ready to start searching for a home. The most important factor is **location, location, location,** specifically the neighborhood, and its ability to meet your needs. It's not just the price. Consider schools, neighbors, crime rates, transportation, zoning, and the general upkeep of the neighborhood. Look at commute time and cost of transportation or a second car. Make a list of likes and dislikes. Do not focus on only one feature.

The art of buying a home is finding one you will be happy in. The science is getting the legal and financial aspects right. Do not chase an exact price. Prices are negotiated. If you cannot afford what you want, where you want it, sacrifice something inside the house rather than location. You can make changes to the house later, but you cannot change the neighborhood by yourself.

Tour the house and make several visits at different times of the day to any house you are seriously considering. Be sure to visit the area during the nighttime and on weekends. That is when you are most likely to be home. Check with police regarding the crime rate in the area. Take a notepad, tape measure, and digital camera. Check the square footage of the lot and the house. Some size claims may be exaggerated. Sketch and measure each room. Is the foundation level? Take note of the age of appliances and major mechanical systems and ask about the property taxes you will have to pay, any assessments, and utility bills. Check out promised facilities and memberships, such as golf, pool, parking, or storage privileges.

Sellers and agents are required by law to warn buyers of material defects. **Always get a professional inspection** before closing on a transaction. They are absolutely worth the cost. Make sure the inspection covers roof, gutters, exterior finish, furnace, electrical, plumbing, foundation, termites, soil assessment, leaks, dry rot, mold, water stains, and cracks in walls or concrete. The seller should pay for repairs or you can negotiate a reduction in the price of the house equal to the cost of repairs.

You are ready to **make the offer**. You know what you are willing and able to pay. Start lower. Check sites such as www.googleearth.com and www.zillow.com. Get **comps** of similar homes sold in the area in the last six months. **Negotiate in writing.** Your agent will present your offer with your price and conditions. One condition may be your **ability to get financing** or to sell your current house. Another condition should cover the **inspection (buyer pays) and repair (seller pays)** of the property. Expect to get a counter offer as part of the process. Negotiations can go on for days or weeks. Stop. Do not get sucked in. Continue to look elsewhere.

Picking the right mortgage is a mechanical, impersonal, and competitive process. Hunt for the best deal. Consider the down payment, payment options, interest rate, points, processing fees, adjustable terms, prepayment penalties, and all other fees. Ask if you are eligible for a **rate lock** to lock in the interest rate so it is guaranteed. You may still have the right to change it one time for a lower rate if interest rates decline while you are in the closing process.

Once you settle on a lender, the lender may get a physical **appraisal** of the property or just rely on online sites or drones. The lender must also give you an **itemized estimate of closing costs** once you complete the loan application. Lender fees may include running credit reports, appraisals, filing fees, and mailing costs. Closing costs may run between $1,000 and $5,000 or more. Some lenders offer loans with no closing costs, but they may make up for it by charging a higher interest rate. It may also depend on the competitiveness of the mortgage market.

Again, make certain you can pay off the loan early without a prepayment penalty. You may want to refinance the loan at a lower rate of interest before the loan matures or move to another house and take out a new mortgage.

Escrow: This is a neutral third party which holds the documentation and money involved in the transaction until the transaction is completed and then distributes the funds and executes the instructions. The escrow company charges a fee for service.

Title search and title insurance guarantees clear ownership of a property to buyers and lenders. You do not want to buy a house from a party who does not own the house. This is your protection against that occurring. However, 25% of titles actually need cleaning up. You do not need to go with your agent's or lender's recommendation, but can shop around for the lowest cost service, which varies by state. Expenses may include such items as FedEx delivery fees, surveying, and recording deeds and mortgages.

Before **closing the deal**, decide how you want to take title to the property. Always get legal advice! Have your name on the title or deed of any property you buy or purchase jointly with another person. There are alternatives.

- **Joint Ownership with Rights of Survival:** If one dies, the other automatically inherits the property.
- **Tenants in Common:** Each of you owns half of the house.

If there is no legal agreement between the parties buying the home together, you should discuss such things as how the property is to be titled and what will happen to it if the relationship of the parties ends for any reason? Is a cohabitation or partnership agreement needed?

When purchasing a condominium or apartment, you are purchasing an individual unit in a multi-tenant building. The basic "art and science" factors which apply to buying a home are quite similar, including financing and inspection. However, there are special issues that apply and may affect the price or your ability to resell. You should check out such items as:

- Are common areas such as hallways, elevators, pools, exercise rooms, and laundry facilities kept clean and operational?
- Are the walls and ceilings soundproof?
- What are the monthly fees to cover repairs, maintenance, and other shared expenses?
- Are all the units owner occupied?
- Are any units in foreclosure?
- Is there a right to sublet units?
- Is there a reserve fund for major repairs?
- Are there any upcoming special assessments?

Welcome to home ownership!

Remodeling or renovating can be a major undertaking. The cost of remodeling has been increasing primarily due to rising material costs and a shortage of skilled labor. A project may involve architects, contractors, and subcontractors, as well as local building permits, inspections, and neighbors' approval. You may want to get references from friends, realtors, and tradesmen, and do check them out. Make sure the contractor is licensed and insured, and familiar with local permits, codes, and inspectors. As you would with any major investment, get multiple bids. Keep in mind **the lowest bid may not be the best bid**.

Consider whether the renovations are cost justified in terms of resale value. Updated kitchens and bathrooms usually generate the best returns on investment. Prepare a budget and time lines but assume it will cost 10% to 20% over the bid price for change orders and cost overruns; and assume it will take 20% to 50% longer to complete the project than planned. It seems most jobs end up costing more and taking longer than planned, never the other way around.

Have a good idea of what you want to achieve in the project, so you can work with architects and contractors to develop the specifications for the job and compare bids when they are submitted. Do not try to guide or pressure bidders to come up with the lowest price. This frequently leads to cheap materials and workmanship. Look out for expensive add-ons which often arise, but be open-minded to recommendations for additions or upgrades.

Carefully discuss scheduling and progress payments with the contractor as work proceeds. Establish appropriate benchmarks and approximate start and complete dates. If possible, try to agree on some incentives for adhering to the schedule. Get a written contract from the contractor, which includes start and completion dates; plans that you have agreed to; and scheduled progress payments. Obtain a written warranty on workmanship and materials for the longest possible period of time. Seek help from qualified professionals if you are unsure about the details.

The job may involve mechanics' liens which are a guarantee of payment to a contractor, subcontractor, laborer, or material provider recorded with the county recorder's office. Left unpaid, liens can affect your ability to borrow against, refinance, or sell the property. So once the contractor, workman, or vendor has been paid, make sure they sign a lien release.

In many cases, for smaller jobs or for specialized skills, you may to prefer to directly hire the worker and not use a general contractor. To get the best advice you might try one of these approaches:

> I heard the story of one property owner who has a "10% rule." For example, whenever he gets a bid he always asks the contractor, "If we add 10% to the cost, what changes would you make?" He claims it's amazing what you can get for an extra 10% regardless of the size of the job.

A property owner I know always asks contractors, "If this was your house what would you do differently?" That is how she finds out how the job really should be done!

Taxes again, but this time some good news.

The government subsidizes and encourages home ownership through the tax code. With some limitations, homeowners can **deduct mortgage interest**, not principal, on federal and state tax returns with a mortgage currently as large as $750,000 on new loans, and up to $1,000,000 on loans in effect prior to December 16, 2017. Homeowners can also include "points" as interest when calculating mortgage interest for tax deduction purposes. "Points" are paid to the lender when the loan is closed and represent prepaid interest. One point equals 1% of the loan amount. Each point will buy down, or lower, the interest rate about 0.25%, thus lowering the monthly payment.

Once you own a home, government subsidies continue. Your **property taxes** may be tax deductible if, when combined with your state and local taxes, the total does not exceed $10,000. Homeowners insurance is not tax deductible.

And there is more good news when you sell your house. Homeowners who sell their house can **exempt from taxes the profits they make up to $250,000 for a single person or $500,000 for a married couple** if they lived in the house **any two** of the prior five years as their primary residence.

Let's look at how we calculate those profits. You will first need to calculate the **cost basis** of the house. Start with the original cost of the property, including fees. Add to that what you spent on **permanent improvements**, not repair or maintenance. Include such items as additional rooms or floor space; and **new** decks, fences, landscaping, fitted draperies, wall-to-wall carpets, shelves, storm windows, and air conditioning. You may also include the cost of preparing the house for sale. These expenses are added to the initial cost of the house to become your **adjusted cost basis** and may reduce any capital gain tax due upon sale.

If you sell the house for more than the adjusted cost bases, you have a profit. If you have owned the house for more than a year the profit is a long-term capital gain. And if you have resided in the house for at least two of the last five years, profits up to $250,000 (single) or $500,000 (married) are exempt from taxes.

However, if you sell the house for a loss, there is no loss for tax purposes. So be sure to keep good records for the IRS.

These benefits will be obvious when you complete your tax Form 1040, though they may be reduced or limited for alternative minimum tax payers.

It is buyer beware but there are some protections built in.

The Consumer Financial Protection Bureau (CFPB), formed by the federal government, reviews mortgage rules and regulations such as prepayment penalties, disclosure forms, credit scores, down payments, debt levels, and income requirements. Its main focus is to ensure that borrowers can repay their loans.

- Banks must carefully **document** and verify a person's income and not allow a borrower's total debt payments to exceed about 43% of their pretax income. Some banks are more conservative than this.

- **Interest-only** loans and **negative amortization** loans **should be eliminated**.

- ARM loans with **low "teaser" interest rates** can only qualify if judged on the highest payment that will apply in the first year of the adjusted market rate.

- 30-year fixed rate mortgages are now more common.

Many of these items have been implemented, while others are being phased in. CFPB's website will keep you updated on the latest consumer protections.

The government is also proposing new, **easier to understand rules for disclosure** to protect homebuyers, including:

- A one-page disclosure document explaining various risk features.
- Disclosure of the annual interest rate, including most fees and costs.
- A list of all the "early" costs.
- The banning of side payments for steering borrowers into higher cost loans with higher fees.
- Comparison of your interest rate with those of higher credit rated borrowers.

Search the website of the Department of Housing and Urban Development (HUD), www.hud.gov/respa, for the **Real Estate Settlement and Procedures Act** (RESPA). It includes the **good faith estimate (GFE) form** a proposed lender must give you with their loan terms and estimated settlement charges. You should also look at **Settlement Statement (HUD-1)** for additional details.

Do's and Don'ts

The DO's

- Shop for your loan.

- Interview real estate agents, mortgage brokers, lenders, and other settlement service providers to find the best professionals for your loan and settlement needs.

- Be sure to read and understand everything before you sign anything.

- Accurately report your debts.

- Be honest about all sources of funds you will use to purchase your home.

- Be upfront about any credit problems you have or have had in the past.

- Be wary of unsolicited loan or refinance offers that you receive in the mail or through email.

- Always pay your mortgage payment on time, even if you are having a dispute with your loan servicer.

- If you are having problems paying your mortgage, contact your loan servicer immediately.

The Don'ts

- Do not sign blank documents.

- Do not overstate your income.

- Do not overstate your length of employment.

- Do not overstate your assets.

- Do not change your income tax returns.

- Do not list fake co-borrowers on your loan application.

- Do not provide false documentation or permit someone to provide false documents about you.

Timeline

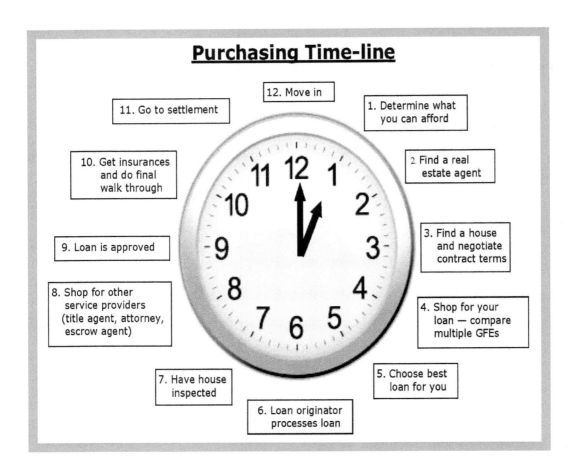

Purchasing Time-line

12. Move in

11. Go to settlement

1. Determine what you can afford

10. Get insurances and do final walk through

2. Find a real estate agent

9. Loan is approved

3. Find a house and negotiate contract terms

8. Shop for other service providers (title agent, attorney, escrow agent)

4. Shop for your loan — compare multiple GFEs

7. Have house inspected

5. Choose best loan for you

6. Loan originator processes loan

Determining what you can afford

Use the following worksheet to calculate your monthly income and expenses. This will help you determine the amount you have left over every month to pay for house- related expenses, including your monthly loan payment, property taxes, and homeowner's insurance.

Determine Your Monthly Income and Expenses	Monthly Amount
Income (what you take home after taxes and other deductions)	
Borrower salary	$
Co-borrower salary	$
Other income	$
INCOME TOTAL	$
Expenses	
Credit cards	$
Car payment	$
Car insurance	$
Health insurance	$
Savings and retirement	$
Medical expenses	$
Child support and alimony	$
Tuition	$
Utilities	$
Clothing	$
Entertainment	$
Other expenses	$
EXPENSES TOTAL	$
TOTAL MONTHLY INCOME	$
SUBTRACT TOTAL MONTHLY EXPENSE	$
EQUALS	$

Notes and Updates

CHAPTER 15

RENTING AN APARTMENT

The Home You Don't Own

For many years, owning a home has been the American dream – one that has been strongly subsidized by our taxing structure. During the Great Recession, that dream was challenged. The Great Recession crushed housing prices and left tens of millions of households overwhelmed with debt. In addition, millions of workers in real estate related occupations including contractors, construction workers, architects, mortgage bankers, real estate brokers, and material suppliers, lost their jobs and were unable to pay their bills.

While many people still aspire to own their own home, many others are questioning whether renting may be a better alternative. So, **what are the advantages** of renting?

Renters are not tied to a particular location beyond the time horizon of their rental agreement. In a more mobile world, many people, especially millennials, want to be flexible. If plans change they do not want to wait around to sell their house. As a renter, if opportunity strikes, it's easier to move.

Many prefer not to tie up their money in a down payment or a long-term mortgage contract. Renters do not have large-debt obligations, or directly pay property taxes, private mortgage insurance, homeowner's insurance, or maintenance and repairs. Some would prefer to use their money to form a start-up business rather than tie it up in an illiquid "investment." Or they may feel other types of investments such as traveling or pursuing a hobby is better use of their money. And in many locations it may be cheaper to rent than to buy.

But whatever the reason, just like when you are purchasing a home, the first thing to think about when renting an apartment is **location, location, and location.** Consider transportation, parking, commute time, schools, crime rates, and security. Visit the neighborhood during the evening and on weekends which are the times you are most likely to be home. Talk to other renters and neighbors about the landlord and the area. Consider the general upkeep of the neighborhood. Are shopping and other services conveniently available nearby?

How much can you afford to pay? Prepare a budget. Consider your disposable income. As a rule of thumb, rent should be in the range of 25% to 35% of your gross monthly pay, but in some attractive areas that could be difficult. The landlord may also want your monthly income to be within that same range but may be willing to include dividends, interest, and other outside income. If it's too much of a stretch, having a roommate(s) to share expenses may be a good alternative.

The landlord may request your credit report and credit score; check you out on "Facebook" and "Google;" or ask for references or other pieces of information. You should bring with you a letter to verify employment and your pay. That can impress a landlord.

A landlord may not discriminate against anyone on the basis of race, religion, color, creed, sex, sexual orientation, age, etc. This is guaranteed by both state and federal laws. The **only exception** is taking a boarder into one's primary residence.

You may not own it, but it is your home.

Because this is the place you're going to call home, even though you're not the owner, it's important to evaluate the condition of the building or complex as well as the unit you plan to rent.

What is the general condition of the neighborhood?
What is the condition of the apartment building or complex?
Are there fire hazards, well-marked exits, sprinklers, and fire escapes?
What about security? Are there deadbolt locks, security guards or burglar alarms?
What are the general amenities, such as a pool or recreation room?
Is there a washer and dryer in the unit or in the building for you to use?
Are children and pets allowed?
What are the rules on noise and smoking? Is there adequate parking?

Check out the specific unit you plan to rent.
What is the general condition of the unit?
Are there built in hook ups for cable, phone lines, and internet access?
Is it relatively soundproof?
Are there cooking odors?
Do all the appliances work?
Will your furniture and other personal items fit?

When signing a rental or a lease agreement remember it is a legal document. Renting or leasing an apartment is a **negotiation**. You can always try to lower the rent or the amount of the deposit. If upgrades have been promised, such as carpeting, drapes, painting, or appliances, make sure it is in writing. You do not have to accept the "asking" price or terms. Do not sign anything without reading it carefully and understanding the terms and conditions.

Among the things you should look for in the agreement:

How much is the rent, and are there any provisions for raising it?
How long will the rental agreement or lease last? Is it renewable?
Are utilities included or do you pay for them separately?
Can you paint the interior walls?
Are there storage facilities, exercise rooms, pool, etc. available for you to use?
Is parking included?
Are there guest facilities such as guest rental units, guest parking, etc.?
What happens if you have to move due to your employment?
If you are on a lease, under what conditions can you change the name on the lease or sublet the unit?

Landlords may require an application fee, first and last month's rent, and a **security deposit** before you move in. They are required to pay you interest on deposits they hold. Some cities have well-defined laws and ordinances regarding **renters' and tenants' rights.** Check them out if you are not familiar with the area.

If you have a roommate each of you should sign the lease and understand your financial obligations. Decide how you will pay bills for utilities, cable, internet, phone, garbage, etc. Decide who will do the cleaning and purchase the cleaning supplies. Decide how you will pay for or share food. Agree on the rules for overnight guests, smoking, and other lifestyle choices.

Consider purchasing **rental insurance** to protect your contents. Contact an insurance agent for coverage and price information, or contact insurers such as State Farm, AAA, or Geico directly.

Before moving in, do a walk through with the landlord. Take pictures and time stamp anything that might be damaged or worn so no one later claims you did the damage. Do the same thing when you move out and have the landlord sign off that there is no additional damage. You are not responsible for normal wear and tear.

If you have trouble getting your deposit back when you move out, contact your state's Department of Real Estate. They can advise you of your options, one of which might be small claims court.

Warning!

A new scam involving rental housing has emerged and is becoming more popular. An imposter posing as the landlord gains access to a vacant apartment or house and advertises it at a below market rate, attracting several anxious renters. The imposter collects from each prospect a security deposit, first and last month's rent, and a completed application, then sets up a move-in date and makes arrangements for providing keys. The imposter then promptly disappears and it is only when everyone finally tries to move in that the scam comes to light. But the imposter and the money are long gone.

One way you can protect yourself is to contact the county assessor's office for the name and phone number of the property owner. If they will not give it to you over the phone, you can go to their office and get the information from public records. You can then better determine if you are talking to the real property owner or their representative. If you are still uncertain ask to see a driver's license or some other form of picture identification.

In rental real estate, just like in every other business transaction, you need to watch out for yourself.

Notes and Updates

CHAPTER 16

HOMEOWNER'S INSURANCE

The Devil is in the Details

Insurance is a way to protect yourself and your family from catastrophic losses. It protects you and your assets from financial disaster. I do not know anyone who gets excited about paying for insurance. You might never even need it. And if you do use it, it probably means something bad happened.

How much risk are you willing to take?

Buying insurance is buying security from the loss of property, large or unexpected medical expenses, loss of income or earning power, and the financial impact of death.

I have owned houses for more than 35 years and spent well over $60,000 insuring them and their contents. All that time I have only had one claim for $3,500. I could have done a lot of other things with that money, but I wouldn't even think about not insuring my house. My insurance has been protecting me from a serious loss well over 20 times the cost for all these years.

Homeowner's insurance is far more than just fire insurance. It's a **package policy** providing financial protection against disasters, including both damage to your property **and** your liability or legal responsibility for injuries or property damage you, or members of your family, cause to other people. Some policies may limit coverage, exclude coverage, or omit coverage for certain risks. So, review them carefully. Acts of nature such as floods, hurricanes, tornadoes, and earthquakes may need to be insured separately, and usually involve additional premiums and deductibles.

The devil truly is in the details.

Shopping for homeowner's insurance can be confusing. There are many companies that offer this kind of insurance, but policies are never identical. Policies are carefully worded, and may be slightly different or very different in coverage and exclusions, which are usually described in "legalese," subject to interpretation. It is quite common for the insurance company to inspect your property at the time of issue to make sure it is well maintained, up to code and there are no unusual hazards in the area that could cause a problem.

When there is a potential claim, the typical first response for both the insured and the insurance company is to look up the terms and conditions of the policy to see if this particular loss or event is covered. The reality is that most insured parties believe they are covered, hope they are covered, or think they should be covered for a loss; while insurance claims departments may be looking for ways to deny or reduce their exposure to the loss.

What you will find is that, in a claim, what is or is not covered can be difficult to understand or agree upon. For example, there may be a difference in coverage for water damage, depending on whether it was caused by a leak, faulty plumbing, a flood, or rain. And what if insured damages were incurred at the house at two different times of day? Are there two deductibles?

Policies can be purchased directly from the company, through an insurance broker, an independent agent, or a captive agent who works exclusively with a specific insurance company. You can ask the agent or broker to explain what is covered and what is not covered, excluded, or omitted. But it is important that you read the policy carefully, ask questions, and understand what you're getting.

The standard homeowner's insurance policy includes **four essential types of coverage:**

- **The structure of your home.** This portion of the insurance pays to repair or rebuild your home if it is damaged or destroyed by fire, hail, lightning, or other disasters listed in the policy. Coverage extends to detached structures such as a garage or tool shed. New building codes requiring upgraded roofing materials or sprinkler systems may add to the cost to repair or rebuild, so it's a good idea to add the feature to your policy that pays for such required upgrades. The incremental cost is usually small.

  To determine the amount of insurance you need, one easy way is to multiply the square footage of the house by the approximate cost per square foot to build a new house in your area, such as, $250/square foot. Local real estate agents, insurance agents, and contractors usually know the approximate cost. The cost of the land itself, or having waterfront property or views can add considerably to the value of the property, but they **are not covered by insurance**.

Always insure at least 80% of the value, otherwise you may be only partially covered if a loss occurs. I always recommend insuring 100% of the estimated **replacement value**, and periodically adjusting that figure for inflation. In the event of a loss, you will be glad you did. Check with your insurance agent, broker, or issuer of the policy.

- **Your personal belongings.** This portion of the insurance covers furniture, clothes, sports equipment, and other personal items if they are stolen or destroyed by fire or other insured disasters. Coverage is typically limited to 50% to 70% of the amount of insurance you have on the structure of your home. You can buy extra coverage above this amount for specific items of higher value such as art or jewelry.

To determine the amount of loss you could incur, take pictures of each room, including furniture, wall hangings, carpeting, and drapes. Open all of your closets, drawers, and cabinets and conduct a periodic home inventory by list or photo, and store it somewhere safe outside of the house, in the "cloud," or at www.knowyourstuff.org. You will want this information to substantiate your claim should a loss occur.

Your **off premises belongings** are also covered worldwide. Coverage is usually limited to 10% of the amount of insurance you have for your possessions. It may even include up to $500 of coverage for unauthorized use of your credit cards, though this risk is usually covered by the credit card company itself. It may also include baggage lost by an airline to the extent it is not covered by the carrier.

Expensive items like jewelry, furs, art and silverware are usually covered up to $1,000 to $2,000 if they are stolen, subject to a deductible amount. To insure these items to a greater value you will need to purchase additional insurance, called a **rider.** In some cases, the insurer will require an independent appraisal of an expensive or rare item you seek to insure. Coverage may even include "accidental disappearance" (you lost it).

- **Liability protection.** This insurance covers you worldwide against lawsuits for bodily injury or property **damage that you or family members cause** to other people. It pays for both the cost of defending you in court and court awards up to the limit of your policy. However, there could be exceptions to liability coverage for gross negligence on your part. Anything beyond your policy limit is your personal responsibility.

The amount of liability coverage you purchase should be more than adequate to protect your assets. As a rule of thumb, I recommend at least 10 times your gross household income. But as your net worth increases, you need to increase this amount to protect your accumulated assets. Usually, additional amounts of coverage are not very expensive. Awards and settlements have been skyrocketing. Discuss this with your insurance representative.

Liability insurance usually provides **no-fault medical coverage** in the amount between $1,000 and $5,000 if a guest is injured in your home. As an additional option, for a small expense, some policies now offer **identity theft coverage.**

- **Additional living expenses.** This coverage pays the additional costs of living away from home if you cannot live in your home for a period of time due to damage from a covered disaster. It should cover reasonable hotel bills, rental housing, meals, and incidentals. Coverage is usually limited to about 20% of the amount of insurance on the structure. If you rent out part of your house, it might reimburse you for the rent that you would have collected.

Insurance companies only pay up to the limits of their policy. Where negligence or inadequate coverage exists, you may become personally and financially responsible.

Following are suggestions for preparing property for insurability. Some of them may be required by local regulations, your insurance company, or your lender in order to complete your mortgage or refinancing:

- Install smoke alarms.
- Install carbon monoxide detectors.
- Install sprinkler systems.
- Install a burglar alarm connected by phone to the police station.
- Bring roofing material up to code.
- Are solar panels required?
- Clear vegetation around the property.
- Put a fence around your pool.

To reduce the cost, consider:

- Increasing deductibles where appropriate

- Consolidating all your personal lines with one or two insurance companies, including homeowner's, auto, life, health, and disability coverage.

Policies all differ in coverage and cost. Read your policy carefully and ask for advice from your agent or broker before purchasing and upon renewal. I recommend you get three quotes. Since each policy may be slightly different, make sure you compare both cost and coverage.

> **When a loss occurs, it is too late to change the wording of the policy.**

Notes and Updates

CHAPTER 17

THE GREAT RECESSION

Bad Decisions . . . . . Bad Consequences

You may be wondering why rehash the Great Recession? It's over. Housing prices have rebounded in most places and even soared in other areas. But the reality is millions of families lost their homes and were devastated. Millions lost their jobs. Unemployment skyrocketed. We need to be on guard to make certain this never happens again; not to our economy and not to you personally. In fact, it never had to happen before. You could point a lot of fingers, but among the culprits there's no denying greed and subprime loans were at the top of the list.

Subprime mortgages were loans given to borrowers with FICO scores of 660 or less. These low scores were due primarily to borrowers not paying bills on time, or because they were already burdened with a high level of debt relative to their income. Because of the higher risk, these loans carried a higher interest rate, usually two percentage points or more above rates offered to those with higher credit scores. This was a major added expense to the borrower, further hurting their creditworthiness.

About 80% of subprime borrowers took out **adjustable rate mortgages (ARM)**. ARMs usually began with a **teaser rate** of interest which was substantially lower than the interest rate the borrower could otherwise get on a comparable fixed rate mortgage. After the 1–5 year introductory period, however, the interest rate would be adjusted, and payments would increase by hundreds, if not thousands, of dollars each month. If the borrower stopped paying, a **default** occurred which led to a short sale or foreclosure, eviction, and forced sale by the lender.

Some loans were **interest-only**, requiring only the payment of the monthly interest on the loan for the first 1-5 years, with no money going toward the actual repayment of principal. At the end of the period, payment of the principal would begin or, worse yet, the entire loan would become due. But paying it off or refinancing it with an affordable new loan was not possible in a bad market.

Prior to the Recession, lenders often made loans of 100% or more of the purchase price of a house with little or no down payment required from the borrower.

They did this under the mistaken assumption that housing prices, and thus their collateral, would continue to rise in value.

In many cases, home buyers were told the loan verification process would take so long that a house would be sold or the price bid higher by the time their loan application could be processed. So it became, "Sign here and I'll fill in the blanks and get you the money right away. We need to move NOW to get the house you want."

Arguments both ways.

Subprime borrowers tended to have the following characteristics:

- They lived in lower-income neighborhoods, and were more likely to be part of a minority group.

- They purchased homes in areas of rising prices that were ultimately overbuilt by developers and speculators.

- They had less formal education or did not understand the transaction or its complex legal paperwork.

- They were more likely to have substantial credit card debt.

- They believed or were told that when the interest rate adjusts, they would have higher income, or interest rates would be lower, and they could refinance the loan with even lower monthly payments. They were also convinced the value of the house would substantially increase and they could sell it for a nice profit.

- They wanted more house than they could afford and didn't seem to consider having to pay far more each month sometime in the future.

Opponents of subprime mortgages believed many subprime lenders knowingly engaged in **predatory lending practices** with borrowers who could never meet the payment terms of their loans, ultimately leading to default, eviction, and foreclosure. They took advantage of people and should have known better.

Proponents of subprime mortgages argue that the practice extended credit to people who would otherwise not be able to get a loan, and thus not be able to own a home, missing out on the American dream.

How did we get into this mess?

Mortgages were generally originated by mortgage brokers, some of whom were owned or controlled by financial institutions, while others were independent businesses. Regardless, mortgage brokers were paid for finding and arranging loans for lenders, serving only as intermediaries in the transaction, sharing none of the risk. Mortgage brokers were paid their commission whether or not a loan ultimately failed or the investor lost money. So naturally, even when loans were beginning to go bad, the brokers kept going. Some originators even falsified their client's income and financial status just to increase their own fees and commissions.

Surprisingly, about 60% of all borrowers who took out subprime loans had credit scores high enough to qualify for conforming loans with lower rates and better terms. But **fees paid to loan originators** for arranging subprime loans were two to three times the fees paid on conforming loans, so there was a financial incentive for the originator to arrange a subprime loan regardless of a borrower's higher credit score.

Separate from the brokers, the financial institutions who actually underwrote the loans were not very careful either since they didn't plan on sticking around for long. Their immediate goal was to collect fees, sell the loans to a third party, and use the proceeds of the sale to start the process all over again by making new home loans with new fees and repeat the cycle.

To do this, financial institutions would make these high risk loans to the borrowers and then bundle them together with good quality loans into packages for sale to "sophisticated" investors, like pension funds, insurance companies, and mutual funds. Somehow these bundled loan packages were rated as high-quality AAA rated investments by the major bond rating agencies, so no one looked too closely. Many of these fraudulent loans with defective paperwork, and loans to poor quality borrowers were owned or guaranteed by governmental agencies such as Fannie Mae and Freddie Mac, thus creating massive losses which were ultimately absorbed by the taxpayers.

The eventual results of faulty lending.

Eventually, the consequences of poor lending decisions began to appear. Those who had taken out ARMs found their monthly payments soaring when the teaser interest rate period ended. Their only options were paying much more each month if they could afford it, or missing payments, thus leading to default, eviction, and foreclosure.

Most of these homeowners were unable to refinance their loans at low interest rates because of poor credit scores or because they did not have enough, or any equity in the property. In most cases the house was worth less than they paid for it and, even worse, less than its loan.

When borrowers reached a point where they could no longer make their adjusted payments, and refinancing alternatives were no longer available, foreclosed properties went up for sale by the dozens, depressing the value of everything else in the neighborhood. Many homeowners just walked away from their houses, depressing home values even further. As the value of the collateral and the stream of interest payments pledged to those who had invested in these loans fell dramatically, attempts to sell these investments found few buyers at any price. The market was frozen, and losses soared into hundreds of billions of dollars.

In the meantime, serious overbuilding had occurred. Bloated housing prices stalled and these too began to fall, creating large losses for home builders, speculators, and adjacent homeowners. Unemployment started to spread across the country. This was a crisis of major proportions resulting in massive losses to homeowners, home builders, contractors, construction workers, appliance and furniture manufacturers, real estate and mortgage brokers, financial institutions, federal, state and local government agencies, pension plans, retirement savings, and sophisticated investors around the world.

In the end, the federal government had to step up with hundreds of billions of dollars of borrowed funds to support and backstop the losses Fannie Mae, Freddie Mac, and other mortgage holders sustained during this period. Steps to prevent such a crisis from reoccurring continue to be made, but the damage that was caused will go down in history as one of near catastrophic proportions.

Could it happen again?

We have been warned. As of this writing, Fannie Mae, Freddie Mac, the Federal Housing Authority, and the Veteran's Administration are being pressured into lowering qualification standards for home mortgages. The focus now seems to be on making it easier for low and middle income households to purchase houses with as little as a 3% down payment.

Even though conforming loans with very low down payments typically require private mortgage insurance, only a small decline in a home's value can wipe out any equity in a very short period of time, driving the loan into negative territory. Is our memory that short? Have we forgotten what boom and bust did to the country's economy? Are lower standards for home loans really the answer?

Notes and Updates

CHAPTER 18

INDIVIDUAL RETIREMENT ACCOUNTS (IRA)

A Gift from Uncle Sam

The tax code is your friend.

Yogi Berra, the iconic Yankee catcher, manager, and philosopher once said, "It's tough to make predictions, especially about the future." But one thing is certain, **retirement** can no longer be thought of as it once was: a gold watch, a small pension, and a check from Social Security. Today, some people retire at age 50, 60, or later, while others may continue working well past 80. If you ask people at age 40 when they plan to retire, most will say they have no idea how long they will keep working or will **have to keep working**.

After all, when people retire, the paycheck stops and income to live on will have to come from somewhere. Most employers have terminated their pension plans, and more will follow. If you are counting on government checks to take care of you, you will probably have to accept the government's level of support, which may not be very high. Even small-to-modest savings can be wiped out in a hurry, especially with skyrocketing medical bills.

Although retirement may mean different things to different people, the real issue is no longer retirement, its **longevity.** It is **living too long.** And here is the bigger problem: to prepare for retirement and longevity, a person needs to have a **long-term horizon.** To even think about this in a world of credit card debt, educational expenses, student loan debt, and home mortgages when 80% of the people live paycheck-to-paycheck, is very difficult. To think about how one will financially survive 20, 30, or 40 years from now when the paychecks stop is even harder to do when just paying each month's bills is stressful enough. But how will you support yourself when paychecks stop, and life continues for another 20 or 30 years?

Until recently, estate planners used age 85 as the target life span for financial planning. Saving 10% of one's income seemed to be an acceptable rate for most people. Now, estate planners have settled on age 95 as the target. That is a big change as it has moved the acceptable rate of savings to 15%.

At these upper age levels, it's not just how long someone lives, but it's also inflation, the rising cost of living, senior housing, nursing care, and medical expenses that deplete one's assets. But there are ways to plan for longevity, and they are available to anyone who is willing to accept a long-term view.

Let's start with individual retirement accounts:

An **individual retirement account** (IRA) is a **tax-sheltered account** ideal for retirement investing. It permits investment earnings such as interest, dividends, and capital gains to **accumulate tax free** and be **reinvested** within the account, super charging the already powerful effect of compound interest.

There are two types of IRAs:

- **Traditional IRA:** The money you contribute to your account is tax deductible in the year it is contributed. But the money you withdraw is fully taxed as ordinary income. All income and earnings within the account are tax sheltered.

- **Roth IRA:** The money you contribute to your account is with after-tax dollars (no tax deduction). But the money you withdraw is tax free. Once contributed to the account this money, even after compounding for many years, may never again be subject to taxation. All income and earnings in the account are tax sheltered.

To put it very simply, in a traditional IRA, you pay no taxes now but pay taxes when you withdraw the money in retirement. In a Roth IRA, it's the reverse. You pay taxes now before contributing, but no more taxes will be due when you withdraw money in retirement.

Which type of IRA you choose depends on many assumptions you will have to make, among the most important are your adjusted gross income, your current tax bracket, and an estimate of what your tax bracket might look like in retirement.

According to projections, you are likely to live well beyond retirement age.

Regardless of the fact that you may never be a participant in a defined benefit plan, it is worth knowing what they are. **Defined benefit plans** are plans in which an employer promises an employee a specific defined **lifetime monthly benefit** upon retirement. The amount usually depends on the employee's age at retirement, their salary, and the number of years on the job. Sometimes, these plans also provide for continuing benefits to a surviving spouse.

Currently, defined benefit plans are most commonly provided to employees of governmental agencies. Many of the benefits were enriched over the years as a trade-off for lower increases in wages and in some cases to help local politicians attract votes at election time. Many of these programs today are vastly underfunded; benefits are in jeopardy as more people are reaching retirement age and living much longer than expected. Most of the private sector has already given up such plans as they were far too expensive to continue.

Some employers do not contribute to any kind of retirement or savings plan. Even if they do, you may want or need more retirement income than your employer or Social Security will provide many years from now. So, the IRA can be a big part of your financial longevity goal.

Anyone who is younger than 70 ½ and has "earned income" can open an IRA. There is no minimum age. **Earned income** is income from a job or self- employment. **Investment income** is dividends, interest, and capital gains. Investment income is not considered earned income and is not used in calculating your contribution to an IRA.

If you qualify to open an IRA, either traditional or Roth, there are a few important rules. You can **contribute only up to a fixed amount.** The current maximum you can contribute is $5,500, (plus $1,000 additional if you are age 50 or more), but the numbers change periodically so always check before funding your IRA. You can contribute to more than one IRA account, but your combined annual contributions cannot exceed the maximum allowed for a single account. Also, you **cannot contribute more than your earned income.**

The detail you need to know.

Traditional IRA Plan Contributions:

- If you are single and **not covered by a retirement plan at work**, you can take a tax deduction up to the amount of your contribution, but not to exceed $5,500. If you are married filing jointly and your spouse is covered at work, see IRS Pub. 590.

- If you are single and **are covered by a retirement plan at work** through your employer's pension, profit sharing, 401(k) or 403(b) retirement plan, you can take a tax deduction up to the amount of your contribution, but not to exceed $5,500 subject to the following:

  o If your adjusted gross income (AGI) is more than $63,000, but less than $73,000 your tax deduction will be proportionally reduced and phased out. For example, if your AGI was $68,000, you would be able to tax deduct a contribution of $2,750 (50% of $5,500).

  o For example, if your AGI exceeds $73,000 (single) you cannot tax deduct your contribution to a Traditional IRA for tax purposes.

  o For those who are married and filing jointly the current phase out begins at begins at $101,000, and if AGI exceeds $121,000 you cannot tax deduct any of your contribution.

These dollar limits are adjusted over time so it is good to **check them annually** before making a contribution. But be careful. Any excess contributions above the maximum allowed are hit with a 6% penalty plus taxes.

If your income exceeds these limits you may still contribute to a separate taxable IRA, but you would not be able to take a tax deduction for the excess contribution, and the money would be better used elsewhere, such as an emergency fund, or to pay down a high interest loan, or invested in a personal investment account.

Traditional IRA Plan Withdrawals:

- After age 59½ you can take out all you want penalty free, but you will pay ordinary income tax on the proceeds in the year of the withdrawal.

- At age 70½ you **must** begin yearly withdrawals using the **IRS required minimum distribution** schedule ("RMD"), which is designed to get all your money out and taxed by the time you die, or your beneficiaries die.

- If you do not take out the RMD, the IRS will claim 50% of the amount you failed to withdraw.

There are **exceptions** for early withdrawals without penalty in extenuating circumstances, but you still must pay the income tax. These exceptions include permanent disability, medical bills that exceed a certain percentage of your AGI, higher education expenses for yourself or your immediate family, and up to $10,000 for the first time purchase of a home, to build or buy.

Roth IRA Plan Contributions.

There are **no tax deductions for contributions to Roth IRAs**. Your contribution is made with after-tax dollars. As you might imagine, if you are covered by a retirement plan at work, there is also an income test to determine if you qualify to contribute to a Roth IRA.

- The right to contribute to a Roth IRA is currently phased out as modified AGI rises between $120,000 and $135,000 on a single return or between $189,000 and $199,000 on a joint return (IRS Pub. 590-A).

  Example:
  If you are single with AGI of $127,500, your maximum contribution to a Roth IRA would be cut in half to $2,750. If your AGI is above $135,000 you cannot contribute to a Roth IRA.

Note that the phaseout amounts differ for traditional and Roth IRAs and the dollar amounts may change periodically.

Roth IRA Plan Withdrawals:

- After age 59½, if the account has been opened for at least five years, you can take out all you want, when you want, **tax and penalty free.**

  Example:
  Had you put $4,000 into a Roth at age 20, at 8% compounded annually, at age 65, that $4,000 would be worth over $125,000, with no tax to pay. It is the magic of compounding along with the "no-tax" benefit.

- Money **converted** into a Roth IRA account from a traditional IRA (after paying the taxes) can only be withdrawn tax-free if held in the account for at least five years.

- Before 59½ you can take your contributions out tax-free, but investment earnings will be taxed. Remember, you have already paid the tax on your contributions.

- Keep accurate records of your Roth contributions (Form 5498) so you can verify you are not liable for paying any tax when you withdraw your own contributions upon which you have already paid the tax.

191

- When you die the money will go to your beneficiary tax free, but the beneficiary will have to take required minimum distributions and must meet the "combined" five-year test for distributions to be tax-free.

- Unlike the Traditional IRA, with a Roth IRA the owner has **no required minimum distributions at age 70½.** However, there are required minimum distributions after death that apply to the beneficiaries.

- As in a Traditional IRA, a Roth has limited exclusions for **early withdrawals** without penalties or taxes if you become permanently disabled; need up to $10,000 for a first-time purchase of a home; or the money is distributed to your heirs after death.

If the Roth account is an inherited Roth IRA, the beneficiary can withdraw tax free an amount equal to the owner's contributions, subject to various regulations.

You can **convert all or part of your Traditional IRA into a Roth IRA.** To do so, you will need to **pay the tax due** on the withdrawal from the Traditional IRA at your ordinary tax rate, but subsequent withdrawals from the Roth IRA will not be taxed. Money converted into a Roth IRA account can only be withdrawn tax- free if held in the account for at least five years. Conversion is subject to specific tax code restrictions so a transaction such as this should never be done without professional advice. For example, you cannot convert an inherited IRA into a Roth IRA. That's why you should **get professional help** if you inherit either type of IRA account.

Spousal account: If you have a job, but your spouse does not work during the year, you may contribute to your spouse's IRA account up to the same amount you contribute to your IRA. If you deduct your contribution, you can also deduct your spouse's contribution.

IRA or Roth?

Much has been written about whether it is better to contribute to a Traditional IRA, a Roth IRA, or a combination of both. There are good arguments on all sides.

For example, some say it is better to contribute to a Roth IRA since demographics indicate tax rates will increase over time. That may or may not be true, but most people who retire see their total income decline when their paycheck days are over. That may put them into a lower tax bracket.

Then again, the Traditional IRA has a required minimum distribution which forces the retiree, upon reaching 70½, to withdraw taxable funds which, when added to other sources of income such as Social Security, might push them into a higher tax bracket. The Roth owner has no RMD.

Here is another scenario. Consider recent college graduates who are just starting their careers burdened with credit card and student loan debt, forming households, and wondering how they will ever afford buying a house or starting a family. They too need to start saving for a long life. Contributing to an IRA and getting the tax deduction now may be far more valuable at this stage of life than getting an unknown tax break 40 years from now.

Personal circumstances change, as do tax laws. Examine your situation before you act, do the best you can, start saving, and do not look back. You win either way.

You are in charge. Be wise.

IRAs are **self-directed accounts**, giving you the flexibility to choose who will manage your account and what will go into it. **You are ultimately responsible for managing the assets in your IRA account, whether you do it yourself or designate someone else.** Some advice for starting and managing your IRA:

- You can open an IRA account with sponsors such as a bank, savings and loan, credit union, brokerage firm, or mutual fund.

- You can have more than one IRA account and you can invest in most kinds of assets, depending upon your tolerance for risk.

- Know what the fees are for account maintenance and brokerage services.

- Stocks, bonds, mutual funds, ETFs, sector funds, and CDs are all eligible investments. There are no annual taxes due on dividends, interest or capital gains within the IRA account so factor that into your strategy.

- Investments in limited partnerships are best held in regular accounts, not IRAs, due to complicated tax reporting.

- Real Estate Investment Trusts ("REIT") and other types of investment trusts are usually best held in IRA accounts because their typically higher dividends are tax sheltered within the account.

- Direct transfers and rollovers let you add or switch sponsors. **Direct transfers from trustee to trustee** are the best way to go. It may take a few weeks to complete the transfer. If you must do the transfer or rollover yourself, be careful not to spend, take possession of, or co-mingle the money as mistakes can lead to taxes and penalties being imposed. If you do personally handle the transfer or rollover you have 60 days to complete the process without taxes or penalty.

- You can make your contributions all at once, monthly or by direct deposit. Consider making your contributions as early in the year as you can to get the maximum benefit of compounding, since investment earnings accumulate tax free within the account.

- If you are self-employed or owner of your own small business, there are other special types of plans such as a SEP-IRA that will allow you to save much more than the Traditional or Roth IRAs. Contact your accountant or investment advisor for further information.

- IRAs are currently protected from bankruptcy up to about $1.3 million. There are very few accounts that are that large

- **If you inherit an IRA or Roth IRA, promptly check the then current rules and regulations before you do anything with the money.**

Always **seek professional advice** on all of these issues. Tax laws and personal circumstances change. Your employer, accountant, or investment professional can update you on IRA tax laws and help you make good decisions. See IRS Pub 590.

Suppose I do not qualify? If you are not able to receive a tax deduction for contributing to a traditional IRA, or you earn too much to contribute to a Roth IRA, consider putting money into a **personal investment account**. Such accounts are not tax sheltered, but money can be contributed and invested in a wide range of assets and you can still benefit from the magic of compounding. It is your money and you can withdraw it any time without paying taxes or incurring a penalty. Funds may be used to pay off a mortgage, cover educational expenses, invested into a business, or for any other purpose, not just retirement.

> **As Yogi said,**
> **"It's tough to make predictions, especially about the future."**

Notes and Updates

CHAPTER 19

401(K) PLAN

A Gift from Your Boss?

More ways to save for retirement.

A **401(k) Plan** is similar in many ways to an individual retirement account (IRA) except that it must be established by an employer. It is a **defined contribution plan**, as opposed to a defined benefit pension plan, which means the contribution, not the benefit, is defined. The law gives a special tax break to employees who are saving primarily for retirement in a 401(k). Like an IRA, contributions can be made with pretax dollars and, like an IRA, investments in the plan are tax-sheltered so that interest, dividends, and capital gains can compound at an accelerated rate. And, depending on the plan, all or a portion of the employee's contribution may be "matched" by the employer, which represents free money to the employee.

401(k) plans are often used to **replace** defined benefit pension plans. Plans are usually funded with pretax salary contributions from the employee and some matching funds from the employer, thus shifting a large part of the cost from the employer to the employee. However, 401(k)s are not used specifically to replace an IRA. Under certain circumstances, those who have 401(k) plans may also have IRA plans.

During the Great Recession, to save money many employers suspended or reduced matching contributions to their plans. Since then, most employers have restored all or partial contributions. However, some employers are using other tactics to keep costs under control, like tying future 401(k) contributions to the company's profits or delaying their matching contributions until the end of the year so that employees who leave during the year will not take with them any partial employer matching funds. To the employee this also means that compounding of the employer's matching funds will not begin until the end of the year.

One requirement of a 401(k) plan is that the employer designates the investments from which employees are allowed to select. This limits the number of choices available to plan participants. The employer or its agent provides employees with information about each opportunity and then the employee selects from the list those with the most appeal. So, the employee is actually managing the account, but only within the scope of investments offered by the employer.

To retain the tax shelter benefit, a 401(k) plan must adhere to certain rules:

- The employer's plan may not discriminate against lower-paid employees.
- Employee contributions to a 401(k) are tax deductible.
- Growth within the 401(k) is tax-sheltered and tax-deferred until the funds are withdrawn.
- When withdrawals are made they become taxable income subject to ordinary tax rates in the year of withdrawal.
- You generally cannot withdraw funds without penalty before age 59½
- except under special circumstances.

Many employers will match a certain percentage of your contribution. A typical match might be 50 cents or $1 for every dollar the employee contributes up to percentage of salary, usually 3% to 6%. **An employee should always make a contribution large enough to attract the maximum employer match.** After all, the match is free money and who doesn't want that?

The IRS sets limits, adjusted periodically for inflation, on how much an employee can contribute to a 401(k) each year. The current maximum annual **tax deductible** contribution is $18,500 ($24,500 for those ages 50 and over). The deductible amounts and regulations change periodically so be sure to check as you plan your level of contribution.

According to current law, if the plan owner dies, the **beneficiary of a 401(k) plan is the spouse,** regardless of who is the named beneficiary. The only exception is if the spouse has waived, in writing, his or her rights. If the plan owner is single, it goes to the named beneficiary regardless of a will.

When signing up for a plan, be sure to check the administrative, investment management, and consulting **fees** of the plan. Under the current law, retirement plan sponsors must disclose fees, expenses, and past performance. Many plans have fees in the range of 0.60% to 0.75%. The total should not exceed 1.00% of assets. Fees may be paid by the employer or passed on to the plan participants.

Evaluate your investment choices in terms of quality and variety. You can select them from a the list of approved investments provided by your employer. You can be moderately aggressive or conservative. You can **diversify and allocate** your contributions even when using monthly payroll deduction, which is essentially a way to dollar-cost average.

Consider what happened during the sharp market decline in 2008 and 2009. Those who continued to invest on a monthly basis were buying more shares at lower prices (dollar-cost-averaging). When the market rallied to higher levels, they owned many more shares at lower prices. That enabled them to recover and earn a profit much faster than those who got so discouraged they either sold virtually everything they owned or stopped buying near the bottom of the market when stocks were "on sale."

Remember, your 401(k) is part of your overall portfolio of assets, so keep diversification in mind. It is usually not a good idea to invest heavily in your company's stock within the 401(k) since you are already depending on your company for your paycheck and benefits. Too much concentration is never good, no matter how much you love your employer!

Following is an example that will clearly show the benefits and power of a 401(k) plan, including an employer "match":

> Assume you earn $50,000 and your employer matches 100% of your contribution, up to 6% of your salary. You contribute $3,000 and your employer matches with $3,000 for a total of $6,000.

> Assume you are in a combined 25% tax bracket for federal and state income taxes. Since you are making your contribution with pretax dollars, it is really only costing you $2,250. After all, had you not contributed the $3,000 to your 401(k), you would have had to pay $750 taxes on it, and been left with only $2,250.

> So, for a $2,250 after tax contribution on your part you now have $6,000 invested, including $3,000 from your employer and the $750 tax dollars which Uncle Sam is allowing you to invest and compound instead of sending it to the US Treasury. A great deal!

In the above example, there were three parties that contributed to your 401(k); you, your employer, and Uncle Sam. On an after-tax basis, you now have $6,000 in your account, but only $2,250 of it came out of your pocket.

Usually, automatic payroll deductions to your account make saving seem easier. The money is taken out before you even see it, so you won't miss it as much.

Significant efforts are being made to encourage participation by all employees. Until now, enrollment in a 401(k) has been voluntary, but new laws enable employers to automatically enroll employees, unless the employee "opts out" of the plan. Employers are also extending enrollment to all employees, old and new, and are offering more and better diversified investment alternatives. Finally, in some cases they are automatically boosting workers' contributions to help them take advantage of the company's matching funds. One law being considered is to go even further, making 401(k) participation mandatory so that those who do not put money aside for retirement would not become a burden on society when they retire.

You will always be **100% vested in your own contributions** to a 401(k) since that is your money and no one can take it away from you. The concept of **vesting** refers to when you will actually own your employer's contributions since your employer does have the right to put conditions around your getting its contributions if you leave, are terminated, or take early retirement. The conditions an employer puts around vesting are one method they have to reduce turnover and save money. When you depart the company any **unvested employer contributions remain with the employer.** Here's how it works.

There are 3 types of vesting:

- **100% Vesting: You own 100%** of your contributions and your employer's matching funds for which you have qualified. If you leave your job tomorrow, you can take these funds with you.

- **Cliff Vesting:** You take ownership of a given year's annual matching funds all at once, but **only after you have worked for the company** for a specified period of time. The maximum period you can be forced to wait is three years. If you leave before three years, the employer's contribution would not have vested, and you couldn't take it with you.

- **Graded Vesting:** You take **ownership of a percentage** of the employer's match each year. It is usually one-third of the employer's contribution per year for three years, but it could be 20% over five years or some other schedule.

When you consider a job change, you should remember to include the impact vesting might have on your 401(k) plan so you are aware of the money you may be leaving behind.

401(k) plans are portable. When you leave your employer, you have options to consider:

- You can roll it tax free into a traditional IRA, sponsor to sponsor, where the fees may be less, and many more investment choices become available.

- You can roll it tax free into a new employer's 401(k) plan if the new plan allows you to do this, sponsor to sponsor.

- You may be able to leave your account with your old employer if you have more than $5,000 invested, but you cannot add to the plan.

- You can withdraw the funds, but if you are under 59½ taxes will be withheld and you will have to pay a 10% penalty for early withdrawal.

If your 401(k) plan allows loans, you can borrow up to 50% of your vested balance, not to exceed $50,000, but:

- **Loans must be repaid** over no more than five years unless used to purchase a first home.
- Interest is 1% to 3% over the prime rate.
- Principal and interest are usually repaid via payroll deduction.

Warning: You should **avoid borrowing from 401(k) accounts** because your repayments are not tax deductible. They are made with after-tax dollars and after other payroll deductions have been made. Worse, when you retire and take withdrawals, you will pay tax again on the same dollars.

In case you are not yet confused enough!

Depending on the type of organization you work for, there are additional plan types such as:

- **403(b) plans** are defined contribution plans established by **nonprofit** organizations. They are similar to 401(k) plans. 403(b) plans allow matching contributions from nonprofit employers. In many such plans the funds are used to purchase an annuity contract whereby one receives payments on an investment for a lifetime or a specified number of years.

- **Section 457 plans** are defined contribution plans established by **governmental agencies.** They are similar to a 401(k) except they are funded only by your contributions. The government does not match contributions since it has its own retirement plan.

- **Roth 401(k) plan:** Companies that have a 401(k) plan are allowed to add a Roth 401(k) plan, but they are not required to. The basic concept is similar to the Roth IRA in that there is no tax deduction for your contribution, but because you paid taxes going in, **no taxes are due on the withdrawals.** If your company has chosen to make a Roth 401(k) available, you can contribute to it if you are eligible to contribute to the company's 401(k) plan.

  Your maximum annual contribution to a 401(k) is currently $18,500 ($24,500 for those over age 50). If your company also offers a Roth 401(k), you can elect to put some or all of your contribution into that plan. However, **your employer may only contribute to your regular 401(k).**

Let's compare.

Similarities between a Traditional 401(k) and a Roth 401(k):

- There is no difference in contribution limits. If your current limit is $18,500 it can be put into either type of account or shared, but the total cannot exceed $18,500 combined for any one year.

- There is no difference in what is an eligible investment.

- There is no difference in the matching contribution percentage. However, since matching contributions made by an employer are tax deductible to the employer, they **must go into a traditional 401(k) account.** This requirement ensures there cannot be a situation where the employer deducts the contribution and the employee deducts the withdrawal.

Comparing the traditional 401(k) with the Roth 401(k):

- Your contributions to a 401(k) are tax deductible, but contributions to a Roth 401(k) are not.

- In both plans, all **earnings are tax-sheltered**, and allowed to grow tax-free as long as the account exists.

- Distributions from a 401(k) are taxable. Distributions from a Roth 401(k) are tax-free.

- Upon termination of employment you can **rollover a 401(k)** into a new employer's 401(k) or into a traditional IRA. A Roth 401(k) can be rolled over into a new employer's Roth 401(k). It can also be rolled over into a Roth IRA without regard to the Roth IRA contribution limits or phase outs.

- If you decide to roll over your 401(k) plans into those of a new employer, you may have to sell the old investments and purchase the eligible investments in the new employer's plan, since they are not likely to be the same.

- **Both traditional 401(k) and Roth 401(k) plans have a required minimum distribution** at age 70½ or retirement if you continue working. You can also avoid the Roth 401(k) RMD by rolling it tax free into your Roth IRA.

401(k) Planning List:

What is the maximum you can contribute?
What percentage will your employer match?
What do I have to do to get the match?
Which vesting plan does your employer use for its contributions?
How often can you transfer money between investment alternatives?
How do you access your account?
Have you allocated assets so you are diversified with dollar-cost averaging, avoiding your own company stock, and reallocating at least once a year?
Do you understand the fees?
What is your current estimated tax bracket? This might help you choose between a Roth and Traditional 401(k).
Have you sought professional advice?

Financial independence, one step at a time.

General recommendations for saving are as follows:

- Contribute enough money to your 401(k) or Roth 401(k) through payroll deductions to **maximize the employer match.** This is free money so do not miss out.

- Select and **diversify** your retirement plan investments. Focus on growth.

- If a 401(k) has **no matching employer contribution**, consider an IRA or Roth IRA of your own. It will give you more investment options with lower fees.

- **Pay off** high interest rate credit card balances.

- Build an **emergency fund** of savings equal to 3 to 6 months living expenses. Consider an online or other type of savings account, cash deposit or money market deposit account that offers the **best interest and easy access** to your money in the event of an emergency.

- **Fund continuing education** that will enhance your career opportunities and enable you to increase your income and pursue your passion.

- Begin a program of **individual investing** in ETFs, sector funds, stocks, real estate, or starting a business, adhering to the **disciplines** we have outlined.

- Seek **professional advice** along the way, especially regarding taxes and investments.

Plans for the self-employed.

If you choose not to work for a large organization or you have a successful "home" business, you do not have to feel left out. There are a number of **retirement plans** available for the **self-employed**, those working alone or with only a few employees. Before selecting and implementing a plan, be sure to **seek professional advice** as you certainly want the plan which will provide you with the best package of benefits based upon your own personal situation.

Following are the examples of two popular plans:

Solo 401(k) plans are strictly for the sole proprietor who has no employees, except possibly a spouse, and who may sometimes contribute to the plan if he or she earns income from the business. This plan **allows the proprietor to save both as an employee, and as an employer,** up to the lesser of 25% of income or $55,000, based on maximum allowable compensation. The maximum will likely increase in future years. Contributions are voluntary. Both **traditional and Roth type variations** are available. See www.irs.gov for publications that cover Solo 401(k) type plans.

A **SEP-IRA** is a **S**implified **E**mployee **P**ension Individual Retirement Account. It is for **self-employed individuals and small businesses** with only a few employees. Business owners can currently contribute up to the lesser of 25% of income or $55,000 to the plan. In future years, the limit may be changed. **Contributions do not have to be made every year**, but if you choose to contribute you must contribute to your own SEP-IRA plan and make at least a modest contribution **to** the SEP-IRA plan of every eligible employee. See IRS Pub 560.

Retirement plans are for everyone. Use them!

Notes and Updates

CHAPTER 20

REAL ESTATE INVESTING
Start Small and Build

Individuals and business enterprises invest in real estate for many different reasons. Usually we think of real estate as purchasing, developing, constructing, or remodeling property for either one's own use, or to sell or rent. There are many other reasons why real estate attracts so much investor interest including:

- To speculate on land appreciation.
- To diversify an investment portfolio.
- To take advantage of financial leverage and tax benefits.
- To manage property as a business.
- To become a broker or agent assisting in the purchase and sale of real estate as a career or part-time employment.
- To provide financing for the purchase, development, construction, and remodeling of property.
- To buy property, increase its value, and sell it for a short-term profit, otherwise known as flipping.
- To form real estate investment trusts (REITs).

Purchasing a home to live in is usually the first real estate investment people make. It may be their first experience with the use of **leverage**. It may be their first opportunity to use **special tax deductions** and to learn about loan origination fees, property taxes, and **tax free capital gains.** Whether it is a "fixer-upper" that needs repairing, remodeling, or updating, or construction of a brand new home, rising prices can increase equity. One can borrow against this equity to finance more real estate, or for other uses.

Real Estate Investing – the good, the bad, and the ugly.

Buying real estate as an investment can be risky. It takes **large amounts of capital** and is **subject to interest rates and the availability of financing**. It can **limit**

an individual's liquidity, not only because of the capital that is tied up to make the purchase, but also because it may not be generating enough income to cover monthly expenses. We call that **negative cash flow**. High vacancy rates, unexpected maintenance, and natural disasters can all create needs for more cash. **Future value is uncertain** and may be impacted by changes in interest rates, the neighborhood, or the overall economy.

But it has its rewards too. Buying your home can also be the start of a small or part-time business. **Strategies** could include:

- Buying a house, possibly in foreclosure, living in it for at least two years as a primary residence, and then selling it for a tax-free profit due to rising home prices in the area, with little maintenance or expense.

- Buying and financing a fixer-upper and, while living in it, contracting or doing much of the work yourself. This is frequently done by a couple with one or both having a full-time job to help generate cash flow for the mortgage, taxes, labor, and materials. When completed, it may be rented and refinanced for a down payment on another property.

- Buying a small residential rental property, living in one unit, and renting out the other unit(s) without major repairs.

- Purchasing rental property, living in one unit, and over time making capital and cosmetic improvements, increasing rents, then selling it and using tax-deferred profits as a down payment on a larger piece of rental property.

The **goal** in real estate is to use the **rental income** to help pay for the mortgage, insurance, taxes, and maintenance, while taking advantage of the **tax benefits** and the use of **borrowed funds.** Ultimately, you will build up your equity or ownership of the property as prices and cash flow appreciate.

Location, location, location. You have heard it before. Location is considered to be the most important factor when investing in real estate. Depending on the type of property, you might want to ask yourself questions such as: Will the neighborhood support the price of the property for as long as you are the owner? How secure is the area? Is it subject to floods, tornados, hurricanes, earthquakes, highway diversion, erosion, pollution, or other environmental issues? Are construction, inspection, and use permits required? Is zoning favorable to your plan? Are there local rent control and tenant's rights issues? Is it attractive rental property in terms of schools, transportation, and other local services?

Some of these concerns can be mitigated. For example, landlord insurance is available to cover physical damage to rental property for events such as fire. It may also cover economic losses such as lost rental income, liability protection, and legal fees. But other issues may not be so easily dealt with such as changes in building codes and environmental laws; re-zoning for new development projects; waste management; etc. These are longer- term issues to consider.

It is all about the taxes.

The Internal Revenue Service (IRS) assigns a tax life to various types of property. **Depreciation** reflects that **gradual loss of value** of rental property as it wears out over its tax life. Even though there is no direct or immediate cash outlay, the IRS requires, for tax purposes, that depreciation be deducted as if it were an actual cash expense. Therefore, like any other allowable expense, it **reduces the operating profit** of a property. It also **reduces, for tax purposes, the cost basis** of the property when it is sold.

The tax code enables the owner to deduct depreciation as an expense under the theory that the owner will use the tax savings to reinvest back into the business or property to maintain its condition. As rule of thumb if, over time, **capital expenditures equal depreciation**, the property is hopefully being appropriately updated and maintained, but there are no guarantees or required inspections made for this purpose, and the IRS has the power to audit all returns for accuracy.

Operating profits derived from renting property are taxable, but certain non-operating items such as mortgage interest and depreciation are recorded as expenses for tax purposes and therefore have the benefit of reducing those profits.

Capital improvements generally refer to permanent structural improvements which either increase the property's value or useful life. They might include restoring the property to its original condition, adding a new addition, physically expanding or enlarging the property, replacing a major component, or increasing its strength.

As you can imagine, defining for tax purposes the difference between a capital improvement and a repair or maintenance project can be difficult and subject to interpretation of the tax code. Calculating depreciation can also be complicated and difficult, especially at the time of sale. The IRS codes dealing with real estate are extensive and complicated. I always recommend getting expert professional **tax and legal advice.**

Short term **capital gains** (or losses) occur when property is sold one year or less from its date of purchase. Long term capital gains (or losses) occur when the property has been owned for more than one year. Either type of gain (or loss) is calculated as the difference between the sale price and the cost basis.

For tax purposes, your IRS cost basis is adjusted to reflect the price you originally paid for the property, plus any capital improvements you made during ownership, minus depreciation expensed during ownership. Here is how to determine your cost basis for tax purposes.

Cost Basis = Purchase Price + Capital Improvements − Depreciation

Ultimately, the higher the cost basis, the lower your taxable profit will be upon sale. Be sure to keep good records and all applicable receipts.

Commercial or Residential

Residential rental property including apartments, houses, condos, flats, duplexes, and lofts, is treated as a business investment. Owners, or "landlords," declare **rent as income** and deduct all the **allowable operating expenses** such as repairs, maintenance, utilities, insurance, interest, and property taxes. **Principal payments** which reduce the amount of the loan **are not tax deductible.**

According to the current IRS rules, residential rental properties are required to be depreciated over 27.5 years or at the rate of 3.6364% of the purchase price each year. This is called straight line depreciation. When the property is sold, the cost basis for tax purposes is reduced by the total amount of depreciation which has already been expensed for tax purposes.

Therefore, if an owner were to own the property for 27.5 years, the cost basis for the property after depreciation would be zero **for tax purposes**. Thereafter, sale of the property by that owner would result in a 100% taxable long-term capital gain in the year of sale. In other words, the purchase price of the property would have been completely written down to zero for tax purposes (excluding any other adjustments).

When the property is sold, the seller will terminate its depreciation, and the new owner will begin expensing its own depreciation and adjusting its cost basis over a new period of 27.5 years **Commercial and industrial property** usually requires

larger amounts of capital and is, therefore, often owned by partnerships or corporations. Projects include office properties, retail space, warehouses, storage facilities, malls, manufacturing plants, post offices, restaurants, and other places of business.

Commercial and industrial property may be **owner-operated,** where the owner of the property actually uses the property in its business. Or, the property may be owned by an **investor**, who leases or rents to a single tenant or multiple tenants. In some cases, the property may be built by a company for its own use but sold to an investor and then leased back. This type of transaction is called a **sale- leaseback.** The company gets a facility that is perfectly suited to its needs but, ultimately, does not have to tie up its own capital in real estate. **Leases** usually include **periodic rent increases and renewal options.**

When referring to commercial and industrial leases, you will often hear the term **triple net lease**. This means in addition to rent the tenant will be responsible for property taxes, insurance, maintenance, repairs, utilities, electricity, and other items.

Depreciation on commercial and industrial property is straight line over 39 years, equal to 1/39th or 2.5641% of the purchase price each year. However, equipment and components within the property are depreciated using different rules over different periods of time. So, for tax purposes, calculations can get very complicated and should only be done by experts.

For tax purposes, the IRS distinguishes between those who are actively involved in real estate activities and those who are only passive investors in real estate.

- **Active** activities in real estate are those in which the individual spends at least 50% of his or her working hours a year, but not less than 750 hours, actively involved in the business of real estate such as a developer, owner-operator, property manager, real estate broker, mortgage broker, etc. In this case the tax code treats the business of real estate like a full-time for- profit operating enterprise.

- **Passive** activities are real estate investments in which the individual does not materially participate in the business but is a part-time participant or a silent partner. According to the IRS, this is a person who spends less than 50% of their working hours involved in real estate activities. Currently, losses from such investments can be used to deduct up to $25,000 from other actively managed rental real estate. However, the ability to deduct these losses is phased out as AGI rises above $100,000 and disappears at $150,000.

The distinction between active and passive taxpayers can be confusing. The IRS believes many real estate owners either under report rental income or over state expenses to reduce taxable income. **Keep meticulous records** and seek advice from a tax professional before filing your return.

IRS Code 1031 Exchange is a unique real estate opportunity available to both commercial and residential property owners, which allows you to trade a property and **defer taxes** on capital gains by exchanging or replacing that property with another property, instead of selling it outright and paying the capital gains tax. As you might expect there are strict IRS regulations on such transactions:

- You must invest at least as much equity in the new property as was in the old property because you are trading your equity.

- You must assume at least as much debt in the new property as was in the old property. Any shortfall of debt is subject to tax.

- Investing excess equity or debt in a qualified new property is okay.

- An independent third party may provide a safe harbor by taking title to the property during the exchange period.

- The period of time in which the exchange must take place is about 180 days, the time limit being set by IRS regulations.

In sum, instead of paying the tax in this transaction you are allowed to **defer your tax payment, keep that money, leverage it, compound it, and invest it** in a new, perhaps bigger piece of property. You can do that several times. The tax will eventually come due when the final property is sold, and the funds are not reinvested. These are complicated transactions; so, **always seek professional advice** from real estate lawyers and accountants when contemplating a 1031 Exchange.

It could be a long slog!

Finding good investment property takes time, connections, and research. Finding enough good properties to rent or lease and becoming a landlord can become a full-time job. It is important to network. Get to know city hall and bank employees to find foreclosures. Join a local landlord or property owner's association. Ask landlords directly to see if they would like to sell their property or if they know of other properties which might be for sale. Cruise neighborhoods looking for "for rent" and "for sale" signs. Contact residential and commercial real estate brokers and developers in the area for leads on potential sellers.

Get your finances in shape. Put a "shine" on your credit rating. Lenders usually require **bigger down payments, higher interest rates, and stronger finances** when buying rental property than when buying a house. They may also require **personal guarantees** from the borrower. The standard belief is that tenants are more likely to default on rental property than on mortgage payments on their own home.

Establish a substantial **cash reserve** to prepare for unexpected repairs and vacancies. Set aside at least one month's rent for each residential unit to fix it up between tenants and to re-rent it. Commercial and industrial properties may require substantially larger reserves. **Arrange a line of credit for major repairs and maintenance.**

Carefully check out the background, goals, objectives, and financial resources of all partners in a project. If an unplanned event occurs, you do not want to be the only one able to come up with needed cash.

Know the numbers and avoid overpaying.

Conventional wisdom is you make your profit when you buy a property, not when you sell it.

Potential buyers should look closely at the numbers to see if their investment will pay off. Specifically:

- Make sure rental income will **cover out-of-pocket costs** such as mortgage payments, taxes, insurance, maintenance, repairs with at least **a 5% to 10% vacancy rate.**

- Know the terms and conditions of **existing leases** on the property so the ability to raise rents is not overestimated.

- Factor in repairs, maintenance, mortgage interest, depreciation, insurance, and other items which are tax deductible.

- Factor in **capital improvements,** which may be depreciated in the future. They will be added to the cost basis, the amount you paid for the property.

- Be aware that the $250K to $500K **primary residence tax exemption does not apply** to residential rental property.

Always get **inspections** before you buy any property, and periodically thereafter. Deferred maintenance can get very expensive very fast. Inspecting and verifying the condition and status of the property is called **due diligence.**

The longer you own a property the larger your investment in repair, maintenance, and improvements. Some rules of thumb apply:

- **Five years or less:** Avoid major improvements unless they can be recovered quickly by increasing rents and the probability of achieving a higher selling price. There is risk. Rents are sensitive to swings in the marketplace.

- **20 years or more:** Assume roof, furnaces, appliances, and other major repairs, replacements, and improvements will be necessary, and start thinking about how they will be financed over time. A 20-year rental will almost certainly appreciate in value unless the property is not well maintained or the neighborhood deteriorates.

The "hype" about buying foreclosures is exaggerated. Expect to spend a lot of time looking around for profitable opportunities and ultimately being a successful bidder. Do your homework:

- Advertised foreclosure and short sale discounts of 30% to 40% are, in reality, more like 10% to 15% when **compared to existing market values** and not previous high prices. Also, bids may get competitive, driving up the price.

- The process begins when a property owner falls behind on mortgage payments. This usually means the property has **deferred maintenance and repairs.**

- The lender may have filed a **notice of default**, called *lis pendens,* which is Latin for default. Search public records for **liens** on the property, including unpaid property taxes and assessments which must be paid to transfer title.

- Check the **comps** of similar properties in the area.

Buying from the lender may be the safest way to buy, because there are no taxes or liens to pay, or tenants to evict. The lender has already gone through that process.

And pay attention to the financial markets:

- Interest rates affect the cost of debt. This means that when interest rates are high, you may not be able to finance the purchase of a very attractive property. Or, a property you would like to sell may not find a qualified buyer at your price.

- Interest rates also affect the price of properties. Because borrowed money funds most real estate, as interest rates rise, prices tend to decline. The reverse is also true, as rates fall, prices tend to escalate.

- Sometimes, due to economic conditions such as unemployment and vacancies, lenders may not be willing to finance real estate, essentially paralyzing the marketplace. This was quite evident during the Great Recession, and it could happen again.

- Real estate investments are **not highly liquid** and may take months or years to sell.

Oh, the joys of being a landlord!

Do you have what it takes to be a landlord? Can you take the hassle that comes with owning rental property? Are you willing to screen tenants, obtain credit reports, chase overdue rents, and field middle of the night calls? Can you handle falling rents, major repairs, or costly evictions? Will you keep complete and accurate records?

Will you learn and obey the regulations in your community? You cannot discriminate on the basis of race, religion, sex, gender, age, disability, or sexual orientation. Laws relating to rent control and tenant's rights must be observed.

Building codes, zoning requirements, and use permits must be adhered to, along with disability access, including ramps and elevators.

There are costs, risks, and a lot of effort involved in successfully investing in real estate, but you may be rewarded by **using rental income to pay off the mortgage, using leverage to increase your equity, and by taking advantage of the deferred tax benefits afforded real estate investors.**

But for those who do not have the time or inclination to invest directly in real estate, there are attractive alternatives.

Real Estate Investment Trusts ("REITs") are publicly traded managed pools of money similar to a mutual fund, which invest in real estate rather than stocks or bonds. REITs are preferred by investors looking to profit in real estate without directly owning or having the responsibility of managing real estate. Publicly owned REIT shares trade like stocks and are liquid.

- **Equity REITs** own and operate income producing real estate.
- **Mortgage REITs** finance property.
- **Hybrid REITs** may own and finance property.

Part of the attractiveness of REITs is that companies that operate as a **REIT pay no tax on corporate income** if they pay at least **90%** of their income to shareholders in the form of a dividend. These **dividends are taxed to the shareholder as short term ordinary income.** The dividends tend to be higher than the 10-year treasury rate or the S & P 500 dividend rate, and also have the potential for growth. Dividends from real estate investment trusts **may be eligible for the 20% pass-through** tax treatment. REITs are probably best owned and held in a **tax-sheltered account** like an IRA or 401(k), where dividends are allowed to compound tax free.

Like all investments, REITs have their risks, essentially those of owning real estate. For example:

- Hotel REITs may wake up to very high vacancy rates on any given day.

- Apartment REITs may have declining rents and vacancies in a soft economy or a highly competitive overbuilt environment.

- Retail REITs can face cyclical and consumer slumps.

- Office building REITs may suffer from vacancies, including the effects of unemployment.

- Storage REITs face overbuilding.

- Healthcare REITs may reflect the growing financial despair of a large aging population.

REITs enable investors to participate in real estate without having the hassle of being a landlord, but with the advantage of liquidity by owning shares traded on exchanges which can be easily bought and sold.

> **Real estate, in one form or another, should be considered as part of a well balanced portfolio of investments.**

Notes and Updates

CHAPTER 21

STUDENT LOANS

An Asset or a Liability?

I do not recall who said it first, but the student loan program is a national disgrace. At over $1.5 trillion, its total debt exceeds that of credit cards and is second only to mortgage debt. Over 40 million borrowers with federal or private student loans are burdened with it, including 140,000 senior citizens who are still trying to pay off their loans.

Perhaps the most striking thing is that it hits young people who can now borrow tens of thousands of dollars with little or no knowledge of personal finances or how the loan will be repaid. These loans will haunt them for years after they begin their careers. And it also hits their parents who wanted nothing more than to have their children live better lives, but instead are saddled with huge debts. Do we really want to hang a huge price tag on something as important as education, innovation, and opportunity?

What started out as a well-meaning concept has morphed into something far more sinister. According to a recent survey, nationally over 50% of students entering four- y e a r colleges and universities are taking out loans. Of those who take out loans it is estimated that 70% will leave school with debts averaging about $33,000. For millions of students now attending colleges and universities, regardless of their major, their minor has become "student loan management" and they will need these skills well into the future. And, for graduate students it can be far more expensive.

And I am not talking about just college students. There are millions more who attend postsecondary vocational schools to become aircraft mechanics, chefs, nurses, designers, medical assistants, artists and auto mechanics, and they too are eligible for student loans.

Years ago, I personally owned a vocational school which trained people in the use of computers, software, and basic programming. It qualified for all the usual student loans including the G.I. bill. I also served on the Board of Directors of one of the nation's top culinary academies and was a consultant to other vocational schools. Trying to understand and keep up with all the rules governing student aid programs is a nightmare and requires the hiring and training of thousands of financial aid specialists across the nation. And who do the students and their families have to deal with? The federal government, Congress, and bank loan officers. It's not a fair fight.

The best way to keep up to date is the federal government website www.studentaid. ed.gov. It also has a good loan calculator. One can search the web for volumes of information. But your best bet may be to contact the Student Aid Department at your institution or, if you already have a loan, your servicer or lender.

Be careful of fraudulent student loan debt relief companies who claim to help desperate students deal with a complex bureaucracy. Their usual method of operation is to collect an upfront fee by promising relief from the current program, debt consolidation, or debt forgiveness, but they tend to cash your check and then disappear. You can do all these things on your own without any cost just by contacting your lender or loan servicer.

Student loans are a serious financial obligation which must be repaid even if your financial situation becomes difficult. One-sixth of all student loans are currently in default, amounting to more than $75 billion dollars. To put this in perspective, that is more than the combined tuition of all the campuses in America for a year.

Be aware that if you miss a few loan payments the servicer will report that fact to the credit bureaus. Under current law, those who default also face having the government contact the credit reporting agencies, garnish their wages, seize their income tax refunds, or reduce their Social Security benefits. In addition, credit scores are damaged, and penalties are assessed. The problem is serious enough that the government pays $1 billion a year to collection agencies who eventually recover about 75% of the defaulted debt.

Borrowing for a college education.

The amount to be borrowed should be given serious thought, beginning with the senior year of high school or earlier when the search for college begins, and continuing throughout the process of selecting a campus, major and a career. Consider whether a prestigious school is worth the extra expense. The same may be said when choosing a major which has limited marketable skills, or which would require additional years of education to qualify for what might be a lower paying profession. This is not to say what choices you should make but make them with your eyes wide open and with a plan.

Contact the financial aid department of schools to which you are applying or already attending to seek their advice on sources of funds and regulations. They are in the best position to help you through the mine field of educational financing.

As a general rule, try to limit borrowings to no more than what you realistically would expect your annual salary to be upon graduation.

If you are a student, your monthly student loan payments should not exceed 10% of your expected monthly gross income once you graduate. For a parent, total debts ideally should not exceed 36% to 43% of gross income, which includes the home mortgage, credit cards, car loans, and education loans.

There are a number of factors to research, all of which could potentially impact the **cost of your education:**

- Check into whether you may be able to get college credits for any of your high school courses, especially advanced placement classes. And research whether there might be less expensive courses online or at a community college for which you may get credit.

- Could you complete your undergraduate degree in 3 to 3½ years by including summer sessions or taking extra credits? This could cut the cost by about 25%.

- On the other end of the spectrum, are required courses overcrowded so that completing your degree requirements might take more than four years?

- Consider taking college courses that might make you more marketable such as accounting, computer science, or a foreign language.

- Apply for every grant, scholarship, or loan for which you might qualify. These might include Pell grants, international grants and scholarships, outside scholarships, state grants, Stafford Loans, parent Plus loans, private loans, and federal work-study.

- Consider part-time work during school years and summers, on or off-campus.

The Student Loan Bill now requires all federal student loans originate directly with the federal government. They are now arranged through each campus's financial aid department. It is your best source of information.

By arranging federal loans directly through each financial aid department, the government eliminated the middleman from the process and estimated it would save $61 billion over 10 years. Part of the savings are directed to Pell grants, increasing them marginally over a 10-year period to about $5,975, including cost of living increases.

Currently, federal student loan interest rates are automatically set by Congress for the academic year beginning on July 1st and ending the following June 30, and are linked to the interest rate on the 10-year Treasury note. Rates are fixed for the life of the loans issued during a given academic year. You can check online for the current rates which are different for undergraduate students, graduate students, and for Direct PLUS Loans.

The legislation guarantees that interest rates will not exceed:

> 8.25% for undergraduates
> 9.50% for graduate students
> 10.50% for Plus loans

Let's take a look at how the math works to help you make some decisions. I like to be conservative so let's assume a relatively high interest rate of 8% on our loan.

> At 8%, each $1,000 borrowed, assuming a 10-year loan, will cost about $12 per month to repay.

> At 8%, a total of $23,000 of undergraduate loans will have a monthly payment of approximately $276.

> Graduates with starting salaries under $30,000 should try to borrow no more than $18,000 over their college career, a $216 monthly payment.

Private loans to students, parents, and other creditworthy parties are also available, but without federal government guarantees. Private lenders such as banks and other financial institutions each have their own terms and conditions, and they may be quite different from those offered by the federal government, so it is worth comparing all of your options.

For example, private loans may have variable interest rates, require a co-signer, may not be tax deductible, and are seldom forgiven. There are some private loans which are currently available at interest rates lower than those offered by federal loans and with extended repayment periods. Although a high credit score is required, the benefits could be substantial. Private loans may be available for consolidation or refinancing.

Federal loans on the other hand have fixed rates, do not usually require a co-signer, may have tax deductible interest, and may qualify for forgiveness programs. They are generally eligible for consolidation, but not refinancing. But be careful because if a federal loan and a private loan are consolidated the student could lose all the benefits of a federal loan such as flexible repayment plans and loan forgiveness.

Because of the many options available and the fact that student and family situations differ, when it comes to student loans you should get help and shop around.

It's Payback time!

There are many options for paying back loans, depending on the type of loan and the balance due. For maximum flexibility, many borrowers choose the longest payback period available. **The longer the term, the lower the monthly payments, but the more you will pay in interest over time.** To show you how it works:

Suppose you borrow $1,000 at 6% and have the option of paying it off monthly over a 6-to-48-month period of time. What will it cost you?

    6 monthly payments of $169.60 = $1,017.60
    12 monthly payments of $88.07 = $1,056.84
    24 monthly payments of $44.32 = $1,063.68
    36 monthly payments of $30.42 = $1,095.12
    48 monthly payments of $23.49 = $1,127.52

If you pay off the loan in **48 months** instead of 12 months you will pay an additional $71 in interest, but you will **save $65 in monthly payments** or $780 over the first 12 months. In the short term, that money might be better used to pay off a high interest credit card or other debts. However, in the longer term you will pay somewhat more in total interest on this loan. There is no right or wrong. It depends on your personal circumstances. This is looking at the total picture and the kind of trade-off you might want to consider. To review the various payment plans, go to: www. studentaid.ed.gov/sa/repay-loans/understand/plans

This concept holds true for student loans too. When it comes to repaying student loans, depending on the type of loan, balance due, your income and choice of career, loan payment periods may be as long as 30 years. For many borrowers, selecting a long payback period makes sense because the lower payments may enable a person to start saving for a down payment on a house, contributing to a retirement plan, or paying off high interest credit card debt. These could be a higher priority than paying off student loans over a shorter time period, even considering the extra interest. However, if you want to pay off your loan faster than required, try paying an extra amount with each payment. Make sure your extra payment is reducing the principal and not going toward interest.

When your "in-school" deferment period ends, you are automatically placed in a standard repayment plan with a ten-year payment period. If you want to be in a federal income- driven repayment plan, **you need to set it up** by contacting your loan servicer.

The federal government offers plans designed to make student loan debt more manageable by reducing the monthly payment amount. According to the Department of Education, "If your outstanding federal student loan debt is higher than your annual income or if it represents a significant portion of your annual income, you may be able repay your federal student loans under an income-driven repayment plan."

The newest forms of student loans are **federal income-driven repayment plans,** which have various requirements and options. These plans, of which there are several, are gaining popularity. In general, the attraction is that the monthly payment is based upon 10%, 15%, or 20% of **disposable income** and the loan may be forgiven after 10, 15, or 25 years, depending on the plan.

The two most popular repayment plans are: (1) Income-Based Repayment Plan ("IBR") and (2) Pay As You Earn Repayment Plan ("PAYE"), which is capped at 10% of your disposable income.

Income-driven federal plans may have the added **benefit of loan forgiveness** after 10 years if you work for the government or a non-profit agency. The goal behind this feature is to incentivize students to pursue careers in teaching, law enforcement, and other public-sector jobs. In this case the forgiven amount is not taxable, while forgiven loan amounts under other plans may be taxed by the IRS as ordinary income, with the tax being due and payable in the year when forgiven.

With income-driven plans you are **required to requalify** with your servicer each year by providing your current financial information. As your disposable income increases, so might your monthly payment. At the same time, you may be able to reduce your monthly payments if your disposable income has decreased or your family size has increased. Failure to requalify annually could result in a confusing array of late payment penalties and additional interest, not to mention the impact it could have on your credit score.

Missing payments can result in damaged credit, withheld tax refunds, or garnished wages. The best way to insure you won't be late is to **authorize automatic payments**. By doing so, many lenders will even reduce the interest rate by a quarter to half a percentage point.

You should check each year with the three major credit reporting agencies to see if overdue payments or other items regarding your student loan have been incorrectly reported by the servicer. As a reminder, you can get a free credit report each year from each of these agencies. Try getting one of the three every four months at: www.annualcreditreport.gov.

Neither the Income-Based Repayment Plan nor the Pay As You Earn Repayment plan applies to **private loans,** whose terms and conditions are constantly changing as private lenders test the marketplace. Financing or refinancing with a private lender may save you interest if you have a high credit score, but it will **cost you** the option of switching later into a federal plan which might include consolidation, forgiveness or restructuring of the loan payments.

Three or four major servicers in the country handle the vast majority of higher education loans. Servicers send out monthly bills, collect payments and counsel borrowers on their options. True or not, servicers have been criticized lately for taking shortcuts, insufficient counseling, and keeping calls short due to an overload of inquiries. The charge is that bad advice and incorrect information have been dispensed, in some cases directing students into programs not in their best interest.

To change plans, contact your servicer. I strongly suggest sending your questions and changes through your servicer's messaging system to provide a valuable paper trail.

Colleges have financial aid departments, many of which offer student loan exit counseling. They will have up to date information and advice.

You should always be thinking of your total debt picture strategically. Student loans are one component of that. Before rushing to pay them off, consider whether the money might be better used by investing in a 401(k) to take advantage of an employer match.

Managing the debt load.

Some suggestions for managing your student debt:

- Pay off loans with the **highest interest rate first.**

- If you plan to make **extra payments** to pay off a loan faster than required, be sure to **notify the lender** that the additional amount is to be used to **reduce the amount of loan**, and not to pay interest or be put toward future payments.

- **Try not to defer interest on student loans**. If possible, at least make interest-only payments while in school. After graduation, deferred interest folds into the principal so borrowers end up paying interest on interest. It can cost you thousands of dollars in finance charges.

- When you start working do not neglect to **save**, especially if your employer will **match** your contributions to a retirement plan.

- Consider getting a **job** that helps pay off your loans or that could qualify you to have your loans forgiven if such jobs exist within your field of interest.

- Take advantage of **tax breaks** that are offered.

- Be sure to update any change of name or address with your servicer.

- Search for **Exit Counseling Guide** for more information at www.studentaid. ed.gov.

Tax deductions for education are available. **Student loan interest** is a tax deductible item found on IRS Form 1040, and you may be able to take the deduction even if you do not itemize. There is a phaseout which begins for a single person at $65,000 AGI and is eliminated at $80,000 AGI. The AGI phaseout is higher for married couples filing jointly.

There is also a line for deducting "tuition and fees". The American Opportunity Tax Credit, the Lifetime Learning Credit, and the Hope Scholarship Credit have been extended, but you will need to get tax advice to see if you qualify. Always go to: www.irs.gov for details and **get professional advice**.

If you find yourself unable to make your payments, there are three options:

- **Forbearance:** Put total payments on hold for a number of months, but **the unpaid interest** is added to the loan principal

- **Interest-only loans:** Defer principal payments until a later date, but **continue to pay the interest**.

- **Increase the borrowing period:** Lower your monthly payments by stretching out the payment period, though you will end up paying more interest.

What happens if your payment is…..

One day late: You will lose any discount for paying on time.

21 to 30 days late: The loan becomes delinquent.

22 to 37 days late: You will be mailed a notice for collection.

60 days late: Your delinquency is reported to the major credit bureaus.

Over 270 days late: The loan goes into default and you will be subject to possible wage garnishment and other serious penalties.

As we go to press, there is no way to know what the government will decide to do with its student loan program in the future. Make sure to check periodically for changes with your financial aid advisor, accountant, and if you have a loan, your lender or servicer. Periodically check the websites of the federal and state departments of education, and the IRS. By all means, be prepared to remain patient when navigating this complex system.

Notes and Updates

CHAPTER 22

PURCHASING OR LEASING A CAR

Let the Buyer Beware

Perhaps the day will come when automobile manufacturers will decide to sell cars in America without forcing their customers to go through the painful process of negotiating with auto dealers and their salespeople. Buyers frequently drive away wondering if they got a fair deal, or were they completely hosed?

Owning and operating cars is one of life's biggest expenses.

When the need arises to make a decision regarding purchasing or leasing a car, there are options. You can keep your old clunker as long as possible, buy a new or used car, or lease a new or used car. Or you might decide to fly, take a bus, rent a car when needed, or use Uber or Lyft. But if you need to own a car, here's where you start.

A decently cared for used vehicle may be your best choice. Today's cars can easily last 100,000 miles, and almost any car can be nursed to 200,000 miles and still be safe. Even a new engine is cheaper than all but the cheapest used cars. Keeping your older vehicle means there are no new car or lease payments. And, insurance, registration and property taxes cost less as cars age.

However, at some point in time the repair bills get to be too much. It is not just tires and brakes, but the electrical system fails, the fuel pump stops, or the transmission wears out. Your lifestyle or job may change, and you may be nervous about driving an unreliable car. Or, maybe you have just gotten tired of having it towed to repair shops.

To begin the **search for a car**, write down the **make, model, and color** of any car you see on the road that appeals to you. **Compare the new car model to a 2 to 3-year old version of the same car.** Sometimes, it may be difficult to tell them apart. Shop alternative nameplates. For example, Camry is similar in many ways to Lexus, and also manufactured by Toyota, but priced much lower. Make the internet your shopping tool of choice. Begin searching the sites of both new and used car dealers in your area; Vehix.com, Autotrader.com, Autoscoop.com,

Edmunds.com, MSN autos, Yahoo autos, Kelly Blue Book, Craig's list, Carfinder, E-bay, and your local newspapers.

Check the **safety records** and compare standard and optional safety equipment such as airbags, antilock brakes, stability control, and traction control. Go online to the National Highway Transport Safety Administration and Insurance Institute for Highway Safety websites.

Check the **warranty, repair records, and consumer satisfaction** at J. D. Power, Consumer Reports, and Alldata. Your last online stop for a used car should be **Carfax.com** where, for a very reasonable price, you can track a specific car by its **vehicle identification number** (VIN). Carfax can tell you if the vehicle was ever reported stolen; declared salvage or a total loss; its odometer readings; the number of owners; and accidents reported. Some dealers have been known to charge $99 to $199 for a Carfax report. Do not let them. It does not cost nearly that much.

Affordability is key. While searching for your car, put together a budget with monthly payments you think you can afford. Include the **down payment, sales tax, insurance, and registration fee.** Consider fuel usage and maintenance costs for tune-ups, brakes, and tires. Go to **www.truecar.com** and search for manufacturer and dealer options and incentives.

For at least three months while you are deciding on a car, set aside the amount you think you can afford each month in a separate car account. This will test your budgeted amount and also help you save money toward a down payment. The bigger the down payment the lower the amount financed and the lower the monthly payment.

Are you going to need financing? If you need financing, first check with banks and credit unions where you have an account. See what kind of a car loan you can get there. Dealers will also want to provide financing since they receive extra fees for originating loans. Their interest rates may be high unless the manufacturer is supporting zero or low interest loans as an incentive to move cars. Now, you have choices. Let the dealer know you already have a loan and see if they can beat it. You might be surprised at the result.

What kinds of terms are best? When financing a car, I **recommend not going longer than 36 months**. The main reason is that if you decide to sell or trade in the car within 36 months you will probably get enough money to repay the remaining loan balance. Selling or trading in the car beyond 36 months could easily force you to come up with additional cash because the automobile has depreciated faster than the reduction of the loan.

Start your engine . . . . It is time to go shopping.

Always test drive the car you are considering buying, new or used. **If used, you should also have the car inspected** before you buy it unless it is **certified** by a qualified dealer or you know the seller and the car's history.

The best deal, buy or lease, is to get the lowest possible price with the most goodies. To do this you must be willing to shop until the price drops. You have heard of "Moore's law?" Well, here is "Fred's law": **The price you pay is inversely related to the amount of the salesperson's time you waste.** The more time you waste, the lower the price tends to go.

Never forget the salesperson is employed by the dealer, represents the dealer, and gets his or her paycheck from the dealer. **The salesperson is not your best friend** fighting with the boss to get you the lowest price and best terms. They play this game every day, and they are good at it. Brace yourself for a well- choreographed effort to maximize the price, which is what they are trying to do.

Keep in mind, you are in the driver's seat. **You have the money. So, you are the boss.** Do not let them shuffle you around between salespeople and the sales manager to confuse you. Try to deal with one person. Do not be misled by "one time" offers, pressuring, or bullying. If you are confronted by these tactics, just get up and leave.

You may find your best buy at a high-volume dealership with a large inventory. Small dealers often buy or trade cars from larger dealers because they cannot finance a big inventory. And you may end up paying a markup between dealers.

What are the best times to buy a car? Most people do not realize there are certain times that are generally better to purchase a car. The first is the last two days of the month. That is because most showroom sales people are paid a commission and have a monthly quota of cars to sell. If they have not yet reached their quota, they have only two days left. Miss your quota for a few months and you might be out of work. The pressure is on. Also, monthly sales over quota usually earn bonuses. This is an added incentive to move more cars at the end of the month.

Other good times are between Christmas and New Year's Day. That is usually a slow period for car sales, people are still in a holiday mood, and it is the last few days to record sales for the month and the year.

Another time is when last year's new models are sitting on the floor after next year's models have started to arrive. Prices on last year's cars start dropping. Check the white label on the driver's side door or door post where it shows the month and year the car was made. The older the car, the longer it has languished on the lot, even new cars. The financial cost of flooring a car for more than 90 days eats into profits. So, this may be a bargaining chip for you as you negotiate a deal to help clear the floor for the highly advertised new models.

Trading-in a car? Be aware that the dealer probably does not want it and would not pay nearly what you already priced it for on the internet. More than likely they will just wholesale it or take it to auction. If you are asked up front if you have a trade in, you might say, "I'm not planning on it" as you turn your head from side to side.

What you want to do is negotiate the best possible price for the new car and then figure out the best way to sell the old car. Once they know you have a trade-in, everything after that becomes a packaged deal. The more they offer for the old car, the less they will discount the new car. You want the best price on both.

Why tell them you are paying cash? This is a mistake even experienced car buyers make. Most people believe they will get a better price if they let the salesperson know they are ready to pay cash. This is not true because **the dealer also wants to sell you financing and insurance for the extra fees and commissions.** That is why they have a separate Finance and Insurance Department (F&I) which is a major profit center. They will also try to sell you high-margin options for just a few more dollars a month.

Let them think you will need financing until you have agreed upon a price. That may get them to come down a little more on price because they feel they can make it up in F&I. When asked early on how I plan to pay for the car, I will say something like, "Do you finance cars?" "Yes." "That's good."

The **MSRP** is the "manufacturer's suggested retail price." I call it the "manufacturer's **shocking** retail price." This is what appears on the **sticker** in the car's window. It' s almost never the price you will need to pay if you purchase that car. Even the salesperson may find a way to offer you a discount off of the MSRP to see if you might believe this is the only or best discount you will get.

You can assume that is not your best deal. It is more like the dealer's starting point.

The **invoice price** is the manufacturer's price to the dealer before various rebates, allowances, discounts, and incentive awards. Touted as the price the dealer paid for the car, the invoice price does not include a typical dealer holdback by the manufacturer of 2% to 3% designed to make sure the dealer makes a profit. On a $20,000 car that would be $400 to $600.

Manufacturers may offer **incentives** by advertising "deals" directly to consumers to sell slow moving inventory or models. These typically run from $500 to $2,500 and can be very effective in stimulating sales. Alternatively, if a car model is "hot" and in demand, the dealer may actually boost the car's selling price based on allocation and a "market adjustment."

Frequently the manufacturer will offer the dealer added incentives of $500 to $4,500 per car, but you would not know that unless the salesperson tells you about it or you see an ad or website that mentions it. Bargain as though the incentive is there and see what happens. You might be surprised at all the discounts that are available.

Try Kelly Blue Book, Edmunds.com, or Consumer Reports to get information on the dealer's net price. My personal experience has been that the best website when shopping for a new car is www.truecar.com. If you're negotiating with a dealer not affiliated with Truecar, bring the truecar.com price quote. You may want to use it as a bargaining tool. Or, if you're a Costco member, you might be surprised to know how many hundreds of thousands of cars their affiliated dealers sell.

The **base price** may not include all the **options** already on the car, or that you may be encouraged to buy. Options can easily add 5% to 10% to the price of the car. Some cars have almost all the available options already installed on the car and included in the purchase price. Sometimes the dealer has already added some options to increase the purchase price and the dealer's profit and wants you to pay for them. It is okay to refuse.

The **prices for options are definitely negotiable**, sometimes by as much as 50%. They too have an MSRP and an invoice price. The dealer may earn a higher commission on options. If you raise your price a little, make it contingent upon the dealer throwing in an option, for example an extended warranty, 2 to 3 years of free maintenance, or a better sound system. Do not let them sell you things like rust proofing, fabric protection, etching, or specialized insurance coverage which you probably do not need and might purchase for a lot less money elsewhere.

You can also use the internet, classified ads, or invoice price for a starting price. One educated guess is there could be a 10% to 12% markup for the dealer on a new car sale based upon the MSRP, or a hoped for 5% to 10% profit based upon the invoice price. But these margins will vary widely subject to the make, model, and market conditions. Consider opening with a **discounted offer that is below your budget** and eliminates the dealer's profit. That will be met with, "You must be kidding" shock and awe. The worst thing they can say is "no." So what? You have to start someplace.

Once you have settled on the new car's price it is time to deal with the trade-in. The salesperson now knows a deal and a commission are close and is likely to be prodded into offering more for the old car if it means risking the new car sale. That is when it is time to look them in the eye and say, "This is a lot more than I ever budgeted for, so I'll have to trade in that car over there after all."

Most of the time, the dealer will still not offer you what you think it's worth. So, if you think you can sell it yourself for much more, tell them you are willing to go ahead and buy the new car at the negotiated price if they agree to **give you 30 days** to bring them the old car, or replace it with a check equal to their trade-in offer. That way, they sell you the new car now, which makes them happy, and if you can sell the old one within 30 days for more than their offer, you will give them a check for the balance, keep the extra money from the sale, and now you are happy too. If you do not sell it, you can still deliver the old car. CarMax may be a good way to sell your car, perhaps as good as a private party.

You are only half-way home.

Do not win the price war in the showroom only to give it back in the **F&I** office where the deal is closed. This is where the dealer can make another good profit. Be prepared:

- **Know your credit score** before entering the showroom if you want them to give you a quote on financing. Some dealers have been known to be less than honest about credit scores and try offering alternative financing meant for subprime buyers at higher rates or with higher commissions.

- If you finance through the dealer the interest rate may increase 0.5% to 1% as a commission to the dealership. Do not let them charge you a fee for **just** handling the paperwork. By the same token, don't let them charge you a fee for financing elsewhere.

- If you finance through the dealer, make certain the loan's interest rate is the same **in writing** as was verbally quoted. Don't let them extend the loan period to lower monthly payments without your approval. Check for any additional financing fees which might have been added to the written contract.

- You may be offered a **choice between a cash rebate and low rate financing.** Do the math! Usually a $1,000 rebate is worth more if the financed amount is $15,000 or less. Consider putting it toward the down payment. At higher-loan levels, low-rate financing is usually best.

- They may try to sell you **credit life insurance,** so they get paid if you die or disability insurance if you cannot work……. all of dubious value.

- You may want to bargain for an **extended warranty** or maintenance contract. Deep discounts up to 50% off the asking price are not unusual.

- Do not let them charge you hundreds of dollars for a **VIN check**.

- Do not let them add anything that was not agreed upon during the negotiation.

- Do not be afraid to get up and **walk out** at any time if you are not comfortable or feel you are not being treated fairly. Just remember; **never give up the keys to your car**. You will need them to get away.

Read and understand all the terms of the contract before you sign. Do not allow anyone to rush you. Get an explanation for everything you do not understand! Do not let them charge you for things you did not request such as prepping or alarms.

Negotiating is a process. You should understand that the dealership and the salesperson are trying to get the highest price they can. They have every right to do so as long as it is done ethically. But you have the money and you can go elsewhere. You have every right to try to purchase the car at the lowest price.

Sometimes it comes down to: "My price… Your terms." Or "Your price… My terms."

By and large, Americans are not good negotiators. We are not used to haggling over price except maybe over a dollar or two at a garage sale. So, many people feel intimidated being put into that kind of situation especially when they're looking to purchase a $20,000 or $40,000 item. Let us go through 10 basic negotiating principles and, as you read them, think about how we have used them to purchase a car based upon what you have just read in this chapter.

1 Know what you want before you start …. and do not be afraid to ask for it.
2 Do your homework so you know what alternatives you have.
3 Know what motivates the person or people on the other side of the table.
4 Do not get caught up in jargon.
5 Do not get talked into something you do not want.
6 Be patient.
7 You do not have to play all your cards at once.
8 Pay attention to details. You may have to live with the outcome for a long time.
9 Terms and conditions are as important as price.
10 You are not done until the deal is signed, sealed, and delivered.

Can I avoid the sales person all together? Many large dealerships have an **internet sales manager** who usually gets a salary plus a bonus based on the number of units sold. You may be able to get your best deal from the internet manager if you know exactly what you want and have done your homework. This approach should enable you to request bids from three or more internet managers. Let them know you're shopping around. If you're a repeat buyer, ask for their "loyalty discount". Get their offers via e-mail. Then take the lowest quote and go back to the others one by one and tell them you will buy the car from them if they can beat that price. The game is over when they will not go lower.

Shopping for a used car. When there is a glut of trade-ins due to 0% financing, rebates and other incentives on new cars, it's an ideal time to shop for a **preowned vehicle**. Do your homework. Start with the manufacturer's franchise dealers in your area. They usually keep only the best used car trade-ins for themselves and wholesale the rest. Many come with **certification**, which means the dealer has inspected and tested the vehicle according to the manufacturer's specifications. A certified vehicle comes with a **warranty** covering at least the major parts for a year or more.

It is not unusual for dealers to **make more money on used cars** than new cars. Part of the equation is the price they paid for the car, and the other part is what they can work out with you. That gives you a lot of room to negotiate.

You do not know what the dealer paid, and every car seems to have been previously owned by a little old lady or is being sold because of a death or divorce, implying there is nothing wrong with the vehicle, only the previous owner. If the car has been listed for more than 2 to 4 weeks, the price has probably been reduced at least once. The longer it sits on the lot the more anxious the seller will be to reduce the price even more.

If you are **buying from an unknown third party**, you need to be careful. Get the VIN and check the car's history at www.carfax.com. Look into whether there is any warranty left. Have the car inspected by a mechanic who works on that make of car and is using a computer to generate information. Use the same negotiating strategy as with a new car, but start at a deep discount based upon the information you gathered searching on the internet.

Leasing a car is like renting it, almost.

People often want to know whether it is better to lease or buy their automobile. Like most things in life, it depends on the situation. In order to make an intelligent informed decision, you need to know exactly what a lease is and how to do some simple math.

The cost of a lease is based upon the amount the vehicle will depreciate in value during the period of the lease, combined with the number of miles driven. In short, what you pay for a lease over the lease period will at least need to cover whatever loss in value the car is expected to have during that time. It is that simple.

Before entering into a lease be familiar with the terminology:

Capitalized cost ("cap" cost) is the price you and the dealer agree upon for the car to be valued at the time of the lease. Just as if you were buying the car, always negotiate the lowest possible capitalized cost first. The lower the cap cost, the lower the monthly payments will be.

Residual value is the predetermined value and purchase price of the car at the end of the lease. It is what the lender who is financing the lease has determined to be the market value of the car when the lease terminates. **The residual value is as important as the capitalized cost of the vehicle.** However, residual values are **not negotiable** when leasing. They are determined by the cache, quality, reliability, and popularity of the car in the marketplace. You can shop for dealers and leases which have the highest residual values and the lowest cap, but the residual value of a particular car set by a lender will be the same to all of its dealers.

Car lease payments are the monthly lease payments and **are** based upon the **difference between the capitalized cost and the residual value.** This is the amount being financed. If you compare two different vehicles with the same capitalized cost, the one with the highest residual value will lease for less money because you are financing less in depreciation. In other words, you will pay less for the one that **loses the least value** during the lease term.

When leasing, you may need to make a **down payment** in addition to the monthly payments you make for the period of the lease, usually two or three years. The higher the down payment, the lower the monthly payment. **Sales tax is included in each monthly payment over the term of the lease.**

At the end of the lease you have the **choice of buying the car at the residual value or returning it**. There may be a small fee for returning the car. Remember, the purchase price was set at the time of the lease, which is a "closed end lease," so now you **either deliver the car or pay the residual price.**

During the term of the lease, **you are responsible for insurance, regular maintenance, and repairs** not covered by a warranty or maintenance contract. You may need to keep records and have the maintenance done at the dealership. Batteries, brakes, wipers, and tires are usually your responsibility.

A major attraction of leasing may be **less cash up front and a lower monthly cost**, in addition to the added flexibility of not having to bother selling the car at the end of the lease. These leasing benefits may not be available in all markets, especially if the dealer or manufacturer is more anxious to sell cars than to lease them. Sometimes a vehicle can be leased for as little as $500 down, plus one month's payment for security, and another month's payment to cover the first month.

Leases include a **mileage allowance**, usually 10,000 to 15,000 miles per year. As you might anticipate, you will pay more for a higher mileage allowance because the car is expected to be driven more and worth less at the end of the lease. If you exceed the selected mileage allowance the charge is normally 10 to 25 cents per mile to be paid at the end of the lease when you return the car. There is **no mileage charge if you purchase the car**. There is no refund if you drive fewer miles than the allowance.

If the car is to be used for **business purposes**, there may be **tax advantages** for leasing rather than purchasing a vehicle. Check with your accountant or the Internal Revenue Service website.

The lease contract must **explicitly** list the capitalized cost of the vehicle, the down payment, registration fees, trade-in allowances or rebates, the interest cost, the monthly payment including taxes, and the residual value of the car at the end of the lease, and all extra charges.

Ultimately, **you are financing the difference between the market value of the car at the time of the lease, and the residual value of the car at the end of the lease term, adjusted for the down payment, a mileage allowance, trade in, and sales tax.**

Re-leasing a car that just came off a lease can be a great way to drive a more expensive car than you would otherwise buy. Someone else has already absorbed the big depreciation, usually over 40% in three years. **The best deal may be to buy or re-lease a car owned and previously leased by the manufacturer with a certified warranty.** Consider buying a bumper-to-bumper warranty (50% discount?) or, better yet, getting it included in the price to close the deal.

Always **read the lease agreement carefully.** Be sure you understand all the charges. Know what every written number means. Make sure they have not added new fees and that the lease **has been approved**, not just applied for.

Before a warranty expires, or before you purchase a used or previously leased car, I always recommend you **have the car inspected by a dealer or other mechanic for defects**, wear and tear, and engine and transmission functions. In today's cars, this usually requires computer diagnostics. Get items repaired while under warranty. I have had two transmissions replaced just before warranty expiration without having any idea that there was a problem.

Negotiating your lease.

- Shop for a lease the same way you would shop for a car. Be prepared for some hard bargaining.

- Negotiate for the car as though you were planning to purchase it. Then, ask about a lease at the price you negotiated.

- The price for the car is your capitalized cost. Add taxes, registration fees, and service contracts to get the gross capitalized cost.

- Subtract any vehicle trade-in value, manufacturer's rebate, and your down payment to get the adjusted capitalized cost which, after subtracting the residual value, is what you are financing.

- A $1,000 difference in the capitalized cost can cut the monthly payment $25 to $30 per month on a 36-month lease ($30 × 36 months = $1,080).

- The monthly payment includes the interest charge. Many dealers will not disclose the actual interest rate being used. If the dealer will tell you only the interest factor, such as 0.0032, multiply this by 24 to get an idea of the interest rate you are being charged (0.0032 × 24 = 7.68%).

- Shop for the best lease you can find. Usually it is when the manufacturer is offering a special deal. Otherwise, you should try to get at least three quotes. Monthly payments may differ $50 to $150/month between leasing companies.

- The less a car depreciates, the lower the relative lease payment because at the end of the lease the car is worth more. This favors luxury and high demand cars.

- Sometimes it is difficult to negotiate the capitalized cost. Lease contracts are always broken down into monthly payments, so it may be easier to negotiate that. For example, take the salesperson's "best lease deal" and tell them your top budgeted monthly payment is $50 less. Ask them to work it out. You really don't care how they get there. That's $1,800 on a 36-month lease. You may get all or part of it or you can still go elsewhere.

A short and sweet reminder.

- Do your homework.

- Line up your credit source/loan before shopping.

- Know your credit score in advance.

- Test drive different cars.

- If possible, go shopping on the last two days of the month when you know what you want to buy. Commissioned sales people may go the extra mile to get a nice commission at the end of the month.

- Be willing to waste hours of sales time so they finally cut the price a little more just to get you out of the showroom.

- Remember, options that improve performance hold their value best. Convenience items such as high-end audio and power gadgets may be worth little once you drive off the lot.

- Warranties, extended warranties, and maintenance contracts are high profit, so dealers will negotiate their price. A 50% discount in price for some options is not unheard of.

- Buying a 2 to 3- year - old pre-owned or preleased certified car may be the best deal if you can live without the new car smell. It has probably depreciated 30% to 40% on average, and still has some warranty left. You can often get a warranty extension for little or nothing through hard bargaining to close a sale. And you can always buy a can of new car smell. Your friends will never know.

- Do not be afraid to get up and walk out of a dealership. Just leave your phone number so, if they change their mind and decide to sell the car to you at your price, they can call you. They just might.

Good luck and drive responsibly!

Notes and Updates

CHAPTER 23

AUTOMOBILE INSURANCE
Steering in the Right Direction

Auto accidents happen nearly 100,000 times a day in the United States. The cost of repairing and replacing cars has increased. Damage done to other types of property in an accident can be costly. Judgments and settlements involving death, disability, and medical expenses, including pain and suffering, have soared. Insurance may be the only thing between you and financial catastrophe.

Insurance is not optional.

Liability coverage is the **most important part of the automobile insurance policy**. If you are at fault, liability coverage protects you from claims resulting from injuries caused to another person or damage to another party's property. It also protects you when another person driving your car, **with your permission**, is at fault and injures or kills another person or damages another party's property. Your liability policy does not cover **your** car, property, or injuries.

Liability coverage also covers the cost of your insurance company defending you in legal actions even if there is no way to determine blame. But if there is an accident for which you are held responsible, financial judgments against you may be awarded for causing death, bodily injury, pain and suffering, lost income, rehabilitation and nursing care, medical and hospital costs, funeral costs, vehicle damage, and property damage.

Liability coverage is **mandatory** in nearly all states and many require proof of insurance.

Auto insurance is governed by state laws, so you need to make certain you are abiding by the laws of the state in which you reside and operate a motor vehicle. Court awards may also vary from state to state.

Each state has its own minimum insurance requirements which tend to be very low. Although there is no standard, a typical mandatory plan might be:

- $20,000 of coverage for bodily injury to one person

- $50,000 of coverage for bodily injury for all people hurt in a single accident

- $25,000 of coverage for property damage

This is commonly expressed as 20/50/25. Obviously, these limits are wholly inadequate, and judgments could easily exceed these amounts. That is why it is imperative that you insure your assets at a much higher level. A more realistic minimum might be 100/300/50. Even that might be wholly inadequate if you have meaningful assets. It's not unusual to see liability limits at or above $1 million.

When a loss occurs, the insurer limits its payments to the amount of insurance you have purchased. Therefore, as your earning power increases and you accumulate more assets over the years, you will need to substantially increase the amount of coverage you have to protect your assets. The cost of excess liability coverage is not that great considering the protection it provides. But if you have a bad driving record, you can expect to be charged more than drivers with clean records. Check with your agent or insurance provider.

As we said before, perhaps the only thing that stands between you and financial ruin is your liability insurance. Your insurance will only cover you up to your policy limits, and **you may be held personally responsible** for losses in excess of that amount.

Make sure you are adequately covered!

No-fault insurance is medical coverage that comes into play when it is **unclear who is to blame**. It is designed to lower the cost of auto insurance by having an accident victim's **minor medical expenses paid by their own insurance company** regardless of who was to blame.

No-fault insurance may also eliminate the costs and delays of legal action. No- fault laws have been adopted by about half of the states. Elements of the law vary greatly but usually require that your insurance company pays you and others covered by your policy for medical bills, lost wages, household help, and funeral expenses up to the policy's limit.

No-fault plans do not cover property damage, which is covered elsewhere. Neither is pain and suffering covered under no-fault. For that you will have to sue or settle with the other party.

Collision coverage pays for the **damage to your car** when the accident was your fault or you are unable to collect from the other party who was at fault. Your insurer may repair your car, then take over your claim and recover from the other party. It is **optional** coverage, usually with a **deductible** of $500 or more, which is meant to eliminate small claims. The insurance company only pays for the loss above the amount of the deductible and up to the value of the car. As you would expect, the higher the deductible, the lower is the cost of the coverage.

The amount of collision coverage recommended, and its cost depends on the car and its value. However, the insurer is obligated to pay you only up to the car's cash value, defined as the cash value before the accident. If the estimated cost of repairs exceeds the cash value, you get the cash value and the insurance company gets the car. For an older car, collision insurance may not be worth the expense.

If you have an accident with a driver without insurance, suing could be pointless.

Medical payment covers medical expenses for **you and your family members** if one or more are in an auto accident or injured by a car while bicycling or walking, regardless of fault. It also covers guests in your car from $1,000 to $10,000 or more. These payments will not duplicate other medical insurance you may have.

Uninsured motorist covers you and your family members who live with you if **hurt by an uninsured driver** while in your car, walking or bicycling or are injured by a hit-and-run driver. Other passengers are also covered while in your car. Despite laws requiring it, there are a lot of people driving without auto insurance, or without enough liability insurance. Uninsured motorist usually covers only **bodily injury**. For it to apply, the **other driver must be at fault**.

Make sure you purchase coverage for both uninsured and underinsured claims.

Comprehensive covers your car against damage from **fire, theft, and forces of nature**, but not from accidents. This insurance usually has a deductible attached; the higher the deductible, the lower the cost. Among the **items covered** are the following:

- Theft of contents, glass breakage, falling objects, animal collisions
- Fire, explosion, windstorm, hail, water, flood, earthquakes
- Malicious mischief, vandalism, rioting

The amount of coverage is usually up to the car's cash value. Premiums may be reduced for installed antitheft systems. For an old car, the expense may not be worth insuring the cash value. Remember to always **take your keys, lock your car, and keep valuable items out of site.**

You Can Keep Your Costs Down.

To reduce the cost of auto insurance, get quotes from at least three carriers, such as AAA, Geico, State Farm, and Allstate. In the past, the cost was based on the type of car, where you lived, age, marital status, and driving record. Now insurers may take into account 30 or more additional factors such as credit history, prior insurance claims, and your credit report information, such as arrests and DUIs. When asking for price quotes **benchmark the same coverage** at each insurance company and compare the premiums.

Be Sure to Ask!

- Some insurers give discounts to college grads, teachers, military personnel, and those who take defensive or senior driving classes.

- Driving less than 35 miles a day or 7,500, 10,000, or 12,000 miles per year may qualify you for a discount.

- If you have an older car, consider not purchasing comprehensive and collision insurance, or increasing the deductibles on comprehensive and collision to reduce costs.

- Insuring all cars and personal lines, such as homeowners and personal liability, with the same insurance company frequently earns a package discount.

- **Good driver status can earn large discounts.** No tickets or accidents for three years could be worth a 20% reduction in your premiums.

In Case of Accident.

In the event of an accident call for assistance from police, fire, and medical aid as necessary. Help injured people as best you can. **Stay at the scene** until police have come and gone.

- **Keep your auto insurance information with the car.** This may be required by state law but you should have it with you in any case. Most keep it in the glove box, but you may find a more secure place.

- Get the **names and badge numbers of the police officers**, and make sure they have your version of what happened for their report. Get the accident report number and get a copy when it is available.

- **Exchange names, addresses, driver's license, and insurance information** with the other driver(s).

- **Do not admit guilt.** Your insurance company will defend you.

- You may want to **take important pictures** at the site with your camera or smart phone for evidence.

- **Contact your insurance company** as soon as possible and supply them with all necessary information.

Automobile rental insurance: Many companies **extend your coverage to rental cars when not used for business**. Check with your insurance company. Let them know where you plan to travel, as coverage may vary or be excluded in certain areas, especially in Canada and Mexico.

If you do not have auto insurance, check with your credit card issuer. It might provide some sort of collision insurance if you use their card to rent the vehicle. However, **credit card auto insurance does not provide liability coverage**. This is potentially a big exposure if another party is killed or injured, or property is destroyed.

Depending on location and company, the cost of insurance on a rental car will vary. There may be a deductible on any type of coverage. Certain types of cars, such as sport utility vehicles, or pricey models, may be excluded. Normally, the cost is about $15 per day for collision coverage and about $12 per day for liability coverage. Make sure the amount of liability coverage is enough to give you reasonable protection.

Many young people and urban dwellers do not own a car. However, if you travel a lot or rent cars frequently, you may be better off **purchasing a no owner collision and liability policy**. This will usually cost $300 or more per year depending on the amount of coverage.

Coverage under auto insurance policies may be limited or excluded altogether in foreign countries. So, before renting a car internationally, check carefully with your credit card issuer and auto insurance provider. You may need to purchase temporary insurance coverage when you rent the car.

Now that you better understand auto insurance, it may be a good time to reread your policy and make sure you have the coverage you really want.

Most importantly, drive responsibly!

Notes and Updates

CHAPTER 24

HEALTH CARE AND INSURANCE

The Good, the Bad, and the Ugly

Get ready for change!

The Health Care Reform Act (also known as "Obamacare" and "The Affordable Care Act") was signed into law by President Obama in March, 2010. Its goal was to provide better healthcare coverage to more people. To do this it had to address a complex and confusing healthcare system facing fiscal, political, judicial, and medical scrutiny. Upon passage it became the target of the opposition party which, as we go to press, has become the majority party. Many states opted out of Obamacare.

The bill, as written, was 2,400 pages long. It addressed areas of health care as diverse as restricting the use of tanning salons to posting nutrition labels at fast food chains. But the heart of the legislation was that every American citizen and legal alien must have health insurance or be fined by the federal government. This part of the bill was declared constitutional by the Supreme Court of the United States in a controversial 5 to 4 decision.

Many parts of the bill have gone into effect. Others continue to be phased in, and still others are being phased out. One thing is certain, **dramatic changes** in medical care are taking place and will continue to **impact the cost and quality of your health care**, and that of your family.

How dramatic are these changes? We are looking at the transition of one-sixth of our total economy. It is estimated that the federal government now pays 40% of all medical care through Medicare and Medicaid. And that number could reach70% in the not-too-distant future as millions of boomers reach age 65. The impact on this nation's budget can no longer be ignored. And the health of its people is at stake.

Medical care and insurance costs continue to skyrocket, seriously impacting individuals, businesses, and the economy. It is estimated, even with Obamacare, nearly 20 million people in America may still have no medical insurance. When they are sick or injured their choice is to go without medical care or to go to an already overwhelmed emergency room, paid for by Medicaid. Of course, this is in addition to the growing number of senior citizens already enrolled in Medicare who are living longer, and consuming more expensive medical services, making it an unsustainable situation.

The financial impact has become so serious that Medicare, insurers, and providers are sharpening their pencils and experimenting with new ways to mitigate the costs. For example, the government and insurers are adjusting their payments to hospitals to reflect such things as readmission rates and patient satisfaction. They do not want patients back in the hospital within 30 days of being released, so hospitals with low numbers of readmission rates and high patient satisfaction are receiving bonus payments, while those with low scores are being penalized. The ultimate goal is to control costs, incentivize quality care, and pay more attention to the customer.

Paying for quality performance, while common practice in business, has not historically been a major concern of our healthcare system. But times have changed. I recently accompanied a close friend to the hospital for outpatient surgery. The doctors and staff could not have been more friendly and caring. Peet's coffee was free. Patient's blankets were preheated. They even paid for my breakfast in the cafeteria while I waited. But, not surprisingly, before being released there was a very long questionnaire to be completed about the service, and pages of medical instructions all signed by the patient to limit liability. After all, medical care is still a business; a very big and sometimes litigious business.

Following the hospital procedure, the staff periodically called my friend at home to make sure medications were taken on time. Considering the circumstances, we both felt good about the personal attention and rated them accordingly. To take it a step further, some hospitals are now marketing their high scores to enhance their reputation in the community.

I have read that in some hospitals doctors are advised not to stand over the patient, but to pull up a chair. Flat screens have replaced the old television tubes. Cable and satellite TV has added channels, including HBO and ESPN. Menus are being upgraded.

Some hospitals are even providing house calls to cut the number and cost of admissions. Besides training caregivers, services include assessing the home as to the risk of falling, monitoring vital signs, monitoring and administering medications, dressing wounds, managing pain, and taking X-rays and electrocardiograms. It is a real effort toward finding a way to meet the expanding consumption of medical services especially by an aging population.

The goal is to provide better quality care more efficiently. Costs must come down and the allocation of medical services needs to be resolved.

Who wants what from whom?

As the process evolves, there are six major groups fighting for their own self-interest. They are health insurers; hospitals; doctors; pharmaceutical companies; government; and politicians seeking election. Sadly, their interests are frequently on a collision course with one another, fiercely competing for the same dollar.

- **Health insurers** historically made money by controlling claims and trying not to insure high-risk individuals. But those days are over because the new healthcare act mandates certain services be provided to all and reduces their ability to cherry pick their customers. They still try to limit services and shift costs to consumers, hospitals, doctors, generic drug providers, and government.

- **Hospitals want higher fees** from consumers, health insurers, and the government, along with lower liability and reduced malpractice insurance costs and awards. Many hospitals overbuilt capacity not foreseeing the upsurge in outpatient surgical, urgent care, and other satellite facilities.

- **Doctors want higher fees** from consumers, insurers, and the government. They also want **less interference** in treating patients, and **lower liability** and malpractice insurance costs. They are very tired of spending huge amounts of money on processing claims.

- Some **pharmaceutical companies want to protect their patents** on high-priced drugs. They also want to preserve their current right to NOT negotiate with the government the price of drugs for Medicare. Other pharmaceutical companies want to produce and sell low cost generic drugs without having to spend money on research and development. Two different business models; both want to maximize profits.

- The **government theoretically wants everyone to have good health care**, but it does not have an unlimited budget or the desire to raise taxes. It already pays for most of Medicare and Medicaid and is facing enormous overall budget deficits.

- For **politicians, it's raising money to get elected**. They consider doctors, hospital organizations, insurance providers, and pharmaceutical companies as potential sources of campaign funds. And voters want good medical care at affordable prices.

Health insurance does not come cheaply.

Health insurance does not come cheaply, and changes are not made easily. A comprehensive individual **healthcare insurance plan for a family of four can easily cost $15,000 to $20,000** a year. And healthcare costs continue to outpace inflation. This is unsustainable and continues to overwhelm the economy. But instead of attempting to solve the problem, the government, "of the people, by the people and for the people" seems to have forgotten the people who need affordable medical care.

What you need to know.

When selecting a medical insurance plan, whether through an employer or on your own, **cost is a key factor, but the quality, access and continuity of care** are also vitally important. Consider the following key elements of coverage:

- **Deductible**: The amount you pay each year before the insurance company makes any payment at all. The higher the deductible, the lower the cost of the policy.

- **Co-payment or co-insurance**: These represent the share of the bill that you pay after you have met your deductible, with insurance paying the rest up to the policy's limits. Co-payments in the range of $5.00 to $40.00 are paid at the time you see the doctor or fill a prescription. Co-insurance is the percentage amount, usually 20% to 30%, which you pay under major medical insurance after the deductible is met. Usually, the higher the co- payment or the co-insurance percentage, the lower the premium or policy cost.

- **Stipulated maximum (or "cap")**: No matter how high the bills, you pay **no more out-of-pocket** than the stipulated maximum amount **in any one year**. In effect, this is a cap on your annual cost for eligible medical services.

- **High Deductible Health Plan** ("HDHP"): A high deductible health plan has a higher annual deductible than typical health plans. In 2018, to qualify as an HDHP, the **minimum deductible** is $1,350 for singles and $2,700 for family coverage; and the **maximum deductible** is $6,550 for singles and $13,100 for families. These limits tend to adjust annually based on the cost of living, usually at the rate of about $50 to $100 per year.

In addition to the cost of the premium, among the most important things to understand when selecting and purchasing your insurance are the following:

> What are the eligible medical services provided under the plan?
> What is required in terms of co-payments and co-insurance?

What is the deductible?

What is the stipulated maximum?

How does the policy treat prescriptions?

Is the network of providers broad enough to meet my needs?

If your health insurance is through your employer and you **leave your job** or no longer qualify for insurance, you **may have to pay substantially more** for individual health insurance. **COBRA**, which stands for Consolidated Omnibus Budget Reconciliation Act of 1985, provides for the availability of medical insurance under certain circumstances after leaving an employer by allowing you to **continue to participate in the employer's group plan** for up to 18 months. However, the cost of continuing insurance under **COBRA** may substantially increase since the employer's contribution ceases upon termination. With the advent of the Health Care Reform Act, **COBRA** is used mainly as a bridge between the former employer's plan and a new employer's plan or coverage purchased through the Health Insurance Marketplace at www.healthcare.gov.

If you do have coverage through your employment, contributions to health care are tax deductible to your employer, but not taxed as income to you. Unfortunately, if you have to buy your own policy, the cost of your individual health insurance may not be tax deductible to you, unless you are self-employed.

Understanding the industry basics.

There are two major types of healthcare insurance providers, **Health Maintenance Organizations** (HMO) and **Preferred Provider Organizations** (PPO). These are very different business models.

HMOs are structured as **nonprofit organizations.** With that come tax benefits from the Internal Revenue Service (IRS), but also certain obligations. Members, the insured, pay a flat **monthly fee** to the HMO for coverage, **regardless of usage**, with little or no deductible or co-payment at the time of service. But if a member goes to a provider outside the plan they may have to pay all or a large part of the bill. Both individual and group plans are available. Kaiser Permanente is one of the best known HMOs in the country. As an HMO it owns and operates some of its own medical facilities where members go for treatment

At an HMO, **doctors are paid a salary** no matter how many patients they see or services they provide. You will usually get to pick your primary care physician from those at the HMO, but if you have been on another plan, you may have to give up your previous doctor and favorite hospital. **Coverage outside of the geographical area may be limited** or nonexistent. Check coverage carefully if you do a lot of traveling.

255

HMOs were among the first to encourage periodic checkups and other preventative measures. Because they are not paid for each individual service, the **goal of an HMO is to keep costs low by keeping members healthy and requiring fewer treatments and procedures.** They learned that preventing a problem is far cheaper than treating it. In fact, the data is so compelling that the Health Care Reform Act requires all medical care providers, whether HMO or PPO, include annual checkups and other select preventive services for free.

Unlike an HMO**, PPOs** allow you to **choose from a group of providers who have their own contracts with your insurance company** to provide services at a predetermined price. The **medical provider must accept these amounts as full payment**, which is usually significantly discounted from what you or I could get on our own.

With a PPO you do **pay some amount for care when it is received**. Co-pays, co-insurance, and deductibles are part of the plan and help to determine the monthly premium. However, the most important part of the plan may be the **large discount afforded to you by the contracts** between the insurer and the medical providers. Both individual and group plans are available.

With a PPO there is **more flexibility** in selecting your doctor, but make sure your preferred doctor, hospital, out-patient surgical and emergency centers are covered by your insurer. There is generally some flexibility when it comes to seeing doctors outside the plan, though you may have to pay a larger co-payment or co-insurance percentage to do so. Some plans may require you to select a primary care physician who then can refer you to various specialists, though many now allow you to self-refer.

Health Savings Accounts (HSA) and **Flexible Savings Accounts** (FSA) are plans that allow you set aside pretax dollars to pay out-of-pocket medical expenses, essentially making many medical expenses **tax deductible**. These include co-payments, co-insurance, deductibles, and many uninsured services, but exclude medical insurance premiums.

HSAs are tax-sheltered accounts (like an IRA) for medical bills. Plans may be set up through your employer or purchased individually with a qualified trustee such as a bank, investment firm, insurance company or Healthcare Exchange Plan. **They must be used in conjunction with high deductible health plans,** and are available in most states.

Your contribution to your HSA is **tax deductible** to you and there is no FICA or Medicare tax on your contribution. Your employer may also contribute to your HSA. The money in the account is used to **pay qualified out-of-pocket medical expenses,** those not covered by insurance. Thus, you are paying for qualified medical expenses with tax free dollars.

In 2018, participants may tax deduct contributions to an HSA of up to $3,450 for an individual and up to $6,900 for a family. These limits tend to rise annually at about $50 to $100 a year. You can contribute more money to your HSA than is needed to cover your deductible since it may also be used to cover other uninsured out-of-pocket medical expenses such as vision or dental care.

Any **money in an HSA you do not use stays in the account, can be invested, and can grow tax-sheltered,** like an IRA. Monies in the account are usually invested in fixed rate assets, ETFs, REITs, or mutual funds. Once in a lifetime you can roll over money from an IRA to an HSA up to the annual maximum, tax free for medical expenses. This can turn into a cash stash for future medical expenses but remember that there can be market risk when invested.

Many employers are now offering a combined HSA and high deductible health plan, along with wellness programs and prescription drug plans, all in an effort to control the rising cost of healthcare.

If you leave your employer, you can take your HSA and transfer it to a new administrator without losing any tax benefits. The new plan can continue, but you cannot make additional contributions without a HDHP.

If you are married when you die, money in the account can pass on to your spouse tax free to be used for medical care. Otherwise, any balance would go to your beneficiary and be taxed.

For more information, see www.ustreas.gov and review "Health Savings Accounts."

FSAs are similar to HSAs, but are an **employer-only sponsored** plan. Money is deducted from your paycheck on a **pretax basis to pay for out-of-pocket health care expenses.** Contributions are not subject to federal income taxes, Social Security or Medicare taxes, or most state taxes.

Funds in the account can be used to pay for co-payments, co-insurance, deductibles, and other qualified medical expenses that are not covered by insurance. Examples of acceptable expenses are dental, vision, and prescription drug expenses, but not toiletries or vitamins.

At the beginning of the year, **you need to estimate the amount you want to contribute into the plan, up to a maximum in 2018 of $2,650**. The money is deducted monthly from your paycheck. However, be aware that **money not spent by the end of the year is forfeited** (use-it-or-lose-it) unless your employer offers one of two options, but not both:

- The time period is extended by the employer, up to March 15th of the following year, or

- The employer may allow you to carry over up to $500 per year to use in the following year.

Words to the Wise.

Check your medical insurance to make certain all the medical providers who treat you are covered by your insurance. Those who are not covered or only partially covered are considered "out-of-network" and can bill whatever they want.... tens to hundreds of thousands of dollars.

Know which hospitals, clinics, labs, and emergency centers in your area are covered under your policy. And, make sure you know whether the doctors and staff who work there are covered employees or independent contractors that bill separately. Make sure someone knows where to take you in the event of an emergency.

Watch your medical charges very, very carefully. Over 70% of hospital bills are estimated to have gross overcharges. Examples I have seen include $90 for a 70-cent intravenous item; $18 for a 5-cent pill; and $129 for a mucus recovery system (Kleenex).

Bring or purchase your own prescriptions when possible. Prescriptions at hospitals are usually very expensive.

Never pay your bill before leaving the hospital, even if you are told it is required. You will lose all your leverage to question charges at a later date. Always get itemized bills, as required by law, and check them carefully. Call the billing department for answers and explanations to your billing questions.

If you are faced with high medical bills, there are some steps you can take to get them reduced or to develop a realistic payment schedule. First, make sure the bills are correct before paying anything. Then, build your case. If a claim is denied by an insurance carrier, you may appeal the decision. Send a letter from your doctor and copies of other records explaining why the procedure was necessary.

You may prefer to consult with a medical billing specialist at www.claims.org, some of whom charge an hourly fee, while others charge a percentage of the amount they recover. You may also get help from your state insurance department. Some have ombudsmen to intercede for you or explain how to contest claims or file an appeal. Negotiate to reduce the bill and set up a payment schedule, if necessary.

Never go naked (on health insurance)!

Always make sure you have medical coverage. The key ingredient is the contract between your insurer and your medical provider which limits the charges for medical services provided. Once again, it can save you tens or hundreds of thousands in medical expenses in the event of a serious illness or injury. Here's a perfect example.

Not long ago, I agreed to go through a long overdue non-life threating surgical procedure. I signed all the papers and made sure everyone treating me was covered by my insurance. Years ago, this would have required a hospital stay. But now it's performed at an out-patient surgical clinic. I arrived at 8:30am and walked to my car at 12:30pm, four hours later. But I almost died.... when I got the bill for $49,000. My insurance provider paid $5,700 and I paid $46. That's it!! All done. Had I not had health insurance, they could have come after me for the entire $49,000. Or they could have billed me $75,000. What recourse would I have?

At a minimum, make sure you always have medical insurance to **cover major expenses**. If you are single and in good health, you might look for a low-cost, high-deductible plan covering major medical procedures and expenses. If you have small children, look for a plan with low or no co-payments, assuming frequent visits.

If you lose your job and thus your health insurance, purchase your own policy for coverage until you are covered by your new employer. Contact the insurance companies directly and research your state healthcare exchange for alternatives. Consider a high deductible low monthly cost policy with either a PPO or an HMO.

The Health Care Reform Act

Currently, all American citizens and legal immigrants must have medical insurance. Along with annual enrollment periods there are special enrollment periods for college graduates, those getting married or divorced, giving birth, adopting a child, moving to a new area, and aging off a parent's plan. Those who do not comply with the mandate are subject to fines, although it's not clear how or if they will be collected in the future.

This law is just the start of dealing with the inefficiencies and soaring costs of a massive broken healthcare system that impacts every life in America, from the doctor's office to the hospital; from the paycheck to the tax return; from political campaigns to the Oval Office. Furthermore, years from now refinements to the healthcare system will still be going on, just as the Social Security program of 1935 has undergone many changes over the years, including major ones like the addition of Medicare.

The Health Care Reform Act has expanded medical coverage to millions of people. Low-income households are eligible for a subsidy to help them purchase insurance. Very low-income people are exempt and are covered by Medicaid

As part of the current law, many important protections have been included. Among them are the following:

- **It is mandated that all US citizens and legal residents buy medical insurance.**

- Insurers may not cancel a policy because an insured person gets sick.

- **Insurers are prohibited from denying or excluding coverage to anyone, including children, with pre-existing conditions**. If someone loses their job and their employer-based insurance, they cannot be denied new medical insurance coverage, or charged higher rates, due to pre- existing conditions.

- Insurers may not impose **annual** or **lifetime limits on coverage.**

- Parents can keep **children up to age 26** covered on their policy.

- Consumers have access to an **appeals process** to appeal decisions by their health insurance plan.

- The law places **strict limits on how much a premium can vary** among people taking out the same coverage. Premium differences due to age can be considered reasonable. Insurers cannot charge more for women than men.

- **Free preventive care services** not subject to a deductible or co-payment include annual physical exams, vaccinations, screening for high blood pressure, diabetes, human immunodeficiency virus (HIV), cholesterol, obesity, depression, colorectal cancer, and the following:

  > **Men**: Screening for abdominal aortic aneurysm.
  > **Women**: Screening for breast and cervical cancer, sexually transmitted diseases (STDs), urinary tract infections, and domestic violence.
  > **Children**: Screening for autism, hearing, vision, lead poisoning, sickle cell, and developmental issues.

- Under the Health Care Reform Act, the **minimum mandated coverage** established by the government must include emergency services, maternity and newborn care, mental health and drug abuse treatments, rehabilitation, chronic disease management, and pediatric services.

- Employers must **disclose the value of health benefits on worker's W-2 forms**. The amount is not taxable to the employee. The purpose is to let employees know how much their employer is paying on their behalf for medical coverage.

- Funds from HSAs and FSAs may not be used for over-the-counter medications unless they are prescribed by a physician. The **penalty** for nonqualified distributions from HSAs is doubled to 20%.

- The **Medicaid** federal-state insurance program covering low-income people is expanded.

- Payments to **primary care physicians** under Medicaid are to be increased.

- **Abortion coverage** is a very sensitive and controversial issue, especially when it involves state or federal funds. To determine if abortion is covered by your employer's policy or a state exchange, you will need to **check with the provider**. Individual states have approached this issue in many different ways. Exceptions to the use of federal funds are currently extended to rape, incest, and danger to the life of the mother.

State Exchanges

State-based exchanges are purchasing pools of health insurance. Under the law, each state is required to establish an exchange and expand Medicaid. The purpose of the exchanges is to enable small businesses, the self-employed and the uninsured to purchase insurance similar in purchasing power to large businesses.

These exchanges can be accessed through **websites** that will guide users to a variety of insurance plans of varying price and coverage. They will also help participants determine if they qualify for subsidies or Medicaid. Any federal subsidy comes from the IRS to each plan each month.

Your premium, which is your cost, is primarily based on your age, medical costs in your area, the number of dependents being insured, and the coverage provided. Your premium will change when your group gets an increase. The insurer cannot change your premium individually.

If a state does not establish an exchange or expand Medicaid, the federal government will step in and create a single statewide exchange. At this time, about two-thirds of the states have **opted not to form an exchange** and thus accept the risk of losing control over the healthcare of their residents and voters.

Those working for larger employers will probably not see any great changes in their plan coverage.

Health Care Reform Act Tax Reporting

Each year when you file your tax return and have had medical insurance all year for yourself and your dependents, all you need to do is to check a box on your 1040 or 1040 EZ form if you were included in these groups: employer-provided insurance, individually owned policies, policies from state or federal exchanges, or if you were covered by Medicare, Medicaid, Tricare, or the Veteran's Administration.

Exchanges using Form 1095-A, and employers using Form 1095-C will provide these forms to the insured and the IRS as evidence of compliance to be attached to their returns as is now done with W-2 forms.

Generally, subsidies are available for coverage purchased through an exchange by taxpayers with household incomes between 100% and 400% of the federal poverty level. Those who are eligible for a subsidy cannot use the 1040 EZ form but will need to file a 1040 Tax Return with Form 8962 attached.

Those who do not have health insurance may continue to be fined unless the current law is changed, or they have an approved exemption, which needs to be filed on Form 8965 and attached to their 1040 Tax Return.

It can be complicated if you have to do more than check a box. If you are uncertain I highly recommend you get help from a qualified tax preparer.

We are all paying for the Health Care Reform Act.

Individuals

To pay for the Health Care Reform Act, the **Medicare payroll tax has been expanded to include a new 3.8% tax on all unearned income for those individuals making more than $200,000,** or married couples making more than $250,000. Unearned income includes dividends, interest, capital gains, royalties, and passive income from real estate, but excludes tax-free interest and distributions from IRA, 401(k) and other qualified retirement plans.

The 3.8% Medicare surtax will also apply to profits from the sale of primary residences in excess of $250,000 (single) or $500,000 (married), but only to the extent AGI exceeds $200,000 (single) or $250,000 (married).

The same high earners will pay a Medicare Part A tax of 2.35% (up from 1.45%) on earned income over the same income thresholds. This incremental 0.9% Medicare surtax is **paid entirely by the employee**.

Employers

Employers with 50 or more employees must provide health insurance or be subject to a nondeductible fine. Employers with less than 50 employees are exempt from the plan, but tax credits will be available for small businesses that do provide coverage.

Hospitals

Hospitals are servicing **more insured patients**, which helps them collect more of their bills. In return, they agreed to contribute about $155 billion over 10 years to the new plan by accepting lower payments under Medicare. The new law does not allow illegal immigrants to buy insurance on the insurance exchanges, so they will continue to receive emergency care.

Doctors

The United States faces a shortage of 100,000 doctors over the next 15 years even taking into account that 27,000 new doctors are trained each year. With the addition of millions newly insured people under the Health Care Reform Act, and 78 million seniors heading toward retirement age and living longer, there will be a **big increase in the patient loads** of many doctors, exacerbating the existing shortage. Doctors are learning how to leverage their time with increased use of physician assistants, nurse practitioners, and other professionals. In return, the bill does raise reimbursement rates for Medicaid to encourage primary care physicians to accept Medicaid patients.

Drug and Medical Device Companies

On the positive side for the drug companies, many more people are now insured for prescription drugs. Drug and biotech companies are absorbing some discounts to the Medicare Part D plan.

Government

The government **will provide subsidies to help purchase insurance** for households earning up to four times the federal poverty level, which is about $46,000 for a single person and $95,000 for a family of 4. These numbers are adjusted annually for inflation.

For additional and updated information on The Health Care Reform Act, please visit www.healthcare.gov.

Notes and Updates

CHAPTER 25

DISABILITY INSURANCE

They've Got Your Back

Disability Insurance is a form of income replacement, which pays an insured person an income when that person is unable to work because of an accident or illness. At age 40, the average worker faces only a 14% chance of dying before age 65, but a 21% chance of being disabled for 90 days or more. Disability insurance provides a safety net should this occur. Broadly defined, disability is a mental or physical injury or illness that prevents one from performing their regular or customary work. **Disability insurance does not cover you if you are not employed.**

What will happen to me if I get sick or hurt and can't work?

In most states, employers provide some type of sick leave. They may also have a short-term plan or informal policy to cover a disability that lasts 30 to 90 days. But many employers are not able to carry even a long-time employee on the payroll for an extended period. This is especially true of small businesses.

Larger employers may provide long-term disability coverage with benefits of up to 70% of salary lasting for two years, five years, to age 65, or in some cases extended for life. The longer the pay period, the higher the cost.

If your employer has no disability plan or only a minimal plan or you are self-employed, you may want to purchase your own individual policy or supplemental coverage should you become disabled on or off the job.

The **definition of disability is not standardized**, but it's **critical** when searching for the best terms of coverage and cost. This applies to both employer-paid policies and individually owned policies.

- Some policies define disability as the **inability to do your job or a similar job**. This is the most liberal definition you will likely find.

- Some policies define disability as the **inability to do any job for which you may be qualified**. This may be adequate for your needs, especially if your

267

job requires specialized training or strength, but it is a narrower definition, making it harder to qualify to collect, because it is not limited to just your job.

- Some policies require permanent or total disability which is the **inability to do any job.** This is a very strict and narrow definition and may not enable you to collect a benefit unless you are severely disabled.

Regardless of the definition, if the coverage is through your employer and you leave your job, you lose your insurance**.**

Benefits received from employer paid policies are **subject to ordinary income tax**. If you pay the premium, the disability **benefits are not taxed**.

An **Individual Disability Income Insurance Policy** provides you income in the event you are disabled. Because it provides income replacement, **you must be employed to receive benefits**. The insurer would not replace all your income because they want you to be incentivized to go back to work. The policy usually replaces 50% to 70% of your income up to a stated maximum.

Individual policies may be noncancelable or guaranteed renewable.

- A **noncancelable** policy means you have the right to renew the policy without an increase in premium.

- A **guaranteed renewable** policy means you have the right to renew, but the rate may go up with others in your classification; for example, your age group or your occupation, but not just for you individually.

There are usually two types of individual disability policies. **Short-term** policies usually have a waiting period of 0 to 14 days before benefits begin, with a maximum benefit period of no longer than two years. **Long-term** policies usually have a waiting period of several weeks or months before benefits begin, with a maximum benefit period of several years, to age 65, or lifetime. You may want to integrate your policy and its waiting period with your employer's plan or your state plan, if applicable, to avoid duplication of coverage.

In summary, when evaluating a disability insurance policy, these are key terms and conditions to consider:

- **The definition of disability is critical.** Pay attention to how narrowly defined it is as this will impact your ability to be paid under the policy.

The most frequently used definition is either you cannot perform your job or any job for which you are suited.

- The **waiting period** refers to the period you will wait before collecting under the plan. The longer the waiting period, the lower the cost of the policy.

- The **benefit period** refers to how long the policy will continue to pay. The longer the benefit period, the higher the cost of the policy.

- A **cost of living increase** in benefits may be available to keep up with inflation. This could be substantial over the years.

Premiums are based on age, sex, occupation, health and the amount of income you are protecting. As you would expect, longer waiting periods, a lower percentage of income replacement, and shorter benefit periods will also reduce your cost.

Always seek assistance from qualified agents or brokers representing high quality insurance companies. They are there to help you work through the maze of alternatives.

Social Security also has a disability benefit for **workers of any age whose disability is expected to last at least 12 months. Its definition of disability is that no gainful employment can be performed** to be eligible for benefits.

Applications for coverage under Social Security are handled by state governments through the judicial system. Since there are no uniform standards applied to the states by which to judge a disability, some states approve far more applications than other states. Recently Puerto Rico was approving well over 60% of its applications, while Massachusetts was approving less than 10%. Stories abound about lawyers who specialize in these types of claims, and people who moved to Puerto Rico for a better chance at a favorable outcome.

Perhaps due to the Great Recession, many more people have been applying for disability benefits from Social Security. The most popular reasons are bad back and depression. Masses of claims and appeals are waiting for processing, especially in locations where the approval rate is high.

Workman's Compensation Insurance is insurance **paid entirely by the employer,** and provides coverage, including disability, if an **injury or illness is job-related**. The rules and benefits vary state by state, so you will need to check the plan offered in your state.

The initial premium for workman's comp is based primarily on your job description and is quoted as a percentage of payroll for that job title. Logically, the cost of insuring an office worker is low compared to that of a roofer even though they may work for the same company. Each business is **experience rated**, which means that employers with a good safety record are eligible for reduced rates or refunds. That is a big reason why many employers have required safety programs.

The system of workman's compensation insurance is designed to **pay a worker rather than having the worker sue his or her employer.** Benefits usually include the cost of medical care and payment of a worker's pay up to a maximum number of weeks or months. In some cases where there is permanent incapacity or death there may be a lump sum settlement.

Factors that influence payment include whether or not the accident or illness was work related, whether it is temporary or permanent, and whether it is total or partial. Some claims are complicated and may involve drugs, alcohol, malingering, or fraud. In some cases, workers and employers may retain doctors and lawyers to help resolve a claim.

Workman's compensation may be written by state agencies as well as private insurance companies. Since workman's compensation is mandatory, the state needs to be there to provide the insurance if private companies won't, or if they are not competitive in price.

State disability insurance: A few states have their own disability program for workers who suffer a loss of wages when they are unable to work due to a **nonwork related illness or injury**. For example, this might be a case of falling off a ladder while cleaning out the gutters at home, or a knee replacement. Currently, only five states provide this kind of coverage. They are California, Hawaii, New York, New Jersey, and Rhode Island.

To give an example of how this works, California has a **mandatory state disability plan** for nonwork-related disabilities, defined as any mental or physical illness or injury which prevents you from performing your regular or customary work. The plan is **paid entirely by the employee** through payroll deductions. The current cost is 1% of payroll up to about $100,000 of annual earned income. Benefits are based upon quarterly wages with a maximum weekly benefit of $840 if you earn about $20,000 a quarter. It has a waiting period of seven days before benefits can begin and a benefit period of up to a maximum of 52 weeks.

Auto insurance in some instances may provide coverage if a disability results from an auto accident, depending on the policy and who was to blame.

The **Department of Veterans Affairs** provides coverage for members of the armed forces who suffer from military-related disabilities.

Stay safe!

Notes and Updates

CHAPTER 26

LIFE INSURANCE

Your Life May Be Worth More Than You Think

Buying life insurance can be one of the most important decisions you may ever make. But it can be confusing when trying to determine the timing, amount, and type of insurance you need. Nearly one-third of households have no life insurance whatsoever, neither private nor from their employer. In many instances, lost jobs, tight budgets, and expense cuts by employers have been the influencing factor.

Whether or not?

When considering life insurance, the first decision is whether you need it. The answer depends on what you are insuring. If you are single and no one financially depends on you for support, you probably don't need life insurance except possibly to cover your own final medical bills and funeral expenses. Married or cohabitating couples with no children may need little or no life insurance, especially if both are working, though they might want to buy some modest amount to help the survivor with mortgage or rent payments, credit card debts, medical expenses, and funeral costs.

On the other hand, a family with young children in need of nurturing and education is the classic "high need," high insurance situation. If the whole family is dependent on one breadwinner for support, and that breadwinner dies, there could be serious financial consequences for the nonworking spouse and children. Sized properly, life insurance can replace that income in whole or in part and help with the costs of raising children, making continuing rent or mortgage payments, and paying for education, medical bills, and health care. Alternatively, should the nonworking spouse die, the survivor will still have income from continuing employment but may also need some additional help from insurance proceeds. Once children are grown and gone, and if you have enough retirement income, you may not need as much life insurance as you once did. Other examples of high-need situations might be providing support for elderly parents, or a special needs person who might be physically or mentally disabled and dependent on outside support.

How much?

How much life insurance you need depends on a number of factors. Consider these:

- **Immediate needs** might include mortgage payments, credit card and other debts and loans, children's educational costs, medical bills, funeral expenses, and estate taxes.

- **Future needs** might include family living expenses, inflation, and the survivor's ability to work and earn.

- **Sources of funds** may include Social Security survivor's benefits, employer paid benefits, and other death benefits. Many employers provide some amount of life insurance for their employees.

- **Other sources** also may include interest income, dividends, real estate, and assets that can be sold.

In determining your needs, I recommend you seek the advice of a qualified life insurance agent or estate planner.

What type?

Term insurance is strictly "death insurance," with rates actuarially calculated. The only time you or your family collect under the policy is if the insured person dies while the policy is in force, subject to any exclusion for suicide. For most people, term insurance is probably the best choice.

Premiums for term insurance are based upon **age** (by year or age bracket), **health, gender, lifestyle** (smoking), **and occupation.** The younger you are when you first purchase the insurance, the lower the cost, as your odds of dying increase with age. The insurance company will evaluate your health before taking you on as a client and may increase the premium due to certain pre-existing health conditions. However, except for your medical condition at the time of purchase, there are no ongoing health requirements to keep the policy in force. Some term life policies guarantee renewal and will establish a level premium for the term of the policy.

Dollar for dollar, term insurance gives you the **most protection for your money.** When purchasing term insurance, it is easy to compare the premiums of different companies. You are insuring the same event….. death.

Whole life insurance combines the cost of death or term insurance with a savings component called the **cash value**, an amount which is accumulated by you, managed and invested by the insurer. The **cash value builds up tax-free and compounds in your account.** Sometimes the insurer will even guarantee a minimum rate of return on the cash.

The conditions for issuing a whole life policy are essentially the same as those for term insurance, including the upfront health evaluation. But the premium per thousand dollars of **insurance is much higher due to the forced saving component and higher commissions.** Once issued, the premium stays the same throughout the period of the policy, which may be for the rest of your life.

With whole life insurance, you can **borrow your policy's accumulated cash value** from the savings component, but in some instances, you made need to pay interest. Any outstanding loans at the time of death will be deducted from the proceeds of the policy. You can also quit the policy after the first several years and get back your accumulated cash value, less any outstanding loans against the policy.

When purchasing a whole life policy, comparisons are more difficult because of varying death rate assumptions, commissions, interest on cash value, and underwriting standards primarily related to health.

Many consumers choose to buy term insurance instead of a whole life policy, and put the difference in cost in an individual retirement account (IRA), 401(k), closed end mutual fund, exchange-traded fund (ETF), real estate, or other investment. This gives them the ability to manage the investments themselves.

Beyond the basics.

One possible way to **keep the proceeds of an insurance policy out of your estate, thus avoiding estate taxes,** is to name someone else, such as your child, as the owner and beneficiary of the policy, and gift them the money to pay the premiums. Upon your death, the proceeds will not go to your estate, but directly to the named beneficiary, in this case your child, thus skipping a generation of potential taxation. Discuss this approach with your insurance agent.

According to the Internal Revenue Service (IRS), "Generally, if you receive the proceeds under a life insurance contract as a beneficiary due to the death of the insured person, the benefits are not includable in gross income and do not have to be reported. Any interest you receive is taxable and you should report it just like any other interest received."

Many small businesses use life insurance to fund **"buy–sell" agreement**s to deal with the death of an owner, a partner, or an executive of a company when he or she dies. Proceeds from the policy are used to purchase from the beneficiary of the deceased their inherited interest or shares in the business.

Businesses also use life insurance, sometimes called **"key man insurance,"** to reimburse the company for the cost of having to hire and train a new person to replace a deceased employee, presumably a key member of the management group.

Notes and Updates

CHAPTER 27

STARTING A SUCCESSFUL BUSINESS

Ask Yourself This . . . .

In our culture, we admire risk takers. When our businesses do not succeed, we get up and try again. We live in a culture where an unsuccessful business is not considered a "failure," but an "exceptional learning experience." In some cases, it is a "badge of honor."

Since many talented people are interested in starting a business, and many financially independent people are self-employed, it makes sense to think about what it takes to create a successful business. Everything starts with an idea and, the good news is:

Ideas are free.

Business is solving problems. One of these days, perhaps sooner than you think, you may have an idea for a business that excites you. Perhaps, it's a problem you can relate to and solve. What is the next step? Is this something you should be serious about? Would you ever think of going out on your own? What are the risks you would be assuming? Is doing nothing even a bigger risk?

For purposes of this discussion we use the term "business" as generic and apply it to all forms of enterprise, including a proprietorship, partnership, corporation, nonprofit organization, or government agency. Whether you start your own business, work in a large or small company, or find yourself in a nonprofit organization, there are certain characteristics that lead to success.

Every enterprise needs funds to operate. Sources may be capital you put up as a founder, money raised from friends and family, debt or capital from other investors or lenders, sales of products or services, or grants and donations. Regardless, the money has to come from somewhere. Likewise, every enterprise, whether public, private, or nonprofit, has expenses to meet, and if it is unable to meet those expenses over an extended period of time, it will eventually cease to exist.

The distinction between a for-profit enterprise and a nonprofit enterprise is a designation made primarily by taxing authorities. It may have little bearing on how the organization operates on a day-to-day or job-to-job basis. For example, in the healthcare industry there are hospitals that are for-profit and hospitals that are nonprofit. In the operating room, they appear quite similar. The American Association of Retired People, United Steel Workers, Salvation Army, and the University of California happen to be organized as nonprofits. In return for the tax benefits, they have other social responsibilities.

To help you along the way, I have put together a checklist of questions I have used with my clients over the years to help them better understand their business; where they are going; and what needs to be done. As you think about your idea for a business, see how you would respond to some of these questions:

- **What is the business?** For example, is McDonalds' goal to sell the greatest burgers or provide a safe and convenient place to eat and have fun?

- **Can you explain your idea to a spouse or friend in 60 seconds?** What is your elevator pitch?

- **Who is the customer?** Is Samsung's customer Best Buy or the end user?

- **Who will be your customer?**

- **What will create value for the customer?** What does the customer want or need, and what is a fair price?

- **How big is the market for the product or service?** How many people or businesses have this problem or will need and be willing to pay for this service or product?

- **Does demand for this product already exist?** If it is a new product or service do you have to create demand? How will you do that?

- **How much do you think it would cost to create, deliver, and support this product or service?** Cost and pricing are critical, along with aftermarket support.

- **What are the innovations?** Does it differ enough from what's available now in the marketplace?

- **Where and how will someone expect to purchase this product or service?** At a wholesaler, distributor, retailer, shopping mall, medical center, online, Wal-Mart, Amazon?

- **Who is the competition?** What are they doing and what can you do better?

- **What will distinguish you from the competition?** Is it price, function, style, marketing, packaging, advertising, or something else?

- **Who will you need to hire?** What level of experience are you seeking?

- **How important is attitude?** What constitutes fair compensation, and how much will benefits and overhead cost? How will you train employees?

- **How will the work flow through the organization?** Will the organization be efficient, productive, and accountable?

- **Who will be in charge of selling the product or service?** Selling is proactive; order taking is reactive. They are two different things. Do you understand the difference?

- **Who will keep the books and records?** Be careful who you hire for bookkeeping and accounting. Check references and backgrounds carefully. A hiring mistake can be very costly.

- **Who will handle administrative issues such as insurance, legal, personnel, and purchasing?** Mistakes in these areas can cause big problems, including law suits.

- **What are the governmental and regulatory issues?** Are there federal, state, or local laws to obey? What about permits, licenses, labor laws, inspections, compliance issues, and health and safety regulations? What about taxes, zoning, waste removal, and environmental issues? And finally, what about human resources and dealing with diversity, sexual harassment, equal pay, and unions?

- **Who will be the boss** and responsible to the owners, directors, elected and appointed officials, agencies, commissioners, department heads, and committee members?

- **How will you prepare for what is coming?** Who will be looking out over the horizon at what is coming, and planning for the future? Who is thinking about trends, fashions, and obsolescence?

Have you noticed that, up to this point, I have not asked about where the money will come from? This is by design. Until you have well thought out answers to these questions, your idea is unlikely to attract investment, either from yourself or anyone else.

Now, with your business idea more clearly defined and developed, it is time to start thinking about going from the page to the "stage." **Money is necessary to fund the operations of any enterprise.** It comes from both external and internal sources, so let's explore your options.

External sources of funds: In the beginning, most ideas are funded by the entrepreneur and his or her extended family and friends. This "seed" or founder money must be characterized as either equity or debt. Either way, it is important to have the transaction in writing so there is no misunderstanding as to what it is and what it represents. Is it ownership or equity, or is it a debt to be repaid; and at what rate of interest and when? Other external sources of capital may come from:

- Partners, either active or passive.
- Contributions or donations of money, equipment, or inventory.
- Investors or institutions providing loans.
- Government loans or subsidies, such as small business administration (SBA) loans.
- Crowdfunding.
- Proceeds from the sale of stock if a corporation is formed.
- Grants and the awards.

Since most external funding will be in the form of either **debt or equity**, it is important that you understand the characteristics of each:

Debt
- Debt is usually in the form of money **borrowed** from a person(s) or a lending institution, **backed by a promise to repay** over a predetermined period of time and rate of interest. **Interest payments are tax deductible**, except for nonprofit organizations.

- Debt is a **liabi**lity of the business which is often personally guaranteed by the assets of the owner or major shareholder(s), as well as being collateralized by the assets of the business.

- Debt does not dilute ownership. It creates leverage, the ability to make (or lose) money with borrowed funds.

- Debt ultimately must be repaid. The inability to do so could cause bankruptcy and a forced sale of the assets to repay the debt.

- The conditions and terms of the debt are spelled out in the loan agreement which should be read carefully and understood by all parties. Before signing, make sure the details work for you and are consistent with your business plan.

Equity
- Equity represents a **permanent ownership** stake in the business. Raising outside equity may mean giving up some percentage of your ownership and control, but the difficulty is defining how much to give in return for the needed cash. This is called **dilution.** Try to minimize it.

- Some owners may want **dividends** to be paid along the way. Others may be willing to leave their prorated share of the cash flow in the business for future investment.

- Eventually, investors will want to **monetize** their stake, turn it in to money, by selling their shares, selling the business, or merging the business. This is called the **exit strategy.** It will most likely be years away.

Internally generated funds: These are the funds generated by the operation of the enterprise itself, basically its cash flow from operations, and any asset sales.

Now that you have identified your sources of funds, you will be asked many more questions. Be prepared to answer them in detail. They are all part of your business plan.

- What kind of property, plant, and equipment is needed?
- What is the best way to purchase it on a budget?
- What kind of information technology (IT) software and hardware is needed?
- Who will supply you with inventory?
- Do you have alternative materials or sources of materials?

- What will you outsource?
- What are your standards of quality?
- What about shipping and receiving?
- What about late deliveries, defects, returns, and complaints?
- What will be your terms of payment?
- What are the safety and environmental issues?

Ideas are free. Let your mind soar. Look around. Be alert. **Think, dream, create, and innovate.**

One success is worth a hundred failures.

Notes and Updates